GO MATH!

HOUGHTON MIFFLIN HARCOURT

D1548915

HOUGHTON
MIFFLIN
HARCOURT

ISBN 978-0-547-58790-5

17 0877 20 19

4500757906   C D E F G

Dear Students and Families,

Welcome to **Go Math!**, Grade 2! In this exciting mathematics program, there are hands-on activities to do and real-world problems to solve. Best of all, you will write your ideas and answers right in your book. In **Go Math!**, writing and drawing on the pages helps you think deeply about what you are learning, and you will really understand math!

By the way, all of the pages in your **Go Math!** book are made using recycled paper. We wanted you to know that you can Go Green with **Go Math!**

Sincerely,

The Authors

Made in the United States
Text printed on 100% recycled paper
By using this paper in a typical print run, we
achieved the following environmental benefits:*
• Trees Saved: 463
• Air Emissions Eliminated: 28,074 pounds
• Water Saved: 311,402 gallons
• Solid Waste Eliminated: 35,816 pounds

*Environmental impact estimates calculated using
 the Environmental Defense Fund Paper Calculator.
 For more information, visit www.papercalculator.org

GO MATH!

Authors

Juli K. Dixon
Professor of Mathematics Education
University of Central Florida
Orlando, Florida

Matt Larson
Curriculum Specialist for Mathematics
Lincoln Public Schools
Lincoln, Nebraska

Miriam A. Leiva
Founding President, TODOS:
    Mathematics for All
Distinguished Professor
    of Mathematics Emerita
University of North Carolina Charlotte
Charlotte, North Carolina

Thomasenia Lott Adams
Professor of Mathematics Education
University of Florida
Gainesville, Florida

Number Sense and Place Value

Math Story: Whales 1

COMMON CORE | **Critical Area** Extending understanding of base-ten notation

CRITICAL AREA

DIGITAL PATH
Go online! Your math lessons are interactive. Use *iTools*, Animated Math Models, the Multimedia *eGlossary*, and more.

Math Story

Whales

Social Studies

Look for these:

REAL WORLD

H.O.T.
Higher Order Thinking

Use every day for Standards Practice.

2 Numbers to 1,000 53

Domain Number and Operations in Base Ten
Common Core Standards CC.2.NBT.1, CC.2.NBT.1a, CC.2.NBT.1b,
CC.2.NBT.3, CC.2.NBT.4, CC.2.NBT.8

Addition and Subtraction

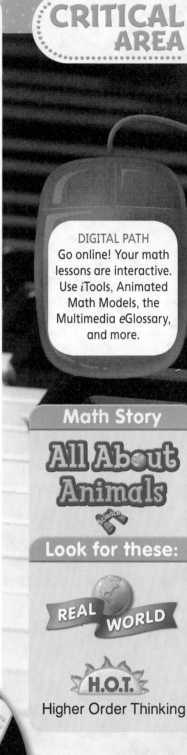

CRITICAL AREA

COMMON CORE — **Critical Area** Building fluency with addition and subtraction

3 Basic Facts and Relationships 117

Domain Operations and Algebraic Thinking
Common Core Standards CC.2.OA.1, CC.2.OA.2, CC.2.OA.4

DIGITAL PATH
Go online! Your math lessons are interactive. Use *iTools*, Animated Math Models, the Multimedia *eGlossary*, and more.

Math Story

All About Animals

Look for these:

REAL WORLD

H.O.T.
Higher Order Thinking

Use every day for Standards Practice.

4 2-Digit Addition 169

Domain Number and Operations in Base Ten
Common Core Standards CC.2.OA.1, CC.2.NBT.5, CC.2.NBT.6, CC.2.NBT.9

CRITICAL AREA

COMMON CORE **Critical Area** Using standard units of measure

DIGITAL PATH
Go online! Your math lessons are interactive. Use *iTools*, Animated Math Models, the Multimedia *eGlossary*, and more.

Math Story

Making a Kite

Look for these:

REAL WORLD

H.O.T.
Higher Order Thinking

Use every day for Standards Practice.

x

CRITICAL AREA

Geometry and Fractions

COMMON CORE   **Critical Area** Describing and analyzing shapes

11 Geometry and Fraction Concepts 505

Domain Geometry
Common Core Standards CC.2.G.1, CC.2.G.2, CC.2.G.3

Whales

by John Hudson

COMMON CORE

CRITICAL AREA **Extending understanding of base-ten notation**

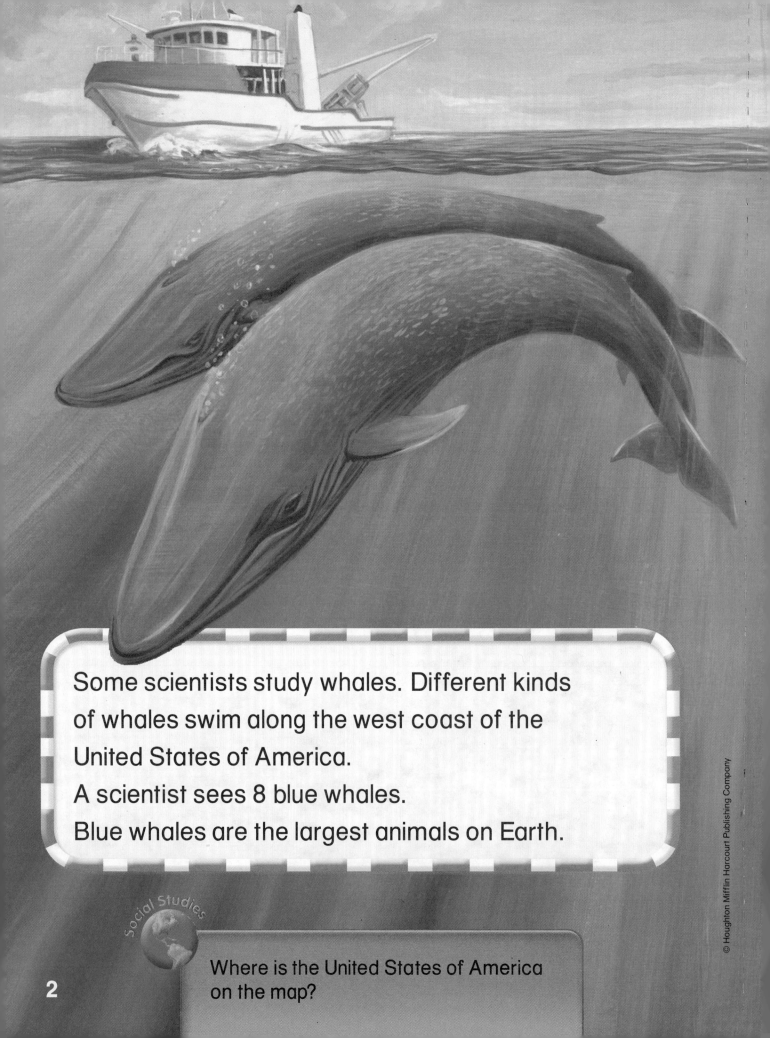

Some scientists study whales. Different kinds of whales swim along the west coast of the United States of America.

A scientist sees 8 blue whales.

Blue whales are the largest animals on Earth.

Social Studies

Where is the United States of America on the map?

North America

Alaska

Pacific
Ocean

Canada

Atlantic
Ocean

N

W E

S

United States
of America

Mexico

0   500   1,000 Miles
0   500 1,000 Kilometers

Map Legend
—— Border

The scientist also sees 13 humpback whales.

Humpback whales sing underwater.

Did the scientist see more humpback whales or

more blue whales?   more _____ whales

Social Studies

Where is the Pacific Ocean on the map?

3

Whales also swim along the east coast of Canada and the United States of America. Pilot whales swim behind a leader, or a *pilot*. A scientist sees a group of 29 pilot whales.

Social Studies

Where is Canada on the map?

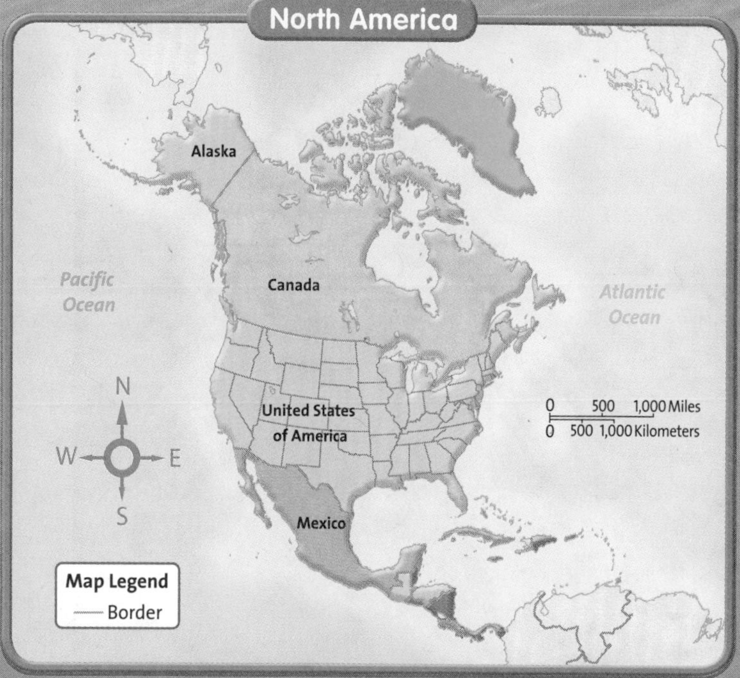

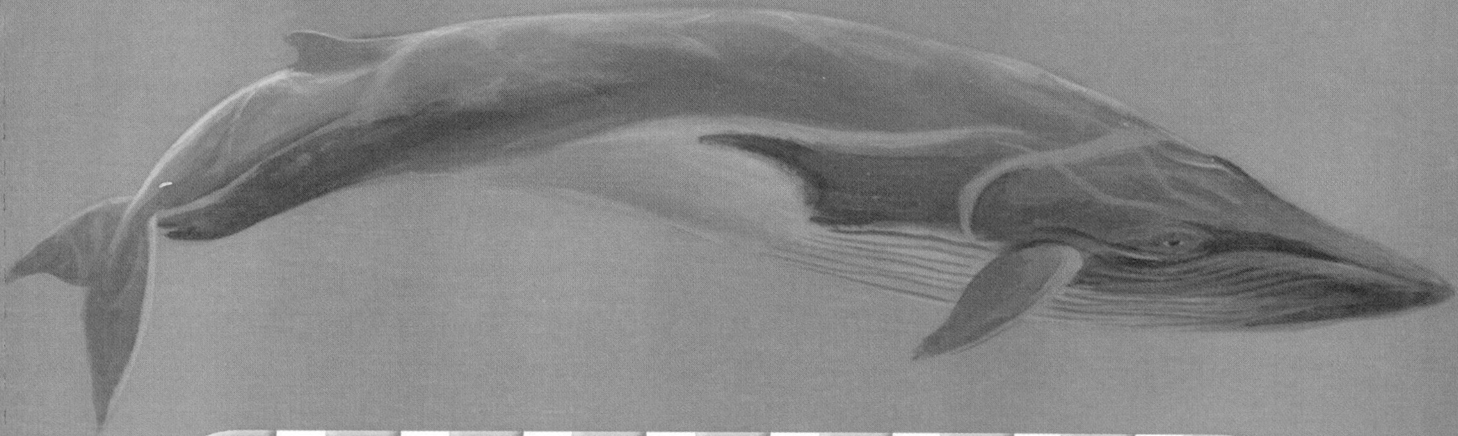

Alaska

Pacific
Ocean

Canada

Atlantic
Ocean

N

W   E

S

United States
of America

0   500 1,000 Miles
0 500 1,000 Kilometers

Mexico

Map Legend
— Border

Fin whales are fast swimmers. They are
the second-largest whales in the world.

A scientist sees a group of 27 fin whales.

How many tens are in the number 27?

_____ tens

Social Studies

Where is the Atlantic Ocean on the map?

Alaska

Pacific
Ocean

Canada

Atlantic
Ocean

United States
of America

N

W ← → E

S

500   1,000 Miles
500 1,000 Kilometers

Mexico

Map Legend
— Border

Humpback whales swim to the warm water near Mexico for the winter. Humpback whales may have as many as 35 throat grooves. In the number 35, the _____ is in the ones place and the _____ is in the tens place.

Social Studies

Where is Mexico on the map?

Write About the Story

Look at the pictures. Draw and write your own story. Compare two numbers in your story.

Vocabulary Review

more	fewer
tens	greater than
ones	less than

_____

_____

_____

_____

_____

The Size of Numbers

The table shows how many young whales were seen by scientists.

Young Whales Seen	
Whale	**Number of Whales**
Humpback	34
Blue	13
Fin	27
Pilot	43

1. Which number of whales has a 4 in the tens place?

   _____

2. How many tens and ones describe the number of young blue whales seen?

   _____ ten _____ ones

3. Compare the number of young humpback whales and the number of young pilot whales seen.

   Write > or <.

   34 ◯ 43

4. Compare the number of young fin whales and the number of young blue whales seen.

   Write > or <.

   27 ◯ 13

Write a story about a scientist watching sea animals. Use some 2-digit numbers in your story.

Number Concepts

Curious About Math with

Curious George

At a farmers' market, many different fruits and vegetables are sold.

If there are 2 groups of 10 watermelons on a table, how many watermelons are there?

Show What You Know ✓

Model Numbers to 20

Write the number that tells how many.

1.  _____

2.  _____

Use a Hundred Chart to Count

Use the hundred chart.

3. Count from 36 to 47. Which of the numbers below will you say? Circle them.

   42   31   48   39   37

1	2	3	4	5	6	7	8	9	10
11	12	13	14	15	16	17	18	19	20
21	22	23	24	25	26	27	28	29	30
31	32	33	34	35	36	37	38	39	40
41	42	43	44	45	46	47	48	49	50
51	52	53	54	55	56	57	58	59	60
61	62	63	64	65	66	67	68	69	70
71	72	73	74	75	76	77	78	79	80
81	82	83	84	85	86	87	88	89	90
91	92	93	94	95	96	97	98	99	100

Tens

Write how many tens. Write the number.

4. _____ tens

   _____

5. 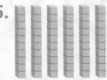 _____ tens

   _____

 Family note: This page checks your child's understanding of important skills needed for success in Chapter 1.

 GO Online   Assessment Options
Soar to Success Math

© Houghton Mifflin Harcourt Publishing Company

Name _____

Vocabulary Builder

Review Words

ones

tens

count on

count back

Visualize It

Fill in the boxes of the graphic organizer.
Write sentences about **ones** and **tens**.

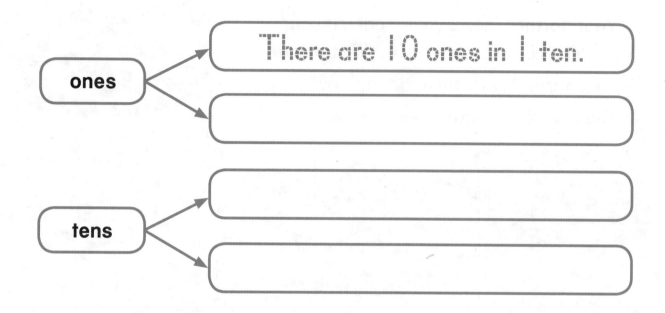

ones → There are 10 ones in 1 ten.

tens →

Understand Vocabulary

1. Start with 1. **Count on** by ones.

   1, ____, ____, ____, ____, ____

_____

2. Start with 8. **Count back** by ones.

   8, ____, ____, ____, ____, ____

GO Online
• eStudent Edition
• Multimedia eGlossary

Game Three in a Row

Materials • 15 • 15 ⬤ • ▭▭▭▭ ▯

Play with a partner.

1. Choose a leaf. Read the number on the leaf. Use ▭▭▭▭ ▯ to model the number.

2. Your partner checks your model. If your model is correct, put your ⬤ on the leaf.

3. Take turns. Try to get 3 ⬤ in a row.

4. The first player with 3 ⬤ in a row wins.

5	21	13	19	20
25	15	7	8	12
11	9	14	16	24
22	23	17	18	10

Name _____

Algebra • Even and Odd Numbers

Essential Question How are even numbers and odd numbers different?

COMMON CORE STANDARD CC.2.OA.3
Work with equal groups of objects to gain foundations for multiplication.

Use 🔲 to show each number.

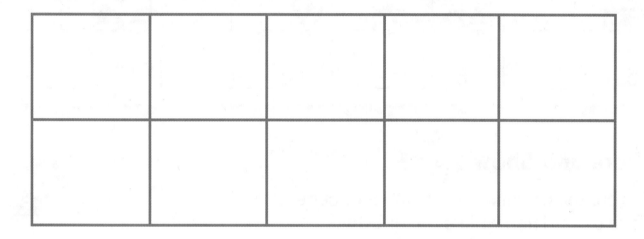

FOR THE TEACHER • Read the following problem. Beca has 8 toy cars. Can she arrange her cars in pairs on a shelf? Have children set pairs of cubes vertically on the ten frames. Continue the activity for the numbers 7 and 10.

Math Talk
When you make pairs for 7 and for 10, how are these models different? **Explain.** MATHEMATICAL PRACTICES

Chapter 1

Count out cubes for each number. Make pairs.
Even numbers show pairs with no cubes left over.
Odd numbers show pairs with one cube left over.

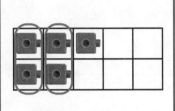 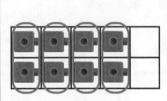 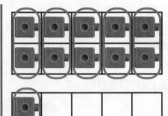 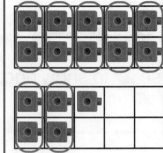

5 __odd__   8 __even__   12 _____   15 _____

Share and Show

Use cubes. Count out the number of cubes.
Make pairs. Then write **even** or **odd**.

1. 6 _____   2. 3 _____

3. 2 _____   4. 9 _____

5. 4 _____   6. 10 _____

7. 7 _____   8. 13 _____

9. 11 _____   10. 14 _____

Name _____

On Your Own

Shade in the ten frames to show the number.
Circle **even** or **odd**.

11. 17
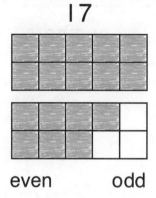
even   odd

12. 16
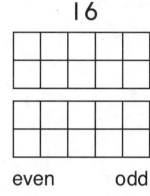
even   odd

13. 19
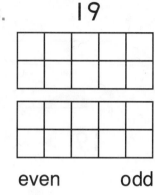
even   odd

14. 15
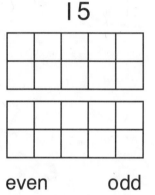
even   odd

15. 20
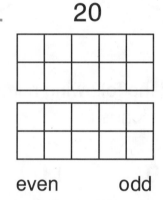
even   odd

16. 18
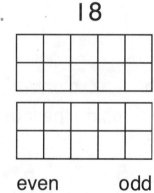
even   odd

17. Which two numbers in the box
are even numbers?

_____ and _____

Explain how you know that they
are even numbers.

_____

_____

_____

PROBLEM SOLVING

Write Math

18. Fill in the blanks to describe the groups of numbers.
Write **even** or **odd**.

_____ numbers   _____ numbers

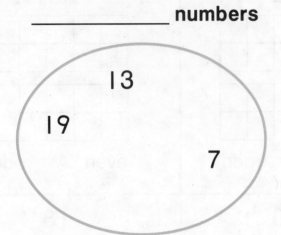

13
19
7

4
12
18

19. H.O.T. Write each of the following numbers
inside the loop that it belongs in.

5   6   10   11   24   25

20. ⭐ **Test Prep** There are an even number
of girls and an odd number of boys in
Gina's class. Which of these choices
could tell about her class?

○ 8 girls and 12 boys

○ 9 girls and 8 boys

○ 10 girls and 7 boys

○ 11 girls and 9 boys

TAKE HOME ACTIVITY • Have your child show you a number, such as 9,
using small objects and explain why the number is even or odd.

16 sixteen

FOR MORE PRACTICE:
Standards Practice Book, pp. P3–P4

Name _____

Algebra • Represent Even Numbers

Essential Question Why can an even number be shown as the sum of two equal addends?

Listen and Draw

Make pairs with your cubes. Draw to show the cubes. Then write the numbers you say as you count to find the number of cubes.

_____ _____ cubes

FOR THE TEACHER • Give each small group of children a set of 10 to 15 connecting cubes. After children group their cubes into pairs, have them draw a picture of their cubes and write their counting sequence for finding the total number of cubes.

Math Talk

Do you have an odd number or even number of cubes? Explain.

MATHEMATICAL PRACTICES

Chapter 1

An even number of cubes can be shown as two equal groups.

You can match each cube in the first group with a cube in the second group.

$$6 = 3 + 3$$

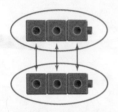

$$10 = 5 + 5$$

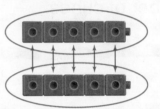

Share and Show

How many cubes are there in all? Complete the addition sentence to show the equal groups.

1. ___ = ___ + ___

2. ___ = ___ + ___

3. ___ = ___ + ___

4. ___ = ___ + ___

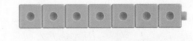

On Your Own

Shade in the frames to show two equal groups for each number. Complete the addition sentence to show the groups.

5. 10

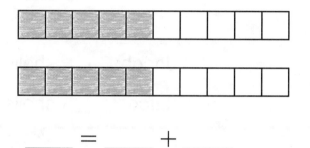

___ = ___ + ___

6. 16

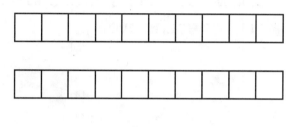

___ = ___ + ___

7. 20

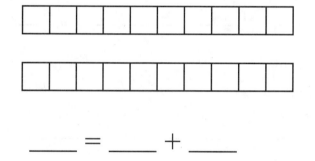

___ = ___ + ___

8. 18

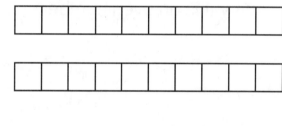

___ = ___ + ___

H.O.T. The number 7 is an odd number. Marc showed 7 with this addition sentence. Use Marc's way to show these odd numbers with addition sentences.

$7 = 3 + 3 + 1$

9. 5 = ___ + ___ + ___

10. 11 = ___ + ___ + ___

11. 9 = ___ + ___ + ___

12. 13 = ___ + ___ + ___

PROBLEM SOLVING REAL WORLD

Write Math

Solve. Write or draw to explain.

13. Jacob and Lucas each have the same number of shells. They have 16 shells altogether. How many shells do Jacob and Lucas each have?

Jacob: _____ shells

Lucas: _____ shells

14. **H.O.T.** Choose an even number between 10 and 19. Draw a picture and then write a sentence to explain why it is an even number.

_____

_____

_____

15. ⭐ **Test Prep** Which sum is an even number?

○ $1 + 2 = 3$

○ $3 + 2 = 5$

○ $5 + 5 = 10$

○ $5 + 6 = 11$

TAKE HOME ACTIVITY • Have your child explain what he or she learned in this lesson.

FOR MORE PRACTICE:
Standards Practice Book, pp. P5–P6

Name _____

Understand Place Value

Essential Question How do you know the value of a digit?

COMMON CORE STANDARD CC.2.NBT.3
Understand place value.

Listen and Draw REAL WORLD

Write the numbers. Then choose a way to show the numbers.

Tens	Ones

Tens	Ones

 FOR THE TEACHER • Read the following problem. Have children write the numbers and describe how they chose to represent them. Tyler collects baseball cards. The number of cards that he has is written with a 2 and a 5. How many cards might he have?

Math Talk
Explain why the value of 5 is different in the two numbers.

MATHEMATICAL PRACTICES

0, 1, 2, 3, 4, 5, 6, 7, 8, and 9 are **digits**.
In a 2-digit number, you know the value of
a digit by its place.

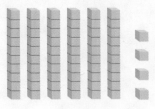

64

Tens	Ones
6	4

6 tens   4 ones

The digit **6** is in
the tens place. It
tells you there are
6 tens, or 60.

The digit **4** is in
the ones place. It
tells you there are
4 ones, or 4.

Share and Show

Circle the value of the red digit.

1. 26

60   (6)

2. 58

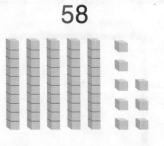

5   50

3. 40

40   4

4. 73

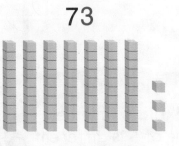

30   3

⊘5. 24

2   20

⊘6. 61

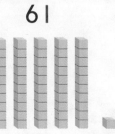

1   10

Name _____

On Your Own

Circle the value of the red digit.

7. **51**

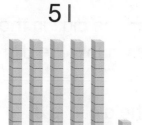

1   10

8. **49**

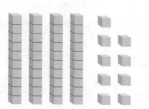

90   9

9. **70**

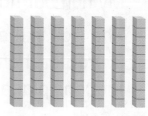

7   70

10. **18**

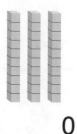

1   10

11. **65**

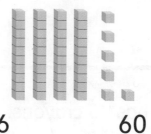

50   5

12. **33**

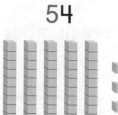

30   3

13. **30**

10   0

14. **46**

6   60

15. **54**

50   5

H.O.T. Look at the digits of the numbers.
Draw quick pictures for the missing blocks.

16. **47**

17. **52**

18. **63**

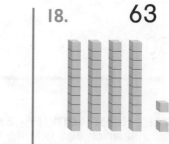

© Houghton Mifflin Harcourt Publishing Company

Chapter 1 • Lesson 3

PROBLEM SOLVING

Write the 2-digit number that matches the clues.

19. My number has 8 tens.

The digit in the ones place is greater than the digit in the tens place.

My number is _____.

20. In my number, the digit in the ones place is double the digit in the tens place.

The sum of the digits is 3.

My number is _____.

21. My number has the same digit in the ones place and in the tens place.

The digit is less than 6.

The digit is greater than 4.

My number is _____.

22. H.O.T. In my number, both digits are even numbers.

The digit in the tens place is less than the digit in the ones place.

The sum of the digits is 6.

My number is _____.

23. ★ **Test Prep** Henry has 45 crayons.
What is the value of the digit 5 in this number?

○ 4
○ 5
○ 9
○ 50

Green

TAKE HOME ACTIVITY • Write the number 56. Have your child tell you which digit is in the tens sense, which digit is in the ones place, and the value of each digit.

24 twenty-four

FOR MORE PRACTICE:
Standards Practice Book, pp. P7–P8

Name _____

Expanded Form

Essential Question How do you describe a
2-digit number as tens and ones?

COMMON CORE STANDARD **CC.2.NBT.3**
Understand place value.

Use ▭▭▭▭▭ ▭ to model each number.

Tens	Ones

FOR THE TEACHER • After you read the following
problem, write 38 on the board. Have children
model the number. Mac used 38 stickers to
decorate a book of photos. How can you model 38
with blocks? Continue the activity for 83 and 77.

Math Talk
Explain how you
know how many tens
and ones are in the
number 29.

MATHEMATICAL
PRACTICES

Chapter 1

What does 23 mean?

Tens	Ones

The 2 in 23 has a value of 2 tens, or 20.
The 3 in 23 has a value of 3 ones, or 3.

__2__ tens __3__ ones

__20__ + __3__

Share and Show

Draw a quick picture to show the number.
Describe the number in two ways.

1. 37

_____ tens _____ ones

_____ + _____

2. 54

_____ tens _____ ones

_____ + _____

✓ 3. 16

_____ ten _____ ones

_____ + _____

✓ 4. 60

_____ tens _____ ones

_____ + _____

On Your Own

Draw a quick picture to show the number.
Describe the number in two ways.

5. 48

_____ tens _____ ones

_____ + _____

6. 31

_____ tens _____ one

_____ + _____

7. 59

_____ tens _____ ones

_____ + _____

8. 75

_____ tens _____ ones

_____ + _____

Write the number.

9. 8 tens 6 ones

_____

10. 40 + 2

_____

11. 70 + 3

_____

12. 9 tens 7 ones

_____

PROBLEM SOLVING

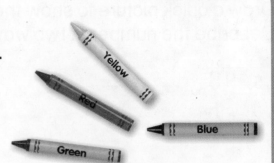

H.O.T. Use crayons. Follow the steps.

13. Start at 51 and draw a green line to 43.

14. Draw a blue line from 43 to 34.

15. Draw a red line from 34 to 29.

16. Then draw a yellow line from 29 to 72.

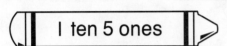

| 1 ten 5 ones |

| 30 + 2 |

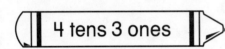

| 4 tens 3 ones |

| 20 + 9 |

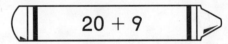

| 3 tens 4 ones |

| 10 + 2 |

| 5 tens 1 one |

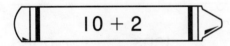

| 70 + 2 |

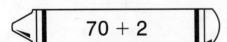

| 7 + 2 |

17. ⭐ **Test Prep** Which of these is another way to describe 85?

- ○ 80 + 5
- ○ 50 + 8
- ○ 8 + 5
- ○ 50 + 80

TAKE HOME ACTIVITY • Ask your child to write 89 as tens plus ones. Then have him or her write 25 as tens plus ones.

FOR MORE PRACTICE:
Standards Practice Book, pp. P9–P10

Name _____

Different Ways to Write Numbers

Essential Question What are different ways to write a 2-digit number?

COMMON CORE STANDARD CC.2.NBT.3
Understand place value.

Listen and Draw REAL WORLD

Write the number. Then write it as tens and ones.

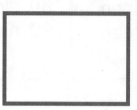

_____ tens _____ ones

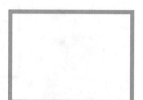

_____ + _____

_____ + _____

_____ tens _____ ones

FOR THE TEACHER • Read the following problem. Taryn counted 53 books on the shelves. How many tens and ones are in 53? Continue the activity with the numbers 78, 35, and 40.

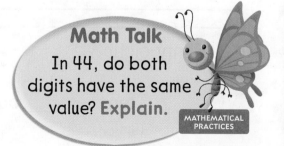

Math Talk
In 44, do both digits have the same value? **Explain.**

MATHEMATICAL PRACTICES

Chapter 1

Model and Draw

A number can be written in different ways.

fifty-nine
5 tens 9 ones
50 + 9
59

ones	teen words	tens
0 zero	11 eleven	10 ten
1 one	12 twelve	20 twenty
2 two	13 thirteen	30 thirty
3 three	14 fourteen	40 forty
4 four	15 fifteen	50 fifty
5 five	16 sixteen	60 sixty
6 six	17 seventeen	70 seventy
7 seven	18 eighteen	80 eighty
8 eight	19 nineteen	90 ninety
9 nine		

Share and Show

Look at the examples above.
Then write the number another way.

1. thirty-two

_____

2. 20 + 7

_____

3. 63

_____ tens _____ ones

4. ninety-five

_____ + _____

5. 5 tens 1 one

_____

6. seventy-six

_____ + _____

✓ 7. twenty-eight

_____ tens _____ ones

✓ 8. 8 tens 0 ones

_____

© Houghton Mifflin Harcourt Publishing Company

Name _____

On Your Own

Write the number another way.

9. 2 tens 4 ones

_____

10. thirty

_____ tens _____ ones

11. eighty-five

_____

12. 54

_____ + _____

13. twelve

_____ + _____

14. 90 + 9

_____ tens _____ ones

15. 7 tens 8 ones

_____

16. forty-one

_____ + _____

17. 39

_____

18. 60 + 2

_____ tens _____ ones

 Fill in the blanks to make the sentence true.

19. Sixty-seven is the same as _____ tens _____ ones.

_____

20. 4 tens _____ ones is the same as _____ + _____.

_____

21. 20 + _____ is the same as _____.

TAKE HOME ACTIVITY • Write 20 + 6 on a sheet of paper. Have your child write the 2-digit number. Repeat for 4 tens 9 ones.

Mid-Chapter Checkpoint

Concepts and Skills

Shade in the ten frames to show the number.
Circle **even** or **odd**. (CC.2.OA.3)

1. 15

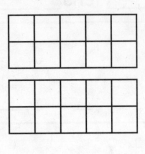

even   odd

2. 18

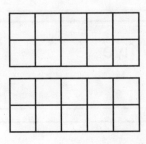

even   odd

Draw a quick picture to show the number.
Describe the number in two ways. (CC.2.NBT.3)

3. 35

_____ tens _____ ones

_____ + _____

4. 53

_____ tens _____ ones

_____ + _____

⭐ Test Prep

5. Which is another way to write 42? (CC.2.NBT.3)

○ 2 tens 4 ones

○ 40 + 2

○ twenty-four

○ 4 + 2

Algebra • Different Names for Numbers

Essential Question How can you show the value of a number in different ways?

COMMON CORE STANDARD CC.2.NBT.3
Understand place value.

Listen and Draw  REAL WORLD

Use ▭▭▭▭▭ ▪ to show the number.
Make trades to show the number a different way.
Record the tens and ones.

_____ tens _____ ones

_____ tens _____ ones

_____ tens _____ ones

FOR THE TEACHER • Read the following problem. Drew has 26 pennies. What are some different ways he can show 26 with blocks? Have children start with 26 ones blocks. Then have them make trades and record the number of tens and ones in each of their models.

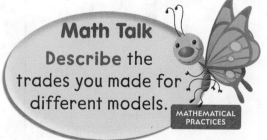

Math Talk
Describe the trades you made for different models.

MATHEMATICAL PRACTICES

These are some different ways to show 32.

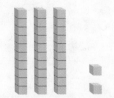

__3__ tens __2__ ones

__30__ + __2__

__2__ tens __12__ ones

__20__ + __12__

__1__ ten __22__ ones

__10__ + __22__

Share and Show

The blocks show the numbers in different ways.
Describe the blocks in two ways.

1. 28

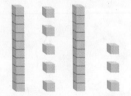

_____ tens _____ ones

_____ + _____

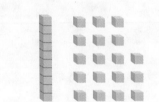

_____ ten _____ ones

_____ + _____

_____ tens _____ ones

_____ + _____

2. 35

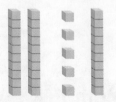

_____ tens _____ ones

_____ + _____

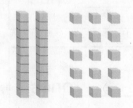

_____ tens _____ ones

_____ + _____

_____ tens _____ ones

_____ + _____

Name _____

On Your Own

The blocks show the numbers in different ways.
Describe the blocks in two ways.

3. 43

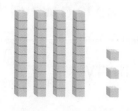 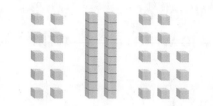 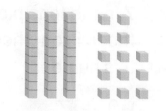

_____ tens _____ ones   _____ tens _____ ones   _____ tens _____ ones

_____ + _____   _____ + _____   _____ + _____

4. 30

  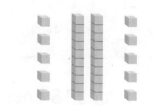

_____ tens _____ ones   _____ tens _____ ones   _____ tens _____ ones

_____ + _____   _____ + _____   _____ + _____

5. 41

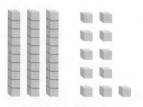 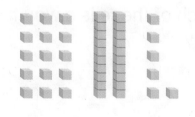 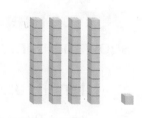

_____ tens _____ ones   _____ tens _____ ones   _____ tens _____ one

_____ + _____   _____ + _____   _____ + _____

6. **H.O.T.** Fill in the blanks to
show 37 in two different ways.

_____ tens _____ ones

_____ tens _____ ones

PROBLEM SOLVING

Write Math

Circle the answer for each riddle.

7. A number has the digit 4 in the ones place and the digit 7 in the tens place. Which of these is another way to write this number?

$$40 + 7 \qquad 70 + 4$$

$$4 + 7$$

8. **H.O.T.** A number is shown with 3 tens and 27 ones. Which of these is a way to write the number?

thirty

thirty-seven

fifty-seven

Fill in the blanks to make each sentence true.

9. _____ tens _____ ones is the same as $90 + 3$.

10. 2 tens 18 ones is the same as _____ + _____.

11. 5 tens _____ ones is the same as _____ + 17.

12. ⭐ **Test Prep** Which of these is a way to show the number 42?

- ○ 1 ten 42 ones
- ○ 2 tens 4 ones
- ○ 3 tens 2 ones
- ○ 3 tens 12 ones

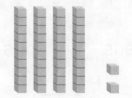

TAKE HOME ACTIVITY • Write the number 45. Have your child write or draw two ways to show this number.

FOR MORE PRACTICE:
Standards Practice Book, pp. P13–P14

Name _____

Problem Solving • Tens and Ones

Essential Question How does finding a pattern help you find all the ways to show a number with tens and ones?

COMMON CORE STANDARD CC.2.NBT.3
Understand place value.

Gail needs to buy 32 pencils. She can buy single pencils or boxes of 10 pencils. What are the different ways Gail can buy 32 pencils?

Unlock the Problem REAL WORLD

What do I need to find?

ways she can buy

32 pencils

What information do I need to use?

She can buy ___single___ pencils

or ___boxes of 10___ pencils.

Show how to solve the problem.
Draw quick pictures for 32. Complete the chart.

Boxes of 10 pencils	Single pencils
3	2
2	12
1	
0	

HOME CONNECTION • Your child found a pattern in the different combinations of tens and ones. Using a pattern helps to make an organized list.

Try Another Problem

Find a pattern to solve.

- What do I need to find?
- What information do I need to use?

1. Sara is putting away a pile of 36 crayons. She can pack them in boxes of 10 crayons or as single crayons. What are all of the different ways Sara can pack the crayons?

Boxes of 10 crayons	Single crayons

2. Mr. Winter is putting away 48 chairs. He can put away the chairs in stacks of 10 or as single chairs. What are all of the different ways Mr. Winter can put away the chairs?

Stacks of 10 chairs	Single chairs

Math Talk
Describe the pattern that helped you solve Exercise 2.

MATHEMATICAL PRACTICES

Share and Show

Find a pattern to solve.

3. Philip is putting 25 markers into a bag. He can put the markers in the bag as bundles of 10 or as single markers. What are all of the different ways Philip can put the markers in the bag?

Bundles of 10 markers	Single markers

4. Stickers are sold in packs of 10 stickers or as single stickers. Miss Allen wants to buy 43 stickers. What are all of the different ways she can buy the stickers?

Packs of 10 stickers	Single stickers

5. Devin is sorting his 29 baseball cards. He can pack them in boxes of 10 cards or as single cards. What are all of the different ways Devin can sort the cards?

Boxes of 10 cards	Single cards

On Your Own

Solve. Write or draw to explain.

6. Mr. Link needs 30 cups. He can buy them in packs of 10 cups or as single cups. What are all of the different ways he can buy the cups?

Packs of 10 cups	Single cups

7. **H.O.T.** Zack has 6 marbles. Olivia gives him some more. Now he has 10 marbles. How many marbles did Olivia give him?

_____ marbles

8. ⭐ **Test Prep** Lee can pack her toy cars in boxes of 10 cars or as single cars. Which of these is a way that she can pack her 24 toy cars?

○ 4 boxes of 10 cars and 2 single cars

○ 1 box of 10 cars and 24 single cars

○ 3 boxes of 10 cars and 14 single cars

○ 2 boxes of 10 cars and 4 single cars

TAKE HOME ACTIVITY · Have your child explain how he or she solved one problem on this page.

© Houghton Mifflin Harcourt Publishing Company

FOR MORE PRACTICE:
Standards Practice Book, pp. P15–P16

Counting Patterns Within 100

Essential Question How do you count by 1s, 5s, and 10s with numbers less than 100?

COMMON CORE STANDARD **CC.2.NBT.2**
Understand place value.

Listen and Draw

Look at the hundred chart. Write the missing numbers.

1	2	3		5	6		8		10
11		13	14	15	16		18	19	20
	22	23	24		26	27	28	29	30
31	32		34	35	36		38	39	
41		43	44	45	46	47		49	50
51		53		55		57		59	60
	62		64	65	66	67	68		70
71	72	73	74		76		78	79	
81		83		85	86	87	88	89	90
	92		94	95	96		98		100

Math Talk

Describe some different ways to find the missing numbers in the chart.

MATHEMATICAL PRACTICES

HOME CONNECTION · Your child completed the hundred chart to review counting to 100.

Model and Draw

You can count on by different amounts.
You can start counting with different numbers.

Count by ones.

1, 2, 3, 4, __5__, __6__, _____, _____

29, 30, 31, 32, __33__, _____, _____, _____

Count by fives.

5, 10, 15, 20, _____, _____, _____, _____

50, 55, 60, 65, _____, _____, _____, _____

Share and Show

Count by ones.

1. 15, 16, 17, _____, _____, _____, _____, _____

Count by fives.

2. 15, 20, 25, _____, _____, _____, _____, _____

☑ 3. 60, 65, _____, _____, _____, _____, _____

Count by tens.

4. 10, 20, _____, _____, _____, _____, _____

☑ 5. 30, 40, _____, _____, _____, _____, _____

On Your Own

Count by ones.

6. 23, 24, 25, _____, _____, _____, _____

7. 77, 78, _____, _____, _____, _____, _____

8. 52, _____, _____, _____, _____, _____, _____

Count by fives.

9. 30, 35, 40, _____, _____, _____, _____

10. 5, 10, _____, _____, _____, _____, _____

11. 70, _____, _____, _____, _____, _____, _____

Count by tens.

12. 20, 30, _____, _____, _____, _____, _____

Count back by ones.

13. 66, 65, 64, 63, _____, _____, _____

14. 18, 17, 16, 15, _____, _____, _____

PROBLEM SOLVING REAL WORLD

Write Math

Solve.

15. Andy counts by ones. He starts at 29 and stops at 45. Which of the following numbers will he say? Circle them.

31   20
    47   35
40   46   39

16. Maya counts by fives. She starts at 5 and stops at 50. Which of the following numbers will she say? Circle them.

55   25
     6   40
10   18   45

17. **H.O.T.** Tina wants to count backward by fives. If she starts at 40, what are the first six numbers she should say?

40, _____, _____, _____, _____, _____

18. ⭐ **Test Prep** Which group of numbers shows counting by fives?

○ 5, 6, 7, 8, 9
○ 20, 25, 30, 35, 40
○ 10, 20, 30, 40, 50
○ 50, 49, 48, 47, 46

TAKE HOME ACTIVITY · With your child, practice counting by ones to 100, starting with numbers such as 58 or 62.

FOR MORE PRACTICE:
Standards Practice Book, pp. P17–P18

Name _____

Counting Patterns Within 1,000

Essential Question How do you count by 1s, 5s, 10s, and 100s with numbers less than 1,000?

COMMON CORE STANDARD CC.2.NBT.2
Understand place value.

Listen and Draw

Write the missing numbers in the chart.

401		403	404		406	407	408		410
411				415	416	417	418	419	
421	422	423	424	425		427	428	429	430
	432		434	435	436	437	438		
441	442	443	444		446	447		449	450
		454	455	456	457	458	459	460	
461	462						468	469	470
	472	473	474	475	476	477		479	480
481	482		484	485	486				490
	492	493		495	496	497	498		

HOME CONNECTION · Your child completed the number chart to practice counting with 3-digit numbers.

Math Talk
What are the next three numbers that follow the counting in this chart? **Explain** how you know.

MATHEMATICAL PRACTICES

© Houghton Mifflin Harcourt Publishing Company

Model and Draw

Counting can be done in different ways.
Use patterns to count on.

Count by fives.

95, 100, 105, __110__, __115__, _____, _____

140, 145, 150, __155__, _____, _____, _____

Count by tens.

300, 310, 320, _____, _____, _____, _____

470, 480, 490, _____, _____, _____, _____

Share and Show

Count by fives.

1. 745, 750, 755, _____, _____, _____, _____

Count by tens.

2. 520, 530, 540, _____, _____, _____, _____

☑ 3. 600, 610, _____, _____, _____, _____, _____

Count by hundreds.

4. 100, 200, _____, _____, _____, _____, _____

☑ 5. 300, 400, _____, _____, _____, _____, _____

Name _____

On Your Own

Count by fives.

6. 215, 220, 225, _____, _____, _____, _____

7. 905, 910, _____, _____, _____, _____, _____

8. 485, _____, _____, _____, _____, _____

Count by tens.

9. 730, 740, 750, _____, _____, _____, _____

10. 160, 170, _____, _____, _____, _____, _____

11. 850, _____, _____, _____, _____, _____

Count by hundreds.

12. 200, 300, _____, _____, _____, _____, _____

Count back by ones.

13. 558, 557, _____, _____, _____, _____, _____

14. 311, 310, _____, _____, _____, _____, _____

PROBLEM SOLVING REAL WORLD

Write Math

Solve.

15. Lisa counts by fives. She starts at 120 and stops at 175. Which of the following numbers will she say? Circle them.

170   135
    151
155   200   180

16. George counts by tens. He starts at 750 and stops at 830. Which of the following numbers will he say? Circle them.

755   780
    690
760   795   810

17. H.O.T. Tony wants to count backward by tens. If he starts at 440, what are the first six numbers that he should say?

440, _____, _____, _____, _____, _____

18. ⭐ **Test Prep** Which group of numbers shows counting by tens?

- ○ 360, 370, 380, 390, 400
- ○ 390, 391, 392, 393, 394
- ○ 395, 400, 405, 410, 415
- ○ 245, 240, 235, 230, 225

TAKE HOME ACTIVITY • With your child, count by fives from 150 to 200.

FOR MORE PRACTICE:
Standards Practice Book, pp. P19–P20

✔️ Chapter 1 Review/Test

Vocabulary

Use a word in the box to complete each sentence.

1. The numbers 3 and 7 are _____ numbers. (p. 14)

2. 5 and 2 are _____ in the number 52. (p. 22)

Concepts and Skills

Draw a quick picture to show the number.
Describe the number in two ways. (CC.2.NBT.3)

3. 37

_____ tens _____ ones

_____ + _____

4. 73

_____ tens _____ ones

_____ + _____

Write the number another way. (CC.2.NBT.3)

5. forty-one

_____ + _____

6. 6 tens 3 ones

_____

Shade in the frames to show two equal groups
for each number. Complete the addition sentence
to show the groups. (CC.2.OA.3)

7. 16

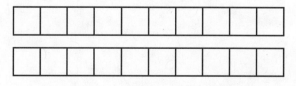

_____ = _____ + _____

8. 14

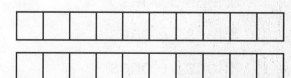

_____ = _____ + _____

Fill in the bubble for the correct answer choice.

9. What is the value of the digit 7 in the number 75? (CC.2.NBT.3)

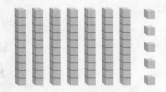

- ○ 7
- ○ 12
- ○ 17
- ○ 70

10. Which group of numbers shows counting by fives? (CC.2.NBT.2)

- ○ 76, 77, 78, 79, 80
- ○ 70, 75, 80, 85, 90
- ○ 20, 30, 40, 50, 60
- ○ 55, 54, 53, 52, 51

11. Which of the following is another way to describe the number 46? (CC.2.NBT.3)

- ○ 2 tens 16 ones
- ○ 3 tens 6 ones
- ○ 3 tens 16 ones
- ○ 4 tens 16 ones

Name _____

Fill in the bubble for the correct answer choice.

12. Wesley has an odd number of red crayons and an even number of blue crayons. Which of these choices could be Wesley's crayons? (CC.2.OA.3)

○ 5 red crayons and 8 blue crayons

○ 6 red crayons and 7 blue crayons

○ 6 red crayons and 8 blue crayons

○ 7 red crayons and 9 blue crayons

13. Mrs. Shaw is buying 26 markers. She can buy them in packs of 10 markers or as single markers. Which of these is a way that she can buy the markers? (CC.2.NBT.3)

Packs of 10 markers	Single markers
2	6
0	26

○ 1 pack of 10 markers and 26 single markers

○ 6 packs of 10 markers and 2 single markers

○ 1 pack of 10 markers and 16 single markers

○ 3 packs of 10 markers and 6 single markers

14. Which group of numbers shows counting by tens? (CC.2.NBT.2)

○ 310, 311, 312, 313, 314

○ 230, 240, 250, 260, 270

○ 405, 410, 415, 420, 425

○ 195, 200, 205, 210, 215

Constructed Response

15. Shawna made a list of ways to write the number 26.

Draw a quick picture for 53. Then list three different ways to write the number 53. (CC.2.NBT.3)

2 tens 6 ones
twenty-six
20 + 6

_____

_____

_____

Performance Task (CC.2.NBT.3)

16. Mrs. Payne is buying 32 pencils. She can buy them in packs of 10 pencils or as single pencils. What are all of the different ways Mrs. Payne can buy the pencils? Find a pattern to solve.

Packs of 10 pencils	Single pencils

Choose two of the ways from the chart. Explain how these two ways show the same number of pencils.

Curious About Math with
Curious George

The White House has 412 doors and 147 windows. Look at the digit 1 in each of these numbers. How do the values of these digits compare?

Show What You Know ✓

Identify Numbers to 30

Write how many.

1.     leaves

2. 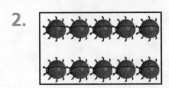 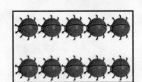    bugs

Place Value: 2-Digit Numbers

Circle the value of the red digit.

3. **47**

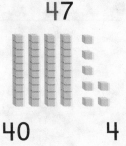

40   4

4. **84**

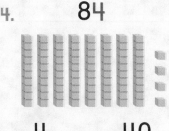

4   40

5. **65**

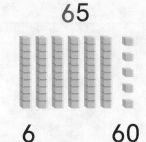

6   60

Compare 2-Digit Numbers Using Symbols

Compare. Write >, <, or =.

6.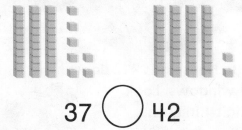

37 ◯ 42

7.

40 ◯ 33

 Family note: This page checks your child's understanding of important skills needed for success in Chapter 2.

GO Online   Assessment Options
Soar to Success Math

Vocabulary Builder

Visualize It

Fill in the boxes of the graphic organizer.
Write sentences using **fewer** and **more**.

fewer

9 pens is fewer than 11 pens.

more

Understand Vocabulary

Use the review words. Complete the sentences.

1. 3 and 9 are _____ in the number 39.

2. 7 is in the _____ place in the number 87.

3. 8 is in the _____ place in the number 87.

Game

Fish for Digits

Materials

- 12 ● • 12 ● • 1 🎲

Play with a partner.

1. Name a place for a digit. You can say **tens place** or **ones place**. Toss the 🎲.

2. Match the number on the 🎲 and the place that you named with a fish.

3. Put a ● on that fish. Take turns.

4. Match all the fish. The player with more ● on the board wins.

14

56

12

46

25

23

32

53

65

61

41

34

Name _____

Group Tens as Hundreds

Essential Question How do you group tens as hundreds?

COMMON CORE STANDARDS CC.2.NBT.1a, CC.2.NBT.1b
Understand place value.

Listen and Draw REAL WORLD

Circle groups of ten. Count the groups of ten.

FOR THE TEACHER • Read the following problem and have children group ones blocks to solve. Bernie dropped 100 pennies. How many groups of 10 pennies can he make as he picks up the pennies?

Math Talk

How many ones are in 3 tens? How many ones are in 7 tens? **Explain.**

MATHEMATICAL PRACTICES

Model and Draw

10 tens is the same as 1 **hundred**.

_____10_____ tens

_____1_____ hundred

_____100_____

Share and Show

Write how many tens. Circle groups of 10 tens.
Write how many hundreds. Write the number.

1.

_____20_____ tens

_____ hundreds

_____

2.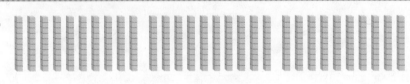

_____ tens

_____ hundreds

_____

☑3.

_____ tens

_____ hundreds

_____

☑4.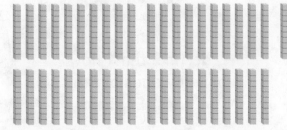

_____ tens

_____ hundreds

_____

On Your Own

Write how many tens. Circle groups of 10 tens.
Write how many hundreds. Write the number.

5.

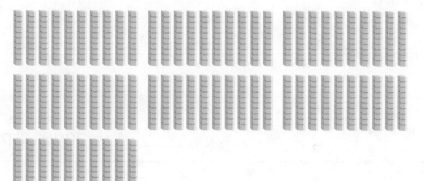

_____ tens

_____ hundreds

_____

6.

_____ tens

_____ hundreds

_____

7.

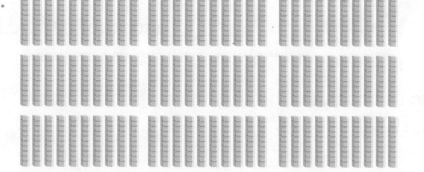

_____ tens

_____ hundreds

_____

8.

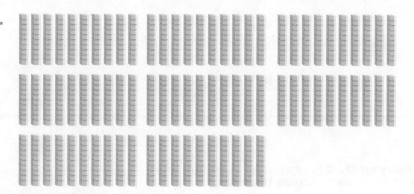

_____ tens

_____ hundreds

_____

PROBLEM SOLVING REAL WORLD

 Write Math

Solve. Write or draw to explain.

9. Mrs. Martin has 20 boxes of paper clips. There are 10 paper clips in each box. How many paper clips does she have?

_____ paper clips

10. H.O.T. Wally has 400 cards. How many stacks of 10 cards can he make? Draw a quick picture to show your work.

_____ stacks of 10 cards

11. ⭐ **Test Prep** Which number has the same value as 30 tens?

- ○ 310
- ○ 300
- ○ 30
- ○ 3

 TAKE HOME ACTIVITY • Ask your child to draw a quick picture of 20 tens and then tell you how many hundreds there are.

FOR MORE PRACTICE:
Standards Practice Book, pp. P25–P26

Name _____

Explore 3-Digit Numbers

Essential Question How do you write a 3-digit number for a group of tens?

COMMON CORE STANDARD **CC.2.NBT.1**
Understand place value.

Listen and Draw REAL WORLD

Circle groups of blocks to show hundreds.
Count the hundreds.

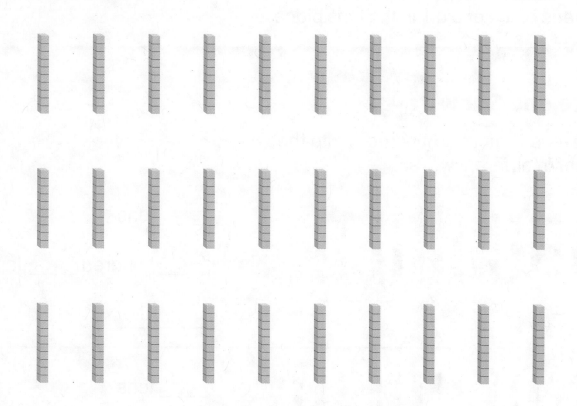

_____ hundreds

_____ straws

FOR THE TEACHER • Read the following problem and have children circle groups of tens blocks to solve. Mrs. Rodriguez has 30 bundles of straws. There are 10 straws in each bundle. How many straws does Mrs. Rodriguez have?

Math Talk

Describe how the number of hundreds would be different if there were 10 more bundles of straws.

MATHEMATICAL PRACTICES

Chapter 2

Model and Draw

What number is shown with 11 tens?

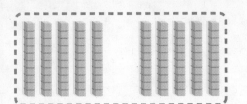

__11__ tens

__1__ hundred __1__ ten

__110__

In the number 110, there is a 1 in the hundreds place and a 1 in the tens place.

Share and Show

Circle tens to make 1 hundred. Write the number in different ways.

1.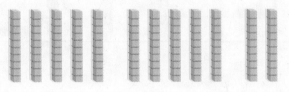

_____ tens

_____ hundred _____ tens

_____

2.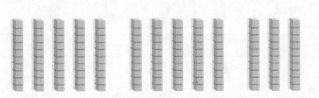

_____ tens

_____ hundred _____ tens

_____

3.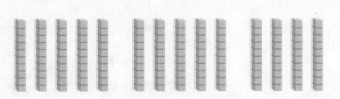

_____ tens

_____ hundred _____ tens

_____

On Your Own

Circle tens to make 1 hundred. Write the number in different ways.

4.

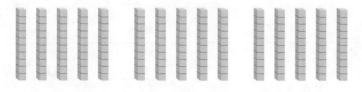

_____ tens

_____ hundred _____ tens

_____

5.

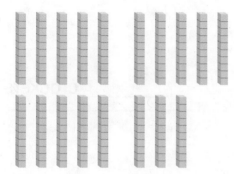

_____ tens

_____ hundred _____ tens

_____

6.

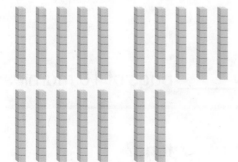

_____ tens

_____ hundred _____ tens

_____

7.

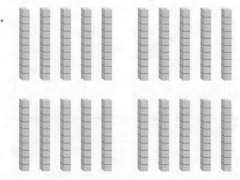

_____ tens

_____ hundreds _____ tens

_____

PROBLEM SOLVING REAL WORLD

Write Math

Solve. Write or draw to explain.

8. Kendra has 120 stickers.
   10 stickers fill a page.
   How many pages
   can she fill?

   _____ pages

9. There are 14 boxes of
   crackers. There are
   10 crackers in each box.
   How many crackers
   are in the boxes?

   _____ crackers

10. **H.O.T.** Ed has 150 marbles.
    How many bags of 10 marbles
    does he need to get so that he
    will have 200 marbles in all?

    _____ bags of 10 marbles

11. ⭐ **Test Prep** Which has the same value as 17 tens?

    ○ 17 ones

    ○ 17 hundreds

    ○ 1 ten 7 ones

    ○ 1 hundred 7 tens

TAKE HOME ACTIVITY • Have your child draw 110 Xs by drawing
11 groups of 10 Xs.

FOR MORE PRACTICE:
Standards Practice Book, pp. P27–P28

Name _____

Model 3-Digit Numbers

Essential Question How do you show a 3-digit number using blocks?

COMMON CORE STANDARD CC.2.NBT.1
Understand place value.

Listen and Draw REAL WORLD

Use ▭▭▭▭▭. Draw to show what you did.

FOR THE TEACHER • Read the following problem. Jack has 12 tens blocks. How many hundreds and tens does Jack have? Have children show Jack's blocks and then draw quick pictures. Then have children circle 10 tens and solve the problem.

Math Talk

If Jack had 14 tens, how many hundreds and tens would he have? **Explain.**

MATHEMATICAL PRACTICES

Model and Draw

In the number 348, the 3 is in the hundreds place, the 4 is in the tens place, and the 8 is in the ones place.

Write the digits in the chart.

Hundreds	Tens	Ones
3	4	8

Show the number 348 using blocks.

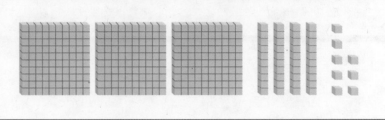

Draw a quick picture.

Share and Show

Write how many hundreds, tens, and ones.

Show with  _____ . Then draw a quick picture.

☑ 1. 234

Hundreds	Tens	Ones

☑ 2. 156

Hundreds	Tens	Ones

Name _____

On Your Own

Write how many hundreds, tens, and ones.

 Show with ▭ ▭▭▭▭ . Then draw a quick picture.

3. 125

Hundreds	Tens	Ones

4. 312

Hundreds	Tens	Ones

5. 245

Hundreds	Tens	Ones

6. 103

Hundreds	Tens	Ones

7. 419

Hundreds	Tens	Ones

8. 328

Hundreds	Tens	Ones

PROBLEM SOLVING

Write Math

Write the number that matches the clues.

9. A model for my number has 2 hundreds blocks, no tens blocks, and 3 ones blocks.

Hundreds	Tens	Ones

My number is _____.

10. A model for my number has 3 hundreds blocks, 5 tens blocks, and no ones blocks.

Hundreds	Tens	Ones

My number is _____.

11. **H.O.T.** How are the numbers 342 and 324 alike? How are they different?

_____

_____

_____

12. ⭐ **Test Prep** What number is shown with these blocks?

- ○ 432
- ○ 342
- ○ 243
- ○ 207

 TAKE HOME ACTIVITY · Write the number 438. Have your child tell you the values of the digits in the number 438.

FOR MORE PRACTICE:
Standards Practice Book, pp. P29–P30

Hundreds, Tens, and Ones

Essential Question How do you write the 3-digit number that is shown by a set of blocks?

COMMON CORE STANDARD CC.2.NBT.1
Understand place value.

Listen and Draw REAL WORLD

Write the number of hundreds, tens, and ones.
Then draw a quick picture.

Hundreds	Tens	Ones

Hundreds	Tens	Ones

FOR THE TEACHER • Read the following to children. Steven has 243 yellow blocks. How many hundreds, tens, and ones are in this number? Repeat for 423 red blocks.

Math Talk
Describe how the two numbers are alike. **Describe** how they are different.

MATHEMATICAL PRACTICES

Model and Draw

Write how many hundreds, tens, and ones there are in the model.
What are two ways to write this number?

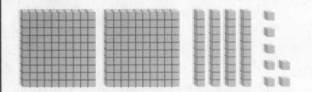

Hundreds	Tens	Ones
2	4	7

247

200 + 40 + 7

Share and Show

Write how many hundreds, tens, and ones are in the model. Write the number in two ways.

1.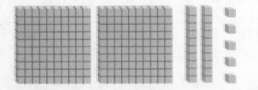

Hundreds	Tens	Ones

_____

_____ + _____ + _____

 2.

Hundreds	Tens	Ones

_____

_____ + _____ + _____

 3.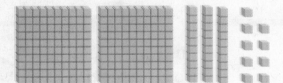

Hundreds	Tens	Ones

_____

_____ + _____ + _____

On Your Own

Write how many hundreds, tens, and ones are in the model. Write the number in two ways.

4.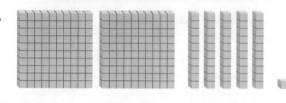

Hundreds	Tens	Ones

_____

_____ + _____ + _____

5.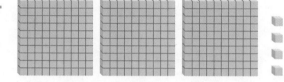

Hundreds	Tens	Ones

_____

_____ + _____ + _____

6.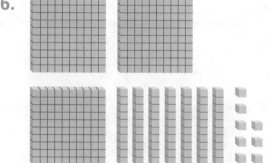

Hundreds	Tens	Ones

_____

_____ + _____ + _____

7.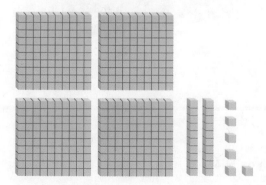

Hundreds	Tens	Ones

_____

_____ + _____ + _____

Chapter 2 · Lesson 4

PROBLEM SOLVING

Write the number that answers
the riddle. Use the chart.

8. A model for my number has
4 ones blocks, 5 tens blocks,
and 1 hundreds block.
What number am I?

Hundreds	Tens	Ones

_____

9. **H.O.T.** The hundreds digit
of my number is greater than
the tens digit. The ones digit is
less than the tens digit. What
could my number be? Write it
in two ways.

_____ + _____ + _____

_____

10. ⭐**Test Prep** Karen has 279 pictures.
How many hundreds are in this number?

○   2 hundreds

○   7 hundreds

○   9 hundreds

○   18 hundreds

TAKE HOME ACTIVITY • Say a 3-digit number, such as 546.
Have your child draw a quick picture for that number.

FOR MORE PRACTICE:
Standards Practice Book, pp. P31–P32

Place Value to 1,000

Essential Question How do you know the values of the digits in numbers?

COMMON CORE STANDARD **CC.2.NBT.1**
Understand place value.

Listen and Draw REAL WORLD

Write the numbers. Then draw quick pictures.

_____ sheets of color paper

Hundreds	Tens	Ones

_____ sheets of plain paper

Hundreds	Tens	Ones

FOR THE TEACHER • Read the following. There are 245 sheets of color paper in the supply closet. There are 458 sheets of plain paper by the computer table. Have children write each number and draw quick pictures to show the numbers.

Math Talk
Describe how 5 tens is different from 5 hundreds.

MATHEMATICAL PRACTICES

Model and Draw

The place of a digit in a number tells its value.

327

The 3 in 327 has a value of 3 hundreds, or 300.

The 2 in 327 has a value of 2 tens, or 20.

The 7 in 327 has a value of 7 ones, or 7.

There are 10 hundreds in 1 **thousand**.

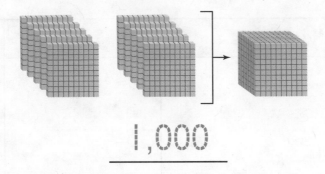

1,000

The 1 is in the thousands place and has a value of 1 thousand.

Share and Show

Circle the value or the meaning of the red digit.

1. 702	2 ones	2 tens	2 hundreds
✓ 2. 459	500	50	5
✓ 3. 362	3 hundreds	3 tens	3 ones

Name _____

On Your Own

Circle the value or the meaning of the red digit.

4. 549	400	40	4
5. 607	7 ones	7 tens	7 hundreds
6. 1,000	1 one	1 hundred	1 thousand
7. 914	90	900	9,000
8. 380	800	80	8
9. 692	6 ones	6 tens	6 hundreds

 Write the number that matches the clues.

10. Clues:

- The value of my hundreds digit is 300.

- The value of my tens digit is 0.

- The value of my ones digit is an even number greater than 7.

The number is _____.

PROBLEM SOLVING REAL WORLD

11. Richard is making a Venn diagram. Where in the diagram should he write the other numbers?

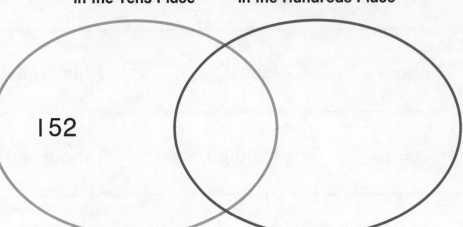

Numbers with a 5 in the Tens Place

Numbers with a 2 in the Hundreds Place

152

~~152~~
215
454
257
352
205
250

12. **H.O.T.** Describe where 752 should be written in the diagram. Explain your answer.

_____

_____

_____

13. ⭐ **Test Prep** Which of these numbers has the digit 4 in the tens place?

○ 64
○ 149
○ 437
○ 504

TAKE HOME ACTIVITY • Ask your child to write 3-digit numbers, such as "a number with 2 hundreds" and "a number with a 9 in the ones place."

FOR MORE PRACTICE:
Standards Practice Book, pp. P33–P34

Name _____

Number Names

Essential Question How do you write 3-digit numbers using words?

COMMON CORE STANDARD CC.2.NBT.3
Understand place value.

Listen and Draw

Write the missing numbers in the chart. Then find and circle the word form of these numbers below.

	12	13		15	16	17	18	19	20
21	22	23	24	25	26	27	28		30
31	32	33	34		36	37	38	39	40
41	42	43	44	45		47	48	49	50
51		53	54	55	56	57	58	59	60

forty-one	ninety-two	fourteen
eleven	thirty-five	forty-six
fifty-three	twenty-nine	fifty-two

Math Talk
Describe how to use words to write the number with a 5 in the tens place and a 7 in the ones place.

MATHEMATICAL PRACTICES

HOME CONNECTION • In this activity, your child reviewed the word form of numbers less than 100.

Chapter 2

Model and Draw

You can use words to write 3-digit numbers.
First, look at the hundreds digit. Then, look at
the tens digit and ones digit together.

245
two hundred forty-five

713
seven hundred thirteen

Share and Show

Write the number using words.

1. 506

five hundred six
_____

2. 189

_____

☑ 3. 328

_____

Write the number.

4. four hundred fifteen

_____

5. two hundred ninety-one

_____

6. six hundred three

_____

☑ 7. eight hundred forty-seven

_____

On Your Own

Write the number.

8. five hundred eighty

_____

9. one hundred fifty-five

_____

10. seven hundred seventeen

_____

11. three hundred ninety

_____

12. six hundred forty-three

_____

13. nine hundred twelve

_____

14. four hundred twenty-six

_____

15. eight hundred seventy-one

_____

Write the number using words.

16. 200

_____

17. 632

_____

18. 568

_____

19. 321

_____

PROBLEM SOLVING REAL WORLD

Write Math

Circle the answer for each problem.

20. Derek counts one hundred ninety cars. Which is another way to write this number?

119

190

910

21. Alma counted two hundred sixty-eight leaves. Which is another way to write this number?

$2 + 6 + 8$

$20 + 60 + 8$

$200 + 60 + 8$

22. **H.O.T.** My 3-digit number has a 4 in the hundreds place. It has a greater digit in the tens place than in the ones place. The sum of the digits is 6. What is my number? _____

Write the number using words.

_____

23. ⭐ **Test Prep** There are five hundred thirty-seven chairs at the school. Which shows this number?

○ 573

○ 537

○ 530

○ 357

 TAKE HOME ACTIVITY · Ask your child to write the number 940 using words.

FOR MORE PRACTICE:
Standards Practice Book, pp. P35–P36

Name _____

Different Forms of Numbers

Essential Question What are three ways to write a 3-digit number?

COMMON CORE STANDARD CC.2.NBT.3
Understand place value.

Listen and Draw REAL WORLD

Write the number. Use the digits to write how many hundreds, tens, and ones.

_____ hundreds _____ tens _____ ones

_____ hundreds _____ tens _____ ones

_____ hundreds _____ tens _____ ones

FOR THE TEACHER • Read the following: Evan has 426 marbles. How many hundreds, tens, and ones are in 426? Continue the activity for 204 and 341.

Math Talk
How many hundreds are in 368? **Explain.**

MATHEMATICAL PRACTICES

Model and Draw

You can use a quick picture to show a number.
You can write a number in different ways.

five hundred thirty-six

__5__ hundreds __3__ tens __6__ ones

__500__ + __30__ + __6__

__536__

Share and Show

Read the number and draw a quick picture.
Then write the number in different ways.

1. four hundred seven

____ hundreds ____ tens ____ ones

_____ + _____ + _____

_____

2. three hundred twenty-five

____ hundreds ____ tens ____ ones

_____ + _____ + _____

_____

3. two hundred fifty-three

____ hundreds ____ tens ____ ones

_____ + _____ + _____

_____

Name _____

On Your Own

Read the number and draw a quick picture.
Then write the number in different ways.

4. one hundred seventy-two

_____ hundred _____ tens _____ ones

_____ + _____ + _____

_____

5. three hundred forty-six

_____ hundreds _____ tens _____ ones

_____ + _____ + _____

_____

6. two hundred sixty-four

_____ hundreds _____ tens _____ ones

_____ + _____ + _____

_____

Use words to write a number that matches the clue.

7. **H.O.T.** In this 3-digit number, there is a zero in the ones place.

_____

TAKE HOME ACTIVITY · Ask your child to show
the number 315 in three different ways.

Chapter 2 · Lesson 7

FOR MORE PRACTICE:
Standards Practice Book, pp. P37–P38

eighty-three **83**

Name _____

✔ Mid-Chapter Checkpoint

Concepts and Skills

Circle tens to make 1 hundred. Write the number
in different ways. (CC.2.NBT.1)

1.

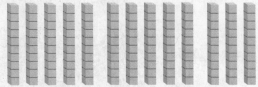

_____ tens

_____ hundred _____ tens

_____

Write how many hundreds, tens, and ones are in
the model. Write the number in two ways. (CC.2.NBT.1)

2.

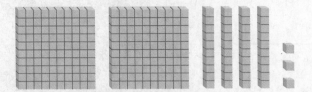

Hundreds	Tens	Ones

_____

_____ + _____ + _____

Circle the value or the meaning of the red digit. (CC.2.NBT.1)

3. 528	5	50	500

4. 674	4 ones	4 tens	4 hundreds

⭐ Test Prep

5. Which is another way to write
the number 645? (CC.2.NBT.3)

○ six hundred forty-five

○ 600 + 4 + 5

○ six hundred fourteen

○ 60 + 40 + 5

Name _____

Algebra • Different Ways to Show Numbers

COMMON CORE STANDARD CC.2.NBT.3
Understand place value.

Essential Question How can you use blocks or quick pictures to show the value of a number in different ways?

Listen and Draw REAL WORLD

Draw quick pictures to solve.
Write how many tens and ones.

_____ tens _____ ones

_____ tens _____ ones

FOR THE TEACHER • Read this problem to children. Mrs. Peabody has 35 books on a cart to take to classrooms. She can use boxes that each hold 10 books and she can also place single books on the cart. What are two different ways she can put the books on the cart?

Math Talk
Describe how you found different ways to show 35 books.

MATHEMATICAL PRACTICES

Model and Draw

Here are two ways to show 148.

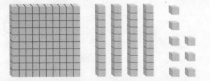

Hundreds	Tens	Ones
1	4	8

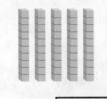

Hundreds	Tens	Ones
0	14	8

Share and Show

Write how many hundreds, tens, and ones are in the model.

✓1. 213

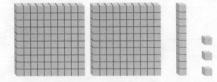

Hundreds	Tens	Ones

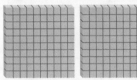

Hundreds	Tens	Ones

✓2. 132

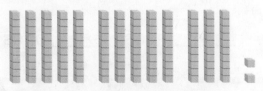

Hundreds	Tens	Ones

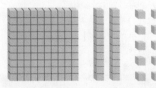

Hundreds	Tens	Ones

Name _____

On Your Own

Write how many hundreds, tens, and ones are in the model.

3. 144

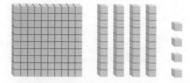

Hundreds	Tens	Ones

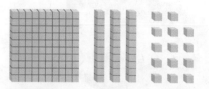

Hundreds	Tens	Ones

4. 204

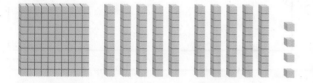

Hundreds	Tens	Ones

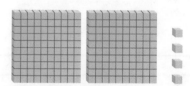

Hundreds	Tens	Ones

5. 157

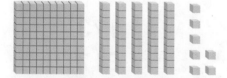

Hundreds	Tens	Ones

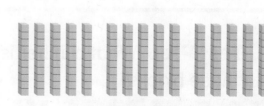

Hundreds	Tens	Ones

PROBLEM SOLVING REAL WORLD

Write Math

Marbles are sold in boxes, in bags, or as single marbles. Each box has 10 bags of marbles in it. Each bag has 10 marbles in it.

6. Draw pictures to show two ways to buy 324 marbles.

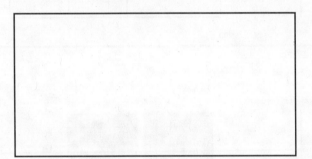 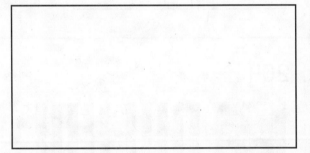

7. **H.O.T.** There is only one box of marbles in the store. There are many bags of marbles and single marbles. Draw a picture to show a way to buy 312 marbles.

8. ⭐ **Test Prep** What number is shown with these blocks?

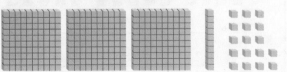

    ○ 173
    ○ 317
    ○ 318
    ○ 327

TAKE HOME ACTIVITY • Write the number 156. Have your child draw quick pictures of two ways to show this number.

FOR MORE PRACTICE:
Standards Practice Book, pp. P39–P40

Name _____

Count On and Count Back by 10 and 100

Essential Question How do you use place value to find 10 more, 10 less, 100 more, or 100 less than a 3-digit number?

COMMON CORE STANDARD CC.2.NBT.8
Use place value understanding and properties of operations to add and subtract.

Listen and Draw REAL WORLD

Draw quick pictures for the numbers.

Girls

Hundreds	Tens	Ones

Boys

Hundreds	Tens	Ones

Math Talk
Describe how the two numbers are different.

MATHEMATICAL PRACTICES

FOR THE TEACHER • Tell children that there are 342 girls at Center School. Have children draw quick pictures for 342. Then tell them that there are 352 boys at the school. Have them draw quick pictures for 352.

Model and Draw

You can show 10 less or 10 more than a number by changing the digit in the tens place.

10 less than 264

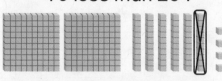

Hundreds	Tens	Ones
2	5	4

10 more than 264

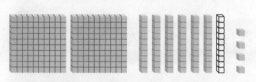

Hundreds	Tens	Ones
2	7	4

You can show 100 less or 100 more than a number by changing the digit in the hundreds place.

100 less than 264

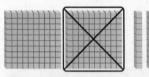

Hundreds	Tens	Ones
1	6	4

100 more than 264

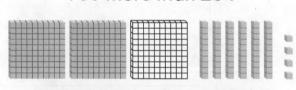

Hundreds	Tens	Ones
3	6	4

Share and Show

Write the number.

1. 10 more than 648

_____

2. 100 less than 513

_____

3. 100 more than 329

_____

4. 10 less than 827

_____

Name _____

On Your Own

Write the number.

5. 10 more than 471

_____

6. 10 less than 143

_____

7. 100 more than 555

_____

8. 100 less than 757

_____

9. 100 more than 900

_____

10. 10 less than 689

_____

11. 100 less than 712

_____

12. 10 less than 254

_____

13. 10 more than 986

_____

14. 100 less than 392

_____

15. 100 more than 485

_____

16. 10 more than 820

_____

 Write numbers to make each sentence true.

17. 854 is _____ more than 844.

18. _____ is 100 less than 352 and 100 more than _____.

19. _____ is _____ more than 751.

PROBLEM SOLVING REAL WORLD

Write Math

Solve.

20. Juan's book has 248 pages. This is 10 more pages than there are in Kevin's book. How many pages are in Kevin's book?

_____ pages

21. There are 217 pictures in Tina's book. There are 100 fewer pictures in Mark's book. How many pictures are in Mark's book?

_____ pictures

22. **H.O.T.** Use the clues to answer the question.

Clues:

- Shawn reads 213 pages.
- Maria reads 100 more pages than Shawn.
- Gavin reads 10 fewer pages than Maria.

How many pages does Gavin read?

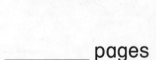

_____ pages

23. ⭐ **Test Prep** Which number is 100 more than 786?

- ○ 686
- ○ 776
- ○ 796
- ○ 886

TAKE HOME ACTIVITY • Write the number 596. Have your child name the number that is 100 more than 596.

FOR MORE PRACTICE:
Standards Practice Book, pp. P41–P42

Name _____

Algebra • Number Patterns

Essential Question How does place value help you identify and extend counting patterns?

COMMON CORE STANDARD CC.2.NBT.8
Use place value understanding and properties of operations to add and subtract.

Listen and Draw  REAL WORLD

Shade the numbers in the counting pattern.

801	802	803	804	805	806	807	808	809	810
811	812	813	814	815	816	817	818	819	820
821	822	823	824	825	826	827	828	829	830
831	832	833	834	835	836	837	838	839	840
841	842	843	844	845	846	847	848	849	850
851	852	853	854	855	856	857	858	859	860
861	862	863	864	865	866	867	868	869	870
871	872	873	874	875	876	877	878	879	880
881	882	883	884	885	886	887	888	889	890
891	892	893	894	895	896	897	898	899	900

FOR THE TEACHER • Read the following problem and discuss how children can use a counting pattern to solve. At Blossom Bakery, 823 muffins were sold in the morning. In the afternoon, four packages of 10 muffins were sold. How many muffins were sold that day?

Math Talk
What number is next in the counting pattern you see? Explain.

MATHEMATICAL PRACTICES

Look at the digits in the numbers. What two numbers are next in the counting pattern?

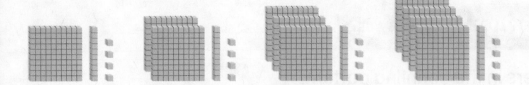

114,   214,   314,   414,   , ▮

The _____ digit changes by one each time.

The next two numbers are _____ and _____.

Share and Show

Look at the digits to find the next two numbers.

1. 137, 147, 157, 167, ▮, ▮

   The next two numbers are _____ and _____.

   _____

2. 245, 345, 445, 545, ▮, ▮

   The next two numbers are _____ and _____.

   _____

☑ 3. 421, 431, 441, 451, ▮, ▮

   The next two numbers are _____ and _____.

   _____

☑ 4. 389, 489, 589, 689, ▮, ▮

   The next two numbers are _____ and _____.

Name _____

On Your Own

Look at the digits to find the next two numbers.

5. 193, 293, 393, 493, ,

The next two numbers are _____ and _____.

6. 484, 494, 504, 514, ▪, ▪

The next two numbers are _____ and _____.

7. 500, 600, 700, 800, ▪, ▪

The next two numbers are _____ and _____.

8. 655, 665, 675, 685, ▪, ▪

The next two numbers are _____ and _____.

H.O.T. Follow the directions. Write your own counting patterns.

9. Write a pattern in which the hundreds digit changes by one from number to number.

_____, _____, _____, _____, _____

10. Write a pattern in which the tens digit changes by one from number to number.

_____, _____, _____, _____, _____

PROBLEM SOLVING REAL WORLD

Write Math

Solve.

11. Luke wrote a number pattern starting with 237. He counted on by hundreds. Write the missing digits to show his pattern.

$\underline{2}\ \underline{3}\ \underline{7}$, $\underline{\ \ }\ \underline{3}\ \underline{\ \ }$, $\underline{\ \ }\ \underline{3}\ \underline{\ \ }$, $\underline{\ \ }\ \underline{5}\ \underline{\ \ }$, $\underline{\ \ }\ \underline{\ \ }\ \underline{7}$

12. **H.O.T.** There were 135 pennies in a jar. After Robin put more pennies into the jar, there were 175 pennies in the jar. How many groups of 10 pennies did she put into the jar?

_____ groups of 10 pennies

Explain how you solved the problem.

_____

_____

_____

13. ⭐ **Test Prep** Sandra wrote a number pattern starting with 806. She counted on by tens. Which of the following numbers could be in her pattern?

○ 706
○ 810
○ 826
○ 960

TAKE HOME ACTIVITY · With your child, take turns writing number patterns in which you count on by tens or by hundreds.

FOR MORE PRACTICE:
Standards Practice Book, pp. P43–P44

Name _____

Problem Solving • Compare Numbers

Essential Question How can you make a model to solve a problem about comparing numbers?

COMMON CORE STANDARD CC.2.NBT.4
Understand place value.

Children bought 217 cartons of chocolate milk and 188 cartons of plain milk. Did they buy more cartons of chocolate milk or plain milk?

Unlock the Problem REAL WORLD

What do I need to find?

if the children bought ___more___
~~cartons of chocolate milk~~
~~or plain milk~~

What information do I need to use?

_____ cartons of chocolate milk

_____ cartons of plain milk

Show how to solve the problem.
Model the numbers. Draw quick pictures of your models.

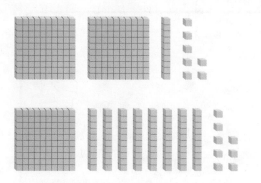

The children bought more cartons of _____ milk.

HOME CONNECTION • Your child used base-ten blocks to represent the numbers in the problem. These models were used as a tool for comparing numbers to solve the problem.

Try Another Problem

Model the numbers. Draw quick pictures
to show how you solved the problem.

- What do I need
  to find?
- What information
  do I need to use?

1. At the zoo, there are 137 birds and
   142 reptiles. Are there more birds
   or more reptiles at the zoo?   more _____

2. Tom's book has 105 pages.
   Delia's book has 109 pages.
   Whose book has fewer pages?   _____ book

Math Talk

Explain what you
did to solve the
second problem.

MATHEMATICAL
PRACTICES

Name _____

Share and Show

Model the numbers. Draw quick pictures
to show how you solved the problem.

☑ **3.** Mary's puzzle has
164 pieces. Jake's puzzle
has 180 pieces. Whose
puzzle has more pieces?

_____ puzzle

☑ **4.** There are 246 children at
Dan's school. There are
251 children at Karen's
school. At which school are
there fewer children?

_____ school

5. There are 131 crayons in a
box. There are 128 crayons in
a bag. Are there more crayons
in the box or in the bag?

in the _____

6. There are 308 books in
the first room. There are
273 books in the second
room. In which room are
there fewer books?

in the _____ room

On Your Own

Choose a way to solve.
Write or draw to explain.

7. Ms. Tyler sold 125 small cards and 118 large cards. Did she sell fewer small cards or fewer large cards?

fewer _____ cards

8. A number has a 1 in the tens place. Which of these could be the number? Circle it.

three hundred fifty-one

one hundred fifty

three hundred fifteen

9. **H.O.T.** Which of these is another way to write the number 257? Circle it.

2 hundreds 57 tens

25 tens 7 ones

25 hundreds 7 ones

10. ⭐ **Test Prep** Corey's book has 256 pages. Which of these numbers is greater than 256?

○ 157
○ 239
○ 281
○ 198

TAKE HOME ACTIVITY · Ask your child to explain how he or she solved one of the problems on this page.

FOR MORE PRACTICE:
Standards Practice Book, pp. P45–P46

Name _____

Algebra • Compare Numbers

Essential Question How do you compare
3-digit numbers?

COMMON CORE STANDARD **CC.2.NBT.4**
Understand place value.

Listen and Draw

Draw quick pictures to solve the problem.

More _____ were at the park.

FOR THE TEACHER • Read the following problem
and have children draw quick pictures to compare
the numbers. There were 125 butterflies and
132 birds at the park. Were there more butterflies
or more birds at the park?

Math Talk

Explain how
you compared
the numbers.

MATHEMATICAL
PRACTICES

Model and Draw

Use place value to **compare** numbers.
Start by looking at the digits in the
greatest place value position first.

Hundreds	Tens	Ones
4	8	3
5	7	0

4 hundreds < 5 hundreds

483 $<$ 570

Hundreds	Tens	Ones
3	5	2
3	4	6

The hundreds are equal.

5 tens > 4 tens

352 $>$ 346

Share and Show

Compare the numbers. Write >, <, or =.

1.

Hundreds	Tens	Ones
2	3	9
1	7	9

239 $\bigcirc$ 179

2.

Hundreds	Tens	Ones
4	3	5
4	3	7

435 $\bigcirc$ 437

✓3. 764
674

764 $\bigcirc$ 674

✓4. 519
572

519 $\bigcirc$ 572

On Your Own

Compare the numbers. Write >, <, or =.

5. 378
    504

    378 ◯ 504

6. 821
    821

    821 ◯ 821

7. 560
    439

    560 ◯ 439

8. 934
    943

    934 ◯ 943

9. 475
    475

    475 ◯ 475

10. 736
    687

    736 ◯ 687

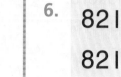 Write a 3-digit number in the box that makes the comparison true.

11. 526 < [ ]

12. 319 > [ ]

13. [ ] > 782

14. [ ] < 131

© Houghton Mifflin Harcourt Publishing Company

PROBLEM SOLVING REAL WORLD

Write Math

Solve. Write or draw to explain.

15. Mrs. York has 358 stickers.
Mr. Reed has 372 stickers.
Who has more stickers?

_____

16. **H.O.T.** Seth has some number cards.
Use the digits on these cards to make
two 3-digit numbers. Use each card
only once. Compare the numbers.

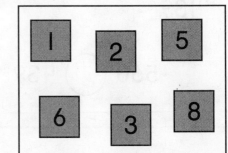

_____ ◯ _____

17. ⭐ **Test Prep** Which of the following is true?

- ◯ 453 > 354
- ◯ 253 < 164
- ◯ 391 > 417
- ◯ 528 < 490

TAKE HOME ACTIVITY • Have your child explain how to
compare the numbers 281 and 157.

FOR MORE PRACTICE:
Standards Practice Book, pp. P47–P48

Name _____

✅ Chapter 2 Review/Test

Vocabulary

Use a word in the box to complete each sentence.

| hundred |
| thousand |
| ten |

1. 10 hundreds is the same as

   1 _____. (p. 74)

2. 10 tens is the same as 1 _____. (p. 58)

Concepts and Skills

Write how many tens. Circle groups of 10 tens.
Write how many hundreds. Write the number. (CC.2.NBT.1a, CC.2.NBT.1b)

3.

   _____ tens

   _____ hundreds

   _____

Read the number and draw a quick picture.
Then write the number in different ways. (CC.2.NBT.3)

4. two hundred thirty-five

   _____ hundreds _____ tens _____ ones

   _____ + _____ + _____

   _____

Look at the digits to find the next two numbers. (CC.2.NBT.8)

5. 267, 367, 467, 567, ▪, ▪

The next two numbers are _____ and _____.

Chapter 2

one hundred five **105**

Fill in the bubble for the correct answer choice.

6. Which is another way to name 14 tens? (CC.2.NBT.1)

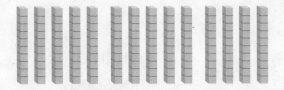

- ○ I ten 4 ones
- ○ I hundred 4 tens
- ○ I thousand 4 hundreds
- ○ 14 ones

7. There is a 3-digit number that has the digit 3 in the ones place, the digit 2 in the tens place, and the digit 4 in the hundreds place. What is the number? (CC.2.NBT.1)

- ○ 324
- ○ 342
- ○ 423
- ○ 432

8. Dylan has 324 baseball cards. Malia has 351 baseball cards.

Which of the following is true? (CC.2.NBT.4)

- ○ 324 > 351
- ○ 324 < 351
- ○ 324 > 432
- ○ 351 < 243

Fill in the bubble for the correct answer choice.

9. **What number is shown with these blocks?** (CC.2.NBT.3)

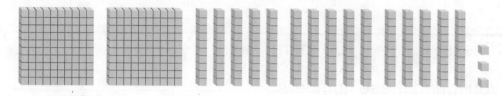

- ○ 173
- ○ 253
- ○ 353
- ○ 380

10. Mr. Grant has 437 sheets of paper. Ms. Kim has 100 fewer sheets of paper than Mr. Grant. How many sheets of paper does Ms. Kim have? (CC.2.NBT.8)

- ○ 337
- ○ 427
- ○ 447
- ○ 537

11. Which is another way to write the number 582? (CC.2.NBT.3)

- ○ five hundred eighteen
- ○ 500 + 8 + 2
- ○ five hundred twenty-eight
- ○ 500 + 80 + 2

Constructed Response

12. Write the number that is 10 less than 357
and the number that is 100 more than 357. (CC.2.NBT.8)

_____   _____
10 less   100 more

Explain how you found these numbers.

_____

_____

_____

Performance Task (CC.2.NBT.1a, CC.2.NBT.3)

13. There are 100 books on the shelves. On the
table, there are 15 stacks of books with
10 books in each stack. What 3-digit number
tells how many books there are? _____

Draw a picture to explain your answer.

What are two other ways to write this number?

_____   _____

All About Animals

by John Hudson

COMMON CORE

CRITICAL AREA Building fluency with addition and subtraction

The giraffe is the tallest land animal in the world. Adult giraffes are 13 to 17 feet tall. Newborn giraffes are about 6 feet tall.

A group of 5 giraffes drinks water at a watering hole. A group of 5 giraffes eats leaves from trees. How many giraffes are there in all?

_____ giraffes

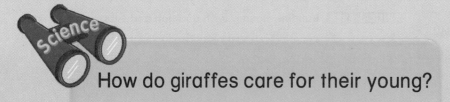

How do giraffes care for their young?

The ostrich is the largest bird in the world. Ostriches cannot fly, but they can run fast. Ostrich eggs weigh about 3 pounds each! Several ostriches will lay eggs in a shared nest.

There are 6 eggs in a nest. Then 5 more eggs are put in that nest. How many eggs are in the nest now?

_____ eggs

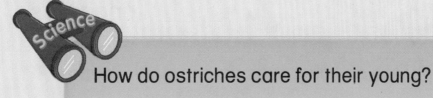

How do ostriches care for their young?

Kangaroos can move quickly by jumping with their two back legs. When they are moving slowly, they use all four legs.

Western gray kangaroos live in groups called mobs. There are 8 kangaroos in a mob. 4 more kangaroos join the mob. How many kangaroos are in the mob in all?

_____ kangaroos

How do kangaroos care for their young?

Wild boars like to eat roots. They use their tough snouts to dig. Wild boars can be up to 6 feet long.

Wild boars live in groups called sounders. There is one sounder of 14 boars. If 7 of the boars are eating, how many boars are not eating?

_____ boars

How do wild boars care for their young?

Moose are the largest kind of deer. Male moose have antlers that may be 5 to 6 feet wide. Moose can trot and gallop. They are also good swimmers!

A ranger saw 7 moose in the morning and 6 moose in the afternoon. How many moose did the ranger see that day?

_____ moose

How do moose care for their young?

Write About the Story

Choose one kind of animal.
Draw a picture and write your own
story about that kind of animal.
Use addition in your story.

Vocabulary Review

add   in all

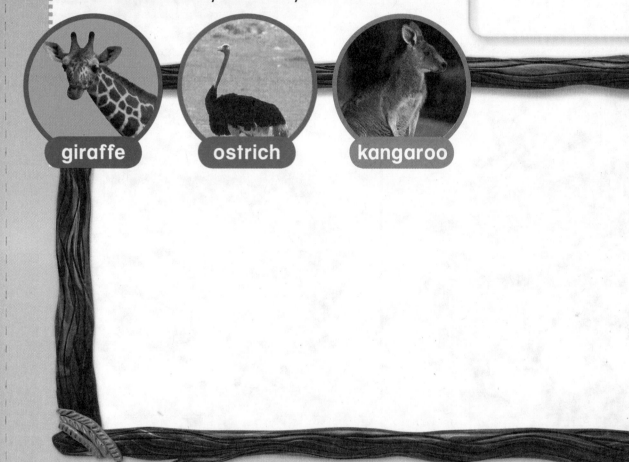

giraffe   ostrich   kangaroo

Write Math

_____

_____

_____

_____

How many eggs are there?

Draw more ostrich eggs in each nest.
Write an addition sentence below each
nest to show how many eggs are in
each nest now.

_____

_____

 Choose a different animal from the story.
Write another story that uses addition.

116

Basic Facts and Relationships

Curious About Math with

Curious George

Parrot fish live near coral reefs in tropical ocean waters. They use their sharp teeth to scrape food off of the coral.

Suppose 10 parrot fish are eating at a coral reef. 3 of the fish swim away. How many fish are still eating?

Show What You Know

Use Symbols to Add

Use the picture. Use + and = to complete the addition sentence.

1.

$3 \bigcirc 1 \bigcirc 4$

2.

$2 \bigcirc 3 \bigcirc 5$

Sums to 10

Write the sum.

3. $\begin{array}{r} 4 \\ +3 \\ \hline \end{array}$ 4. $\begin{array}{r} 5 \\ +0 \\ \hline \end{array}$ 5. $\begin{array}{r} 2 \\ +7 \\ \hline \end{array}$ 6. $\begin{array}{r} 6 \\ +2 \\ \hline \end{array}$ 7. $\begin{array}{r} 9 \\ +1 \\ \hline \end{array}$

Doubles and Doubles Plus One

Write the addition sentence.

8.

___ $\bigcirc$ ___ $\bigcirc$ ___

9.

___ $\bigcirc$ ___ $\bigcirc$ ___

 Family note: This page checks your child's understanding of important skills needed for success in Chapter 3.

 GO Online   Assessment Options
Soar to Success Math

Vocabulary Builder

Review Words
addition
subtraction
plus
minus
equals
count on
count back

Visualize It

Sort the review words in the graphic organizer.

Addition Words   **Subtraction** Words

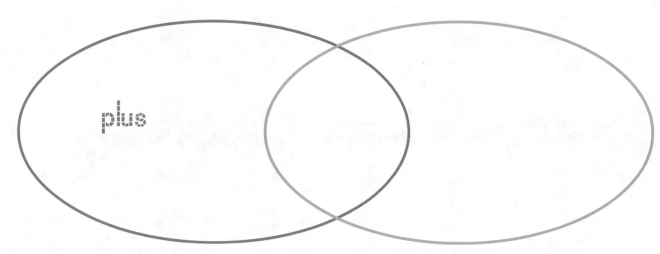

plus

Understand Vocabulary

1. Circle the **addition** sentence. $3 + 6 = 9$ $9 - 6 = 3$

2. Circle the **subtraction** sentence. $8 + 2 = 10$ $10 - 2 = 8$

3. Circle the **count on** fact. $5 - 1 = 4$ $4 + 1 = 5$

4. Circle the **count back** fact. $8 - 2 = 6$ $6 + 2 = 8$

GO Online
• eStudent Edition
• Multimedia eGlossary

Game Caterpillar Chase

Materials

- 1
- 1
- 1

Play with a partner.

① Put your cube on START.

② Toss the , and move that many spaces.

③ Say the sum or difference. Your partner checks your answer.

④ Take turns. The first person to get to FINISH wins.

FINISH

$$7 + 3$$

$$3 - 1$$

$$3 + 4$$

$$6 - 0$$

$$5 + 2$$

$$2 + 4$$

$$1 + 6$$

$$4 - 1$$

$$3 + 0$$

$$6 - 3$$

$$5 - 2$$

$$5 - 5$$

$$7 - 4$$

$$3 + 5$$

$$0 + 4$$

$$7 - 5$$

$$2 + 3$$

$$5 - 3$$

START

$$4 + 4$$

$$6 - 1$$

$$2 + 2$$

$$5 + 3$$

$$8 - 2$$

Use Doubles Facts

Essential Question How can you use doubles facts to find sums for near doubles facts?

COMMON CORE STANDARD CC.2.OA.2
Add and subtract within 20.

Listen and Draw REAL WORLD

Draw a picture to show the problem. Then write an addition sentence for the problem.

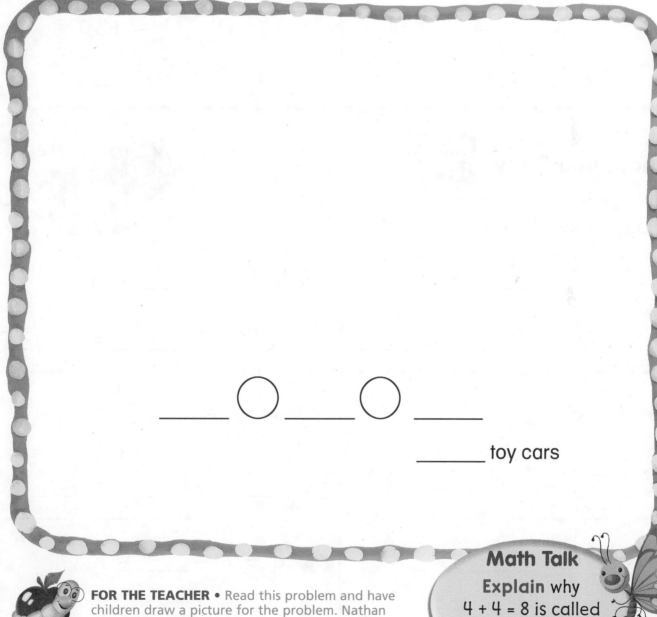

_____ ◯ _____ ◯ _____

_____ toy cars

FOR THE TEACHER • Read this problem and have children draw a picture for the problem. Nathan has 6 toy cars. Alisha gives him 6 more toy cars. How many toy cars does Nathan have now? After children write an addition sentence, have them name other doubles facts that they know.

Math Talk
Explain why 4 + 4 = 8 is called a doubles fact.
MATHEMATICAL PRACTICES

Chapter 3

You can use doubles facts to find **sums** for other facts.

$3 + 4 = ?$

$3 + 3 + 1 = ?$

$3 + 3 = 6$

$6 + 1 = 7$

So, $3 + 4 =$ _____.

$7 + 6 = ?$

$7 + 7 - 1 = ?$

$7 + 7 = 14$

$14 - 1 = 13$

So, $7 + 6 =$ _____.

Share and Show

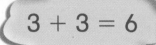

Write a doubles fact you can use to find the sum. Write the sum.

1. $2 + 3 =$ _____

   _____ + _____ = _____

2. $4 + 5 =$ _____

   _____ + _____ = _____

3. $4 + 3 =$ _____

   _____ + _____ = _____

4. $6 + 7 =$ _____

   _____ + _____ = _____

5. $5 + 6 =$ _____

   _____ + _____ = _____

6. $8 + 7 =$ _____

   _____ + _____ = _____

Name _____

On Your Own

Write a doubles fact you can use
to find the sum. Write the sum.

7. 3 + 2 = _____

_____ + _____ = _____

8. 6 + 5 = _____

_____ + _____ = _____

9. 5 + 4 = _____

_____ + _____ = _____

10. 3 + 4 = _____

_____ + _____ = _____

11. 6 + 7 = _____

_____ + _____ = _____

12. 7 + 8 = _____

_____ + _____ = _____

13. 8 + 9 = _____

_____ + _____ = _____

14. 5 + 6 = _____

_____ + _____ = _____

15. 7 + 6 = _____

_____ + _____ = _____

16. 9 + 8 = _____

_____ + _____ = _____

PROBLEM SOLVING REAL WORLD

Write Math

Solve. Write or draw to explain.

17. Andrea has 8 red buttons and 9 blue buttons. How many buttons does Andrea have?

_____ buttons

18. Henry sees 3 rabbits. Callie sees double that number of rabbits. How many rabbits does Callie see?

_____ rabbits

19. H.O.T. Mr. Norris wrote a doubles fact. It has a sum greater than 6. The numbers that he added are each less than 6. What fact might he have written?

_____

20. ⭐ **Test Prep** There are 7 blue hats and 6 red hats on a store shelf. How many hats are on the shelf?

○ 14
○ 13
○ 12
○ 10

TAKE HOME ACTIVITY • Ask your child to write three different doubles facts with sums less than 17.

124 one hundred twenty-four

FOR MORE PRACTICE:
Standards Practice Book, pp. P53–P54

Practice Addition Facts

Essential Question What are some ways to remember sums?

COMMON CORE STANDARD CC.2.OA.2
Add and subtract within 20.

Listen and Draw REAL WORLD

Draw pictures to show the problems.

FOR THE TEACHER • Read the following two problems. Have children draw a picture and write a number sentence for each. On Monday, Tony recycled 3 cans and 6 bottles. How many containers did he recycle? On Tuesday, Tony recycled 6 cans and 3 bottles. How many containers did he recycle?

Math Talk
Explain how the two problems are alike. **Explain** how they are different.
MATHEMATICAL PRACTICES

Model and Draw

These are some ways to remember facts.

> You can count on
> 1, 2, or 3.

$6 + 1 = \underline{7}$

$6 + 2 = \underline{8}$

$6 + 3 = \underline{9}$

> Changing the order of the **addends** does not change the sum.

$\underline{8} = 2 + 6$

$\underline{8} = 6 + 2$

Share and Show

Write the sums.

1. $2 + 2 = \underline{}$

   $2 + 3 = \underline{}$

2. $5 + 0 = \underline{}$

   $2 + 0 = \underline{}$

3. $3 + 8 = \underline{}$

   $8 + 3 = \underline{}$

4. $\underline{} = 4 + 4$

   $\underline{} = 4 + 3$

5. $5 + 7 = \underline{}$

   $7 + 5 = \underline{}$

6. $\underline{} = 7 + 7$

   $\underline{} = 7 + 8$

7. $\underline{} = 3 + 7$

   $\underline{} = 7 + 3$

8. $9 + 3 = \underline{}$

   $3 + 9 = \underline{}$

9. $\underline{} = 6 + 6$

   $\underline{} = 6 + 5$

On Your Own

Write the sums.

10. 7 + 1 = ____

    1 + 7 = ____

11. ____ = 4 + 0

    ____ = 9 + 0

12. 5 + 5 = ____

    5 + 4 = ____

13. 8 + 2 = ____

    2 + 8 = ____

14. 3 + 3 = ____

    3 + 4 = ____

15. 7 + 8 = ____

    8 + 7 = ____

16. ____ = 4 + 1

    ____ = 1 + 4

17. 0 + 7 = ____

    0 + 6 = ____

18. 8 + 8 = ____

    8 + 9 = ____

19. 5 + 3 = ____

    3 + 5 = ____

20. ____ = 9 + 9

    ____ = 9 + 8

21. 6 + 7 = ____

    7 + 6 = ____

Find the addends for each shaded box in the addition table. Write the facts for the shaded boxes.

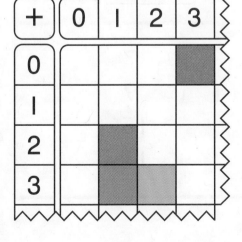

+	0	1	2	3
0				▓
1				
2		▓		
3		▓	▓	

22. ☐ + ☐ = ☐

23. ☐ + ☐ = ☐

24. ☐ + ☐ = ☐

25. ☐ + ☐ = ☐

PROBLEM SOLVING REAL WORLD

Write Math

Solve. Write or draw to explain.

26. Roger builds 4 toy airplanes. Then he builds 3 more toy airplanes. How many toy airplanes does he build?

_____ toy airplanes

27. Joanne made 9 clay bowls last week. She made the same number of clay bowls this week. How many clay bowls did she make in the two weeks?

_____ clay bowls

28. **H.O.T.** Sam painted 3 pictures. Ellie painted twice as many pictures as Sam. How many pictures did they paint?

_____ pictures

29. ⭐ **Test Prep** Chloe draws 8 pictures. Reggie draws 1 more picture than Chloe. How many pictures do they draw?

○ 7
○ 9
○ 15
○ 17

TAKE HOME ACTIVITY · Ask your child to explain how he or she solved Exercise 28.

FOR MORE PRACTICE:
Standards Practice Book, pp. P55–P56

Name _____

Algebra • Make a Ten to Add

Essential Question How is the make a ten strategy used to find sums?

COMMON CORE STANDARD CC.2.OA.2
Add and subtract within 20.

Listen and Draw REAL WORLD

Write the fact below the ten frame when you hear the problem that matches the model.

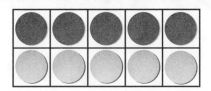

_____

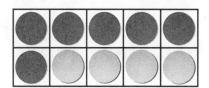

_____

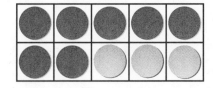

_____

_____

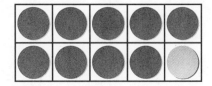

_____

FOR THE TEACHER • Read the following problem. There are 6 dog bones and 4 dog biscuits. How many dog treats are there? Have children find the ten frame that models the problem and write the addition sentence. Repeat by revising the story for each addition fact represented by the other ten frames.

Math Talk
Describe a pattern you see in these make a ten facts.

MATHEMATICAL PRACTICES

© Houghton Mifflin Harcourt Publishing Company

Chapter 3

Model and Draw

$7 + 5 = ?$

You need to add 3 to 7 to make a ten.
Break apart 5 as 3 and 2.

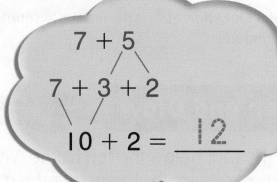

So, $7 + 5 =$ _____.

Share and Show

Show how you can make a ten to find the sum.
Write the sum.

1. $8 + 3 =$ _____

2 1

$10 +$ _____ $=$ _____

2. $2 + 9 =$ _____

1 1

$10 +$ _____ $=$ _____

3. $8 + 5 =$ _____

$10 +$ _____ $=$ _____

4. $4 + 7 =$ _____

$10 +$ _____ $=$ _____

✓ 5. $3 + 9 =$ _____

$10 +$ _____ $=$ _____

✓ 6. $7 + 6 =$ _____

$10 +$ _____ $=$ _____

On Your Own

Show how you can make a ten to find the sum.
Write the sum.

7. $4 + 9 =$ _____

3   1

$10 +$ _____ $=$ _____

8. $9 + 8 =$ _____

1   7

$10 +$ _____ $=$ _____

9. $8 + 6 =$ _____

$10 +$ _____ $=$ _____

10. $5 + 9 =$ _____

$10 +$ _____ $=$ _____

11. $7 + 9 =$ _____

$10 +$ _____ $=$ _____

12. $8 + 4 =$ _____

$10 +$ _____ $=$ _____

13. $9 + 9 =$ _____

$10 +$ _____ $=$ _____

14. $8 + 7 =$ _____

$10 +$ _____ $=$ _____

H.O.T. Write the missing addend that makes
the number sentence true.

15. $9 + 6 =$ _____ $+ 5$

16. $8 + 5 = 10 +$ _____

17. $7 +$ _____ $= 10 + 2$

18. _____ $+ 6 = 10 + 4$

PROBLEM SOLVING REAL WORLD

Write Math

Solve. Write or draw to explain.

19. There are 9 red bicycles at the store. There are 6 yellow bicycles at the store. How many bicycles are at the store?

_____ bicycles

20. There were 5 bees in a hive. Then 9 more bees go into that hive. How many bees are in the hive now?

_____ bees

21. **H.O.T.** Max is thinking of a doubles fact. It has a sum that is greater than the sum of 6 + 4 but less than the sum of 8 + 5. What fact is Max thinking of?

_____ + _____ = _____

22. ⭐ **Test Prep** Natasha had 8 shells. Then she found 5 more shells. How many shells does she have now?

○ 3
○ 12
○ 13
○ 14

TAKE HOME ACTIVITY · Ask your child to name pairs of numbers that have a sum of 10. Then have him or her write the addition sentences.

FOR MORE PRACTICE:
Standards Practice Book, pp. P57–P58

Name _____

Algebra • Add 3 Addends

Essential Question How do you add three numbers?

COMMON CORE STANDARD CC.2.OA.2
Add and subtract within 20.

Listen and Draw

Write the sum of each pair of addends.

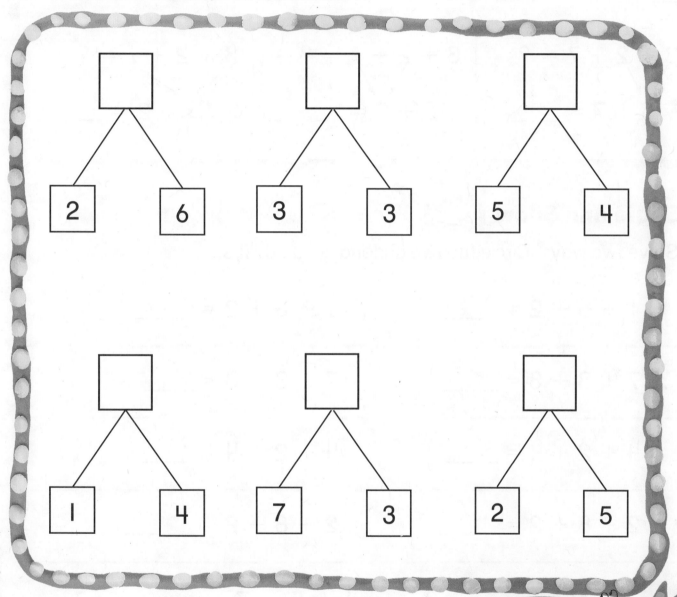

FOR THE TEACHER • After children have recorded the sum of each pair of addends, have them share their answers and discuss the strategies used.

Math Talk
Describe how you found the sum of 5 and 4.

MATHEMATICAL PRACTICES

Chapter 3

one hundred thirty-three **133**

Model and Draw

You can group numbers in different ways to add.

Choose two numbers.
Look for facts you know.

Changing the way the numbers are grouped does not change the sum.

$3 + 2 + 7 = ?$

$5 + 7 = \underline{12}$

$3 + 2 + 7 = ?$

$3 + 9 = \underline{}$

$3 + 2 + 7 = ?$

$10 + 2 = \underline{}$

Share and Show

Solve two ways. Circle the two addends you add first.

1. $1 + 8 + 2 = \underline{}$ $1 + 8 + 2 = \underline{}$

2. $7 + 3 + 3 = \underline{}$ $7 + 3 + 3 = \underline{}$

3. $4 + 2 + 4 = \underline{}$ $4 + 2 + 4 = \underline{}$

☑ 4. $2 + 8 + 2 = \underline{}$ $2 + 8 + 2 = \underline{}$

☑ 5.
$$\begin{array}{r} 3 \\ 2 \\ + 6 \\ \hline \end{array} \qquad \begin{array}{r} 3 \\ 2 \\ + 6 \\ \hline \end{array}$$

6.
$$\begin{array}{r} 7 \\ 0 \\ + 2 \\ \hline \end{array} \qquad \begin{array}{r} 7 \\ 0 \\ + 2 \\ \hline \end{array}$$

Name _____

On Your Own

Solve two ways. Circle the two addends you add first.

7. $4 + 1 + 6 = $ _____ $4 + 1 + 6 = $ _____

8. $4 + 3 + 3 = $ _____ $4 + 3 + 3 = $ _____

9. $1 + 5 + 3 = $ _____ $1 + 5 + 3 = $ _____

10. $6 + 4 + 4 = $ _____ $6 + 4 + 4 = $ _____

11. $5 + 5 + 5 = $ _____ $5 + 5 + 5 = $ _____

12. $7 + 0 + 6 = $ _____ $7 + 0 + 6 = $ _____

13.
```
   5        5
   3        3
 + 4      + 4
```

14.
```
   4        4
   2        2
 + 5      + 5
```

 H.O.T. Write the missing addend.

15.
```
   5
   5
 + ☐
 ───
  14
```

16.
```
   4
   ☐
 + 4
 ───
  12
```

17.
```
   3
   ☐
 + 7
 ───
  11
```

18.
```
   5
   3
 + ☐
 ───
  13
```

PROBLEM SOLVING REAL WORLD

Write Math

Choose a way to solve.
Write or draw to explain.

19. Beth eats 4 green grapes. Lin eats 3 red grapes and 6 purple grapes. How many grapes do they eat?

_____ grapes

20. There are 5 green grapes and 4 red grapes in a bowl. Eli puts 4 more red grapes in the bowl. How many grapes are in the bowl now?

_____ grapes

21. **H.O.T.** Nick, Alex, and Sophia eat 15 raisins in all. Nick and Alex each eat 4 raisins. How many raisins does Sophia eat?

_____ raisins

22. ⭐**Test Prep** Mrs. Morgan has 2 red apples, 7 yellow apples, and 2 green apples. How many apples does she have?

○ 4
○ 9
○ 10
○ 11

TAKE HOME ACTIVITY • Have your child describe two ways to add 3, 6, and 4.

FOR MORE PRACTICE:
Standards Practice Book, pp. P59–P60

Name _____

Algebra • Relate Addition and Subtraction

COMMON CORE STANDARD CC.2.OA.2
Add and subtract within 20.

Essential Question How are addition and subtraction related?

Listen and Draw REAL WORLD

Complete the bar model to show the problem.

8	7

_____

_____ soccer balls

_____	7

15

_____ soccer balls

FOR THE TEACHER • Read the following problems. Have children complete the bar model for each. The soccer team has 8 red balls and 7 yellow balls. How many soccer balls does the team have? The soccer team has 15 balls inside the locker room. The children took the 7 yellow balls outside. How many soccer balls were inside?

Math Talk
Explain how the bar models for the problems are alike and how they are different.

MATHEMATICAL PRACTICES

Model and Draw

You can use addition facts to remember **differences**. Related facts have the same whole and parts.

> Think of the addends in an addition fact to find the difference for a related subtraction fact.

6	7

13

$6 + 7 = \underline{13}$

____	7

13

$13 - 7 = \underline{}$

Share and Show

Write the sum and the difference for the related facts.

1. $5 + 4 = \underline{}$

   $9 - 4 = \underline{}$

2. $2 + 7 = \underline{}$

   $9 - 2 = \underline{}$

3. $3 + 8 = \underline{}$

   $11 - 8 = \underline{}$

4. $5 + 8 = \underline{}$

   $13 - 5 = \underline{}$

5. $1 + 8 = \underline{}$

   $9 - 1 = \underline{}$

6. $9 + 9 = \underline{}$

   $18 - 9 = \underline{}$

7. $8 + 7 = \underline{}$

   $15 - 8 = \underline{}$

8. $4 + 7 = \underline{}$

   $11 - 7 = \underline{}$

9. $7 + 5 = \underline{}$

   $12 - 7 = \underline{}$

On Your Own

Write the sum and the difference for the related facts.

10. $4 + 3 =$ ___

    $7 - 3 =$ ___

11. $2 + 6 =$ ___

    $8 - 6 =$ ___

12. $6 + 4 =$ ___

    $10 - 6 =$ ___

13. $7 + 3 =$ ___

    $10 - 7 =$ ___

14. $8 + 6 =$ ___

    $14 - 6 =$ ___

15. $3 + 9 =$ ___

    $12 - 9 =$ ___

16. $6 + 5 =$ ___

    $11 - 5 =$ ___

17. $7 + 7 =$ ___

    $14 - 7 =$ ___

18. $9 + 6 =$ ___

    $15 - 9 =$ ___

19. $5 + 9 =$ ___

    $14 - 9 =$ ___

20. $4 + 8 =$ ___

    $12 - 4 =$ ___

21. $9 + 7 =$ ___

    $16 - 7 =$ ___

H.O.T. Write a related subtraction fact for each addition fact.

22. $7 + 8 = 15$

    _____

23. $5 + 7 = 12$

    _____

24. $6 + 7 = 13$

    _____

25. $9 + 8 = 17$

    _____

PROBLEM SOLVING REAL WORLD

Write Math

Solve. Write or draw to explain.

26. Trevor has 7 kites. Pam has 4 kites. How many more kites does Trevor have than Pam?

_____ more kites

27. H.O.T. Mr. Sims has a bag of 7 pears and a bag of 6 pears. His family eats 5 pears. How many pears does he have now?

_____ pears

28. Describe how you solved Exercise 27.

_____

_____

_____

29. ★ **Test Prep** Carmen has 11 balloons. She gives 6 balloons to Mark. How many balloons does Carmen have now?

○ 5
○ 6
○ 7
○ 17

TAKE HOME ACTIVITY · Ask your child to name some subtraction facts that he or she knows well.

FOR MORE PRACTICE:
Standards Practice Book, pp. P61–P62

Practice Subtraction Facts

Essential Question What are some ways to remember differences?

COMMON CORE STANDARD CC.2.OA.2
Add and subtract within 20.

Listen and Draw REAL WORLD

Use Gina's model to answer the question.

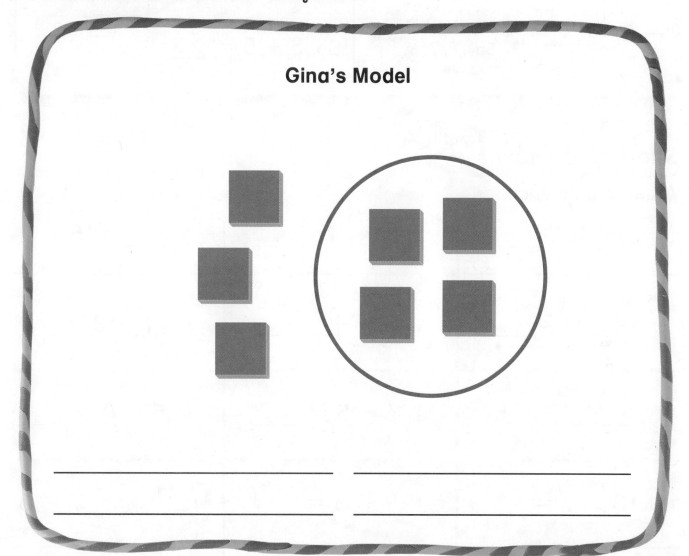

Gina's Model

_____   _____

_____   _____

FOR THE TEACHER • Tell children that Gina put 4 color tiles inside the circle and then put 3 color tiles outside the circle. Then ask: What addition fact could be written for Gina's model? Repeat with stories for the three facts that are related to this addition fact.

Math Talk
Explain how the different facts for Gina's model are related.

MATHEMATICAL PRACTICES

Model and Draw

These are some ways to find differences.

You can count back by 1, 2, or 3.

$7 - 3 =$ ___

> Start with 7.
> Say: 6, 5, 4.

$9 - 3 =$ ___

> Start with 9.
> Say: 8, 7, 6.

You can think about a missing addend to subtract.

$8 - 5 = \blacksquare$

> $5 + 3 = 8$

So, $8 - 5 =$ ___.

Share and Show

Write the difference.

1. $6 - 4 =$ ___

2. $10 - 7 =$ ___

3. ___ $= 5 - 2$

4. $14 - 6 =$ ___

5. $8 - 4 =$ ___

6. $11 - 3 =$ ___

7. ___ $= 7 - 5$

8. $6 - 5 =$ ___

9. $5 - 0 =$ ___

10. $13 - 9 =$ ___

11. $9 - 3 =$ ___

12. ___ $= 7 - 6$

13. $12 - 3 =$ ___

14. $6 - 3 =$ ___

15. $9 - 5 =$ ___

16. $10 - 4 =$ ___

☑ 17. ___ $= 8 - 3$

☑ 18. $13 - 5 =$ ___

Name _____

On Your Own

Write the difference.

19. $11 - 2 =$ ____	20. $9 - 7 =$ ____	21. ____ $= 7 - 4$
22. $12 - 5 =$ ____	23. $8 - 6 =$ ____	24. $7 - 0 =$ ____
25. ____ $= 10 - 5$	26. $15 - 8 =$ ____	27. $13 - 7 =$ ____
28. $10 - 8 =$ ____	29. $8 - 5 =$ ____	30. ____ $= 9 - 6$
31. ____ $= 9 - 4$	32. $11 - 8 =$ ____	33. $12 - 7 =$ ____

H.O.T. Write the differences. Then write the next fact in the pattern.

34. $10 - 1 =$ ____	35. $12 - 9 =$ ____	36. $18 - 9 =$ ____
$8 - 1 =$ ____	$13 - 9 =$ ____	$17 - 8 =$ ____
$6 - 1 =$ ____	$14 - 9 =$ ____	$16 - 7 =$ ____
$4 - 1 =$ ____	$15 - 9 =$ ____	$15 - 6 =$ ____
_____	_____	_____

TAKE HOME ACTIVITY • With your child, practice saying subtraction facts from this lesson.

Chapter 3 • Lesson 6   FOR MORE PRACTICE: Standards Practice Book, pp. P63–P64   one hundred forty-three **143**

Name _____

 Mid-Chapter Checkpoint

Concepts and Skills

Write the sum. (CC.2.OA.2)

1. 3 + 6 = ___	2. 8 + 0 = ___	3. 7 + 7 = ___
4. 9 + 4 = ___	5. ___ = 5 + 6	6. 2 + 8 = ___
7. 3 + 7 + 2 = ___		8. 4 + 4 + 6 = ___

Show how you can make a ten to find the sum.
Write the sum. (CC.2.OA.2)

9. 9 + 7 = ___

10 + ___ = ___

10. 6 + 8 = ___

10 + ___ = ___

Write the sum and the difference for the related facts. (CC.2.OA.2)

11. 5 + 4 = ___	12. 3 + 9 = ___	13. 8 + 7 = ___
9 − 4 = ___	12 − 9 = ___	15 − 8 = ___

 Test Prep (CC.2.OA.2)

14. There are 9 flute players and 4 trumpet
players in the band. How many flute players
and trumpet players are there?

○ 14
○ 13
○ 11
○ 5

Use Ten to Subtract

Essential Question How does getting to 10 in subtraction help when finding differences?

COMMON CORE STANDARD CC.2.OA.2
Add and subtract within 20.

Listen and Draw

Circle to show the amount you subtract for each problem.

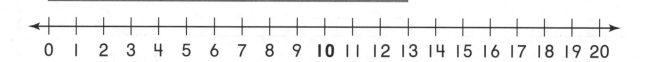

0 1 2 3 4 5 6 7 8 9 **10** 11 12 13 14 15 16 17 18 19 20

0 1 2 3 4 5 6 7 8 9 **10** 11 12 13 14 15 16 17 18 19 20

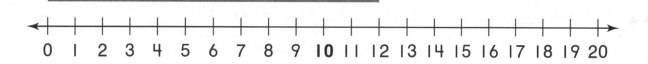

0 1 2 3 4 5 6 7 8 9 **10** 11 12 13 14 15 16 17 18 19 20

FOR THE TEACHER • Read the following problem. Scott has 13 crayons. He gives 3 crayons to Tyler. How many crayons does Scott have now? Have children circle the part of the blue line segment that shows what is subtracted from the total. Repeat for two more problems.

Math Talk
Describe a pattern in the three problems and answers.

MATHEMATICAL PRACTICES

Model and Draw

You can subtract in steps to use a tens fact.

14 − 6 = ?

4   2

Subtract in steps:
14 − 4 = 10
10 − 2 = 8

− 2   − 4

0 1 2 3 4 5 6 7 8 9 10 11 12 13 14 15 16 17 18 19 20

So, 14 − 6 = __8__.

Share and Show

Show the tens fact you used. Write the difference.

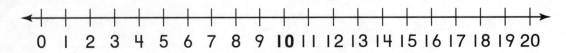

0 1 2 3 4 5 6 7 8 9 **10** 11 12 13 14 15 16 17 18 19 20

1. 12 − 5 = _____

  2   3

10 − _____ = _____

2. 11 − 6 = _____

  1   5

10 − _____ = _____

☑ 3. 15 − 7 = _____

10 − _____ = _____

☑ 4. 13 − 7 = _____

10 − _____ = _____

146 one hundred forty-six

Name _____

On Your Own

Show the tens fact you used. Write the difference.

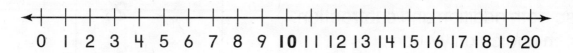

0 1 2 3 4 5 6 7 8 9 **10** 11 12 13 14 15 16 17 18 19 20

5. $13 - 5 =$ _____

10 − _____ = _____

6. $15 - 6 =$ _____

10 − _____ = _____

7. $12 - 8 =$ _____

10 − _____ = _____

8. $14 - 8 =$ _____

10 − _____ = _____

9. $12 - 6 =$ _____

10 − _____ = _____

10. $16 - 7 =$ _____

10 − _____ = _____

H.O.T. Write the missing number that makes the number sentence true.

11. $15 - 6 = 10 -$ _____

12. $11 - 7 = 10 -$ _____

13. $13 - 6 = 10 -$ _____

14. $16 - 8 = 10 -$ _____

PROBLEM SOLVING

H.O.T. Write number sentences that use both addition and subtraction. Use each choice only once.

15. $\dfrac{9 - 2}{7}$ = $\dfrac{3 + 4}{7}$

7 = 7

16. _____ = _____

17. _____ = _____

18. _____ = _____

~~9   2~~
~~3 + 4~~
1 + 4
14 − 6
5 + 4
15 − 6
10 − 5
4 + 4

19. ⭐ **Test Prep** Andy scored 13 points in the first game and 7 points in the second game. How many more points did he score in the first game than in the second game?

○ 9
○ 6
○ 4
○ 3

TAKE HOME ACTIVITY · Ask your child to name pairs of numbers that have a difference of 10. Then have him or her write the number sentences.

FOR MORE PRACTICE:
Standards Practice Book, pp. P65–P66

Name _____

Algebra • Use Drawings to Represent Problems

COMMON CORE STANDARD CC.2.OA.1
Represent and solve problems involving addition and subtraction.

Essential Question How are bar models used to show addition and subtraction problems?

Listen and Draw  REAL WORLD

Complete the bar model to show the problem.
Complete the number sentence to solve.

_____	_____

_____

_____ + _____ = _____   _____ pennies

_____	_____

_____

_____ − _____ = _____   _____ pennies

FOR THE TEACHER • Read each problem and have children complete the bar models. Hailey has 5 pennies in her pocket and 7 pennies in her wallet. How many pennies does she have? Blake has 12 pennies in his bank. He gives 5 pennies to his sister. How many pennies does he have now?

Math Talk

Explain how the problems are alike and how they are different.

MATHEMATICAL PRACTICES

Model and Draw

You can use bar models to show problems.

Ben eats 14 crackers. Ron eats 6 crackers. How many more crackers does Ben eat than Ron?

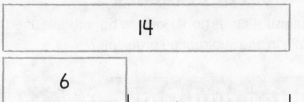

$$14 - 6 = 8$$

_____ more crackers

Suzy had 14 cookies. She gave 6 cookies to Grace. How many cookies does Suzy have now?

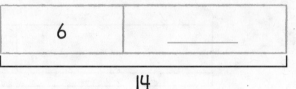

_____

_____ cookies

Share and Show

Complete the bar model. Then write a number sentence to solve.

☑ 1. Mr. James bought 15 plain bagels and 9 raisin bagels. How many more plain bagels than raisin bagels did he buy?

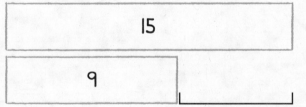

_____

_____ more plain bagels

Name _____

On Your Own

Complete the bar model. Then write
a number sentence to solve.

---

2. Cole has 5 books about dogs
and 6 books about cats. How
many books does Cole have?

5	6

_____

_____

_____ books

---

3. Miss Gore had 18 pencils.
She gave 9 pencils to Erin.
How many pencils does
Miss Gore have now?

	9

18

_____

_____ pencils

---

4. Anne has 16 blue clips and
9 red clips. How many more
blue clips than red clips does
she have?

16

9	

_____

_____

_____ more blue clips

PROBLEM SOLVING REAL WORLD

Write Math

Use the information in the table to solve. Write or draw to explain.

Flowers Jenna Picked	
Flowers	Number
roses	6
tulips	8
daisies	11

5. Jenna put all of the roses and all of the tulips into a vase. How many flowers did she put into the vase?

_____ flowers

6. **H.O.T.** Four of the daisies are white. The other daisies are yellow. How many daisies are yellow?

_____ yellow daisies

7. ⭐ **Test Prep** Mrs. Johnson wants to put 18 flowers into a vase. She put 9 flowers into the vase. How many more flowers does she need to put into the vase?

○ 6
○ 8
○ 9
○ 15

TAKE HOME ACTIVITY • Ask your child to describe one way to solve this problem. There are 7 pennies in one pocket and 9 pennies in another pocket. How many pennies are there?

FOR MORE PRACTICE:
Standards Practice Book, pp. P67–P68

Name _____

Algebra • Use Equations to Represent Problems

COMMON CORE STANDARD CC.2.OA.1
Represent and solve problems
involving addition and subtraction.

Essential Question How are number sentences used to show addition and subtraction situations?

Listen and Draw REAL WORLD

Write a story problem that could be solved using this bar model.

	9
15	

_____

_____

_____

_____

FOR THE TEACHER • Discuss with children how this bar model can be used to represent an addition or a subtraction situation.

Math Talk
Would you add or subtract to solve your story problem? **Explain.**
MATHEMATICAL PRACTICES

A number sentence can be used to show a problem.

There were some girls and 4 boys at the playground.
There were 9 children in all. How many girls were
at the playground?

$$\blacksquare + 4 = 9$$

Think: $5 + 4 = 9$

So, there were ___5___ girls at the playground.

> The ▪ is a placeholder for the missing number.

Share and Show

Write a number sentence for the problem.
Use a ▪ for the missing number. Then solve.

✓ 1. There were 14 ants on the
sidewalk. Then 6 ants went into
the grass. How many ants were
still on the sidewalk?

_____

_____ ants

✓ 2. There were 7 big dogs and
4 little dogs at the park. How
many dogs were at the park?

_____

_____ dogs

On Your Own

Write a number sentence for the problem.

Use a ▇ for the missing number. Then solve.

3. There were 13 girls flying kites.
   Some of the girls went home.
   Then there were 7 girls flying
   kites. How many girls went
   home?

   _____

   _____ girls

4. There are 18 boys at the field.
   9 of the boys are playing soccer.
   How many boys are not playing
   soccer?

   _____

   _____ boys

5. There were some ducks in a
   pond. Four more ducks joined
   them. Then there were 12 ducks
   in the pond. How many
   ducks were in the
   pond at first?

   _____

   _____ ducks

6. Matthew found 9 acorns.
   Greg found 6 acorns. How
   many acorns did the two
   boys find?

   _____

   _____ acorns

PROBLEM SOLVING REAL WORLD

Write Math

Read the story. Write or draw to show how you solved the problems.

> At camp, 5 children are playing games and 4 children are making crafts.
> 5 other children are having a snack.

7. How many children are at camp?

_____ children

8. **H.O.T.** Suppose 7 more children arrive at camp and join the children playing games. How many more children are playing games than children not playing games?

_____ more children

9. ⭐ **Test Prep** Jon counted 12 butterflies and Tessa counted 7 butterflies. How many fewer butterflies did Tessa count than Jon?

- ○ 5
- ○ 7
- ○ 12
- ○ 19

TAKE HOME ACTIVITY · Ask your child to explain how he or she solved one of the problems on this page.

156 one hundred fifty-six

FOR MORE PRACTICE:
Standards Practice Book, pp. P69–P70

Problem Solving • Equal Groups

Essential Question How can acting it out help when solving a problem about equal groups?

COMMON CORE STANDARD CC.2.OA.4
Work with equal groups of objects to gain foundations for multiplication.

Theo puts his stickers in 5 rows.
There are 3 stickers in each row.
How many stickers does Theo have?

🔑 Unlock the Problem

What do I need to find?	**What information do I need to use?**
how many stickers	5 rows of stickers
Theo has	3 stickers in each row

Show how to solve the problem.

© Houghton Mifflin Harcourt Publishing Company

HOME CONNECTION · Your child used counters to act out the problem. Counters are a concrete tool that helps children act out the problem.

Try Another Problem

Act out the problem.
Draw to show what you did.

- What do I need to find?
- What information do I need to use?

1. Maria puts all of her postcards in 4 rows. There are 3 postcards in each row. How many postcards does Maria have?

   _____ postcards

2. Jamal puts 4 toys in each box. How many toys will he put in 4 boxes?

   _____ toys

Math Talk

Explain how acting it out and skip counting helped you solve the second problem.

MATHEMATICAL PRACTICES

Share and Show

Act out the problem.
Draw to show what you did.

✓ **3.** Mr. Fulton puts 3 bananas on each tray. How many bananas are on 4 trays?

_____ bananas

✓ **4.** There are 3 rows of apples. There are 5 apples in each row. How many apples are there?

_____ apples

---

5. Dexter puts 5 grapes on each plate. How many grapes in all does he put on 4 plates?

_____ grapes

On Your Own

Choose a way to solve.
Write or draw to explain.

6. Jon has 6 marbles. Amy gives him some more marbles. Now he has 13 marbles. How many marbles did Amy give to him?

_____ marbles

7. H.O.T. Angela used these counters to act out a problem.

Write a problem about equal groups that Angela could have modeled with these counters.

_____

_____

_____

8. ⭐ **Test Prep** Brett has 3 rows of shells. There are 4 shells in each row. How many shells does he have?

- ○ 6
- ○ 7
- ○ 12
- ○ 15

TAKE HOME ACTIVITY · Ask your child to explain how he or she solved the problem in Exercise 8.

FOR MORE PRACTICE:
Standards Practice Book, pp. P71–P72

Name _____

Algebra • Repeated Addition

Essential Question How can you write an addition sentence for problems with equal groups?

COMMON CORE STANDARD CC.2.OA.4
Work with equal groups of objects to gain foundations for multiplication.

Listen and Draw REAL WORLD

Use counters to model the problem.
Then draw a picture of your model.

Math Talk

Describe how you found the number of counters in your model.

MATHEMATICAL PRACTICES

FOR THE TEACHER • Read the following problem and have children first model the problem with counters and then draw a picture of their models. Clayton has 3 rows of trading cards. There are 5 cards in each row. How many trading cards does Clayton have?

Chapter 3

Model and Draw

You can use addition to find the total
amount when you have equal groups.

3 rows of 4

Write: __4__ + __4__ + __4__ = ____

____ in all

Share and Show

Find the number of shapes in each row.
Complete the addition sentence to find the total.

1.

3 rows of ____

___ + ___ + ___ = ____

☑ 2.

4 rows of ____

__ + __ + __ + __ = ____

☑ 3.

5 rows of ____

___ + ___ + ___ + ___ + ___ = ____

On Your Own

Find the number of shapes in each row.
Complete the addition sentence to find the total.

4.

2 rows of _____

____ + ____ = _____

5.

3 rows of _____

____ + ____ + ____ = _____

6.

4 rows of _____

__ + __ + __ + __ = _____

7.

4 rows of _____

__ + __ + __ + __ = _____

8.

5 rows of _____

____ + ____ + ____ + ____ + ____ = _____

PROBLEM SOLVING   REAL WORLD

Write Math

Solve. Write or draw to explain.

9. Mrs. Chen makes 5 rows of chairs. She puts 2 chairs in each row. How many chairs does Mrs. Chen use?

_____ chairs

10. Jorge has 3 fish bowls. There are 4 fish in each bowl. How many fish are in the bowls?

_____ fish

11. **H.O.T.** There are 6 photos on the wall. There are 2 photos in each row. How many rows of photos are there?

_____ rows

12. ⭐ **Test Prep** Donna has 3 rows of toys. There are 5 toys in each row. How many toys does she have?

   ○ 15
   ○ 12
   ○ 8
   ○ 2

TAKE HOME ACTIVITY • Have your child use small objects to make 2 rows with 4 objects in each row. Then have your child find the total number of objects.

FOR MORE PRACTICE:
Standards Practice Book, pp. P73–P74

✔️ Chapter 3 Review/Test

Vocabulary

1. Circle the **sum**. (p. 122)

$$4 + 6 = 10$$

2. Circle the **difference**. (p. 138)

$$8 - 5 = 3$$

Concepts and Skills

Write the sum and the difference for the related facts. (CC.2.OA.2)

3. $8 + 4 =$ _____

   $12 - 4 =$ _____

4. $5 + 9 =$ _____

   $14 - 9 =$ _____

5. $6 + 5 =$ _____

   $11 - 6 =$ _____

6. Complete the bar model. Then write a number sentence to solve. (CC.2.OA.1)

   Hudson had 13 grapes. He gave 5 grapes to his sister. How many grapes does Hudson have now?

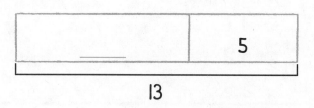

   | | 5 |

   13

   _____   _____ grapes

Find the number of shapes in each row.
Complete the addition sentence to find the total. (CC.2.OA.4)

7.

   2 rows of _____

   _____ + _____ = _____

8.

   3 rows of _____

   _____ + _____ + _____ = _____

Fill in the bubble for the correct answer choice.

9. There are 8 peaches in a basket. Mrs. Dalton puts 7 more peaches in the basket. How many peaches are in the basket now? (CC.2.OA.2)

- ○ 11
- ○ 13
- ○ 15
- ○ 16

10. Mr. Brown hiked 5 miles in the morning. He hiked 6 miles in the afternoon. How many miles did he hike? (CC.2.OA.2)

- ○ 9
- ○ 10
- ○ 11
- ○ 12

11. Erin put 3 apples, 4 bananas, and 5 oranges in a basket. How many pieces of fruit did she put in the basket? (CC.2.OA.2)

- ○ 7
- ○ 9
- ○ 11
- ○ 12

Name _____

Fill in the bubble for the correct answer choice.

12. It rained on 14 days in January. It rained on 8 days in February. On how many more days did it rain in January than in February? (CC.2.OA.2)

○ 6
○ 8
○ 14
○ 22

13. Chase saw 4 ladybugs and 9 ants on a rock. How many more ants than ladybugs did he see? (CC.2.OA.1)

○ 5
○ 6
○ 13
○ 15

14. Tina put some cups into 4 rows. There are 5 cups in each row. How many cups are there? (CC.2.OA.4)

○ 9
○ 10
○ 16
○ 20

Constructed Response

15. Kyle and Luis together have the same number of fish as Mary. How many fish does Luis have?

Kyle 5 fish	**Luis** ? fish	**Mary** 11 fish

Write a number sentence with a ▪ for the missing number. Solve. Then explain how the number sentence shows the problem. (CC.2.OA.1, CC.2.OA.2)

_____

_____

_____

Performance Task (CC.2.OA.1, CC.2.OA.2)

16. Morgan counts 6 ducks in a pond and some ducks on the grass. There are 14 ducks in all. How many ducks are on the grass? Draw or write to show how you found your answer.

How many more ducks are on the grass than in the pond? Draw or write to show how you found your answer.

Chapter 4

2-Digit Addition

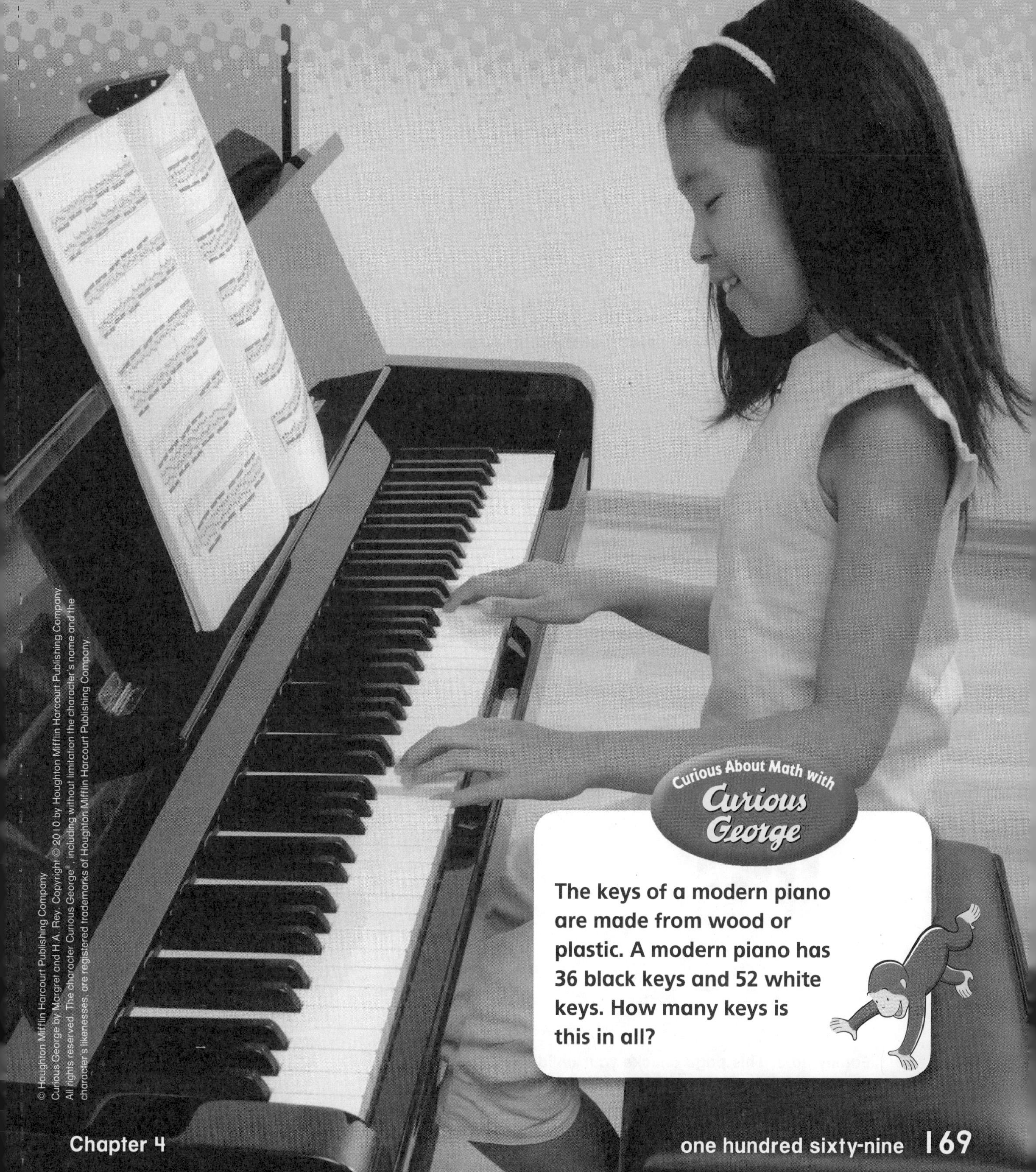

Curious About Math with Curious George

The keys of a modern piano are made from wood or plastic. A modern piano has 36 black keys and 52 white keys. How many keys is this in all?

Show What You Know ✓

Addition Patterns

Add 2. Complete each addition sentence.

1. 1 + __2__ = __3__

2. 2 + ____ = ____

3. 3 + ____ = ____

4. 4 + ____ = ____

5. 5 + ____ = ____

6. 6 + ____ = ____

Addition Facts

Write the sum.

7. 7
   +3

8. 8
   +8

9. 6
   +7

10. 4
    +4

11. 9
    +5

12. 8
    +7

Tens and Ones

Write how many tens and ones for each number.

13. 43

____ tens ____ ones

14. 68

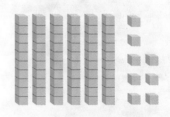

____ tens ____ ones

 Family note: This page checks your child's understanding of important skills needed for success in Chapter 4.

 GO
Online

Assessment Options
Soar to Success Math

Name _____

Vocabulary Builder

Review Words

sum

addend

digit

tens

ones

Visualize It

Use review words to fill in the graphic organizer.

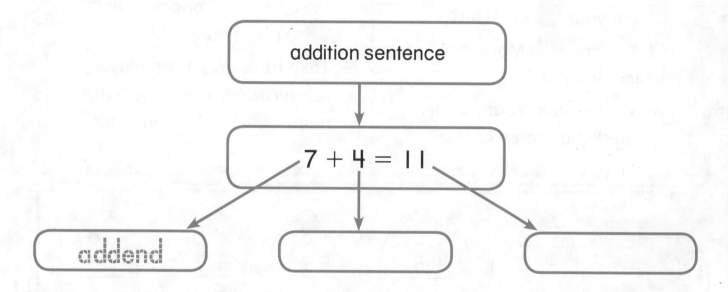

addition sentence

$7 + 4 = 11$

addend

Understand Vocabulary

1. Write a number with the **digit** 3 in the **tens** place. _____

2. Write a number with the **digit** 5 in the **ones** place. _____

3. Write a number that has the same **digit** in the **tens** place and in the **ones** place. _____

4. Write a number with **digits** that have a **sum** of 8. _____

© Houghton Mifflin Harcourt Publishing Company

Chapter 4

GO Online
• eStudent Edition
• Multimedia eGlossary

one hundred seventy-one **171**

Game What is the Sum?

Materials

- 12 ● • 12 ○ • 1 🎲

Play with a partner.

① Put your ● on START.

② Toss the 🎲. Move that many spaces.

③ Say the sum. Your partner checks your answer.

④ If your answer is correct, find that number in the middle of the board. Put one of your on that number.

⑤ Take turns until both players reach FINISH. The player with more on the board wins.

START

$$\begin{array}{r} 2 \\ +7 \\ \hline \end{array}$$ $$\begin{array}{r} 6 \\ +5 \\ \hline \end{array}$$ $$\begin{array}{r} 3 \\ +9 \\ \hline \end{array}$$ $$\begin{array}{r} 0 \\ +7 \\ \hline \end{array}$$ $$\begin{array}{r} 8 \\ +6 \\ \hline \end{array}$$

FINISH

$$\begin{array}{r} 9 \\ +8 \\ \hline \end{array}$$

7	18	9	11	15
13	6	17	8	10
16	4	12	14	5

$$\begin{array}{r} 6 \\ +2 \\ \hline \end{array}$$

$$\begin{array}{r} 1 \\ +4 \\ \hline \end{array}$$

$$\begin{array}{r} 8 \\ +7 \\ \hline \end{array}$$

$$\begin{array}{r} 5 \\ +8 \\ \hline \end{array}$$ $$\begin{array}{r} 9 \\ +9 \\ \hline \end{array}$$ $$\begin{array}{r} 7 \\ +9 \\ \hline \end{array}$$ $$\begin{array}{r} 2 \\ +2 \\ \hline \end{array}$$ $$\begin{array}{r} 4 \\ +6 \\ \hline \end{array}$$ $$\begin{array}{r} 5 \\ +1 \\ \hline \end{array}$$

Break Apart Ones to Add

Essential Question How does breaking apart a number make it easier to add?

COMMON CORE STANDARD CC.2.NBT.6
Use place value understanding and properties of operations to add and subtract.

Listen and Draw  REAL WORLD

Use ▭▭▭▭ ▭. Draw to show what you did.

 FOR THE TEACHER • Read the following problem. Have children use blocks to solve. Griffin read 27 books about animals and 6 books about space. How many books did he read?

Math Talk
Describe what you did with the blocks.

 MATHEMATICAL PRACTICES

Break apart ones to make a ten.
Use this as a way to add.

$27 + 8 =$ ___?___

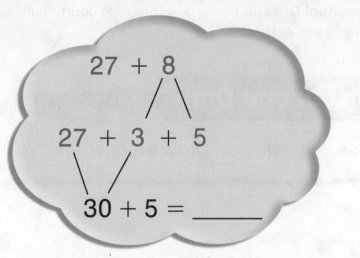

$27 + 8$

$27 + 3 + 5$

$30 + 5 =$ _____

$27 + 8 =$ _____

Share and Show

Draw quick pictures. Break apart ones to
make a ten. Then add and write the sum.

1. $15 + 7 =$ _____

2. $26 + 5 =$ _____

3. $37 + 8 =$ _____

4. $28 + 6 =$ _____

On Your Own

Break apart ones to make a ten.
Then add and write the sum.

5. 23 + 9 = _____

6. 48 + 5 = _____

7. 18 + 5 = _____

8. 33 + 9 = _____

9. 27 + 6 = _____

10. 49 + 4 = _____

11. 24 + 8 = _____

12. 58 + 7 = _____

13. 36 + 8 = _____

14. 47 + 9 = _____

 Write the missing digit.

15. 49 + 7 = □6

16. 35 + □ = 44

17. □5 + 7 = 62

18. 2□ + 8 = 35

19. 74 + 9 = 8□

20. □6 + 5 = 81

PROBLEM SOLVING REAL WORLD

Write Math

Solve. Write or draw to explain.

21. Megan has 38 animal pictures and 8 people pictures. How many pictures does she have?

_____ pictures

22. Bruce counts 25 trees at the park and 7 trees on the way home. How many trees does he count?

_____ trees

23. H.O.T. Jamal has a box with some toy cars in it. He puts 3 more toy cars into the box. Now there are 22 toy cars in the box. How many toy cars were in the box before?

_____ toy cars

24. ⭐ Test Prep Alicia puts 25 books on the shelf. Trenton puts 8 books on the shelf. How many books do they put on the shelf?

- ○ 17
- ○ 23
- ○ 33
- ○ 37

TAKE HOME ACTIVITY • Say a number from 0 to 9. Have your child name a number to add to yours to have a sum of 10.

FOR MORE PRACTICE:
Standards Practice Book, pp. P79–P80

Name _____

Use Compensation

Essential Question How can you make an addend a ten to help solve an addition problem?

COMMON CORE STANDARD CC.2.NBT.6
Use place value understanding and properties of operations to add and subtract.

Listen and Draw REAL WORLD

Draw quick pictures to show the problems.

FOR THE TEACHER • Have children draw quick pictures to solve this problem. Kara has 47 stickers. She buys 20 more stickers. How many stickers does she have now? Repeat for this problem. Tyrone has 30 stickers and buys 52 more stickers. How many stickers does he have now?

Math Talk

Describe how you found how many stickers Tyrone has.

MATHEMATICAL PRACTICES

Take ones from an addend to make the other addend the next tens number.

$$25 + 48 = ?$$

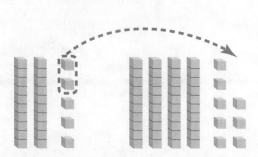

Adding can be easier when one of the addends is a tens number.

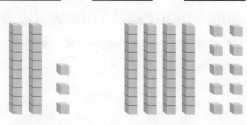

$$\underline{\text{ }23\text{ }} + \underline{\text{ }50\text{ }} = \underline{\text{ }\text{ }}$$

Share and Show Math Board

Show how to make one addend the next tens number.
Complete the new addition sentence.

1. $37 + 25 = ?$

$$\underline{\text{ }40\text{ }} + \underline{\text{ }\text{ }} = \underline{\text{ }\text{ }}$$

2. $27 + 46 = ?$

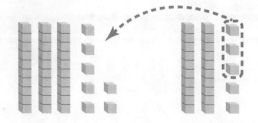

$$\underline{\text{ }\text{ }} + \underline{\text{ }\text{ }} = \underline{\text{ }\text{ }}$$

3. $14 + 29 = ?$

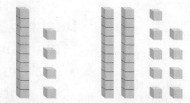

$$\underline{\text{ }\text{ }} + \underline{\text{ }\text{ }} = \underline{\text{ }\text{ }}$$

On Your Own

Show how to make one addend the next tens number.
Complete the new addition sentence.

4. 18 + 13 = ?

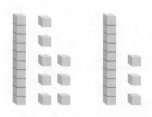

_____ + _____ = _____

5. 24 + 18 = ?

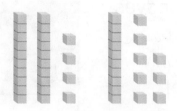

_____ + _____ = _____

6. 39 + 19 = ?

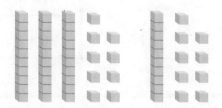

_____ + _____ = _____

7. 27 + 24 = ?

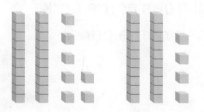

_____ + _____ = _____

8. 19 + 32 = ?

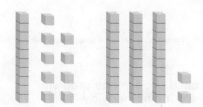

_____ + _____ = _____

PROBLEM SOLVING REAL WORLD

Write Math

Solve. Write or draw to explain.

9. Zach finds 38 twigs. Kelly finds 27 twigs. How many twigs do the two children find?

_____ twigs

10. **H.O.T.** The chart shows the leaves that Philip collected. He wants a collection of 52 leaves, using only two colors. Which two colors of leaves should he use?

Leaves Collected	
Color	Number
green	27
brown	29
yellow	25

_____ and _____

11. ⭐ **Test Prep** Keisha sees 28 small trees at the park. She sees 14 tall trees at the park. How many trees does she see at the park?

- ○ 52
- ○ 44
- ○ 42
- ○ 40

TAKE HOME ACTIVITY · Have your child choose one problem on this page and explain how to solve it in another way.

FOR MORE PRACTICE:
Standards Practice Book, pp. P81–P82

Name _____

Break Apart Addends as Tens and Ones

COMMON CORE STANDARD CC.2.NBT.6
Use place value understanding and properties of operations to add and subtract.

Essential Question How do you break apart addends to add tens and then add ones?

Listen and Draw

Write the number. Then write the number as tens plus ones.

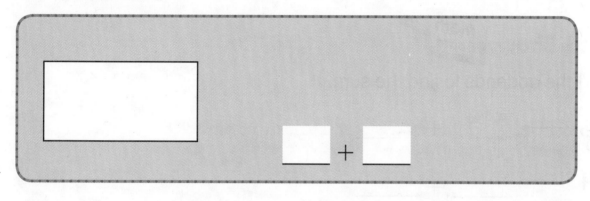

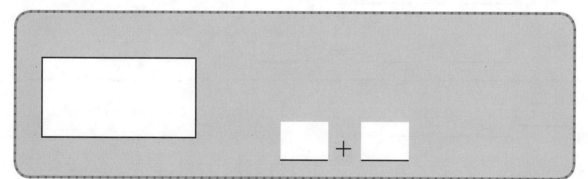

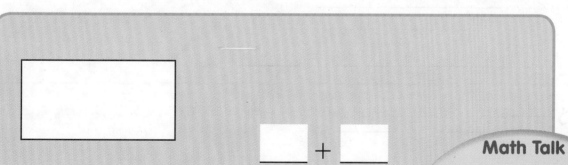

FOR THE TEACHER • Direct children's attention to the orange box. Have children write 25 inside the large rectangle. Then ask children to write 25 as tens plus ones. Repeat the activity for 36 and 42.

Math Talk
What is the value of the 6 in the number 63? **Explain** how you know.

MATHEMATICAL PRACTICES

© Houghton Mifflin Harcourt Publishing Company

Chapter 4

Model and Draw

Break apart the addends into tens and ones.
Add the tens and add the ones.
Then find the total sum.

$$27 \longrightarrow 20 + 7$$
$$+48 \longrightarrow 40 + 8$$

$$\underline{} + \underline{15} = \underline{}$$

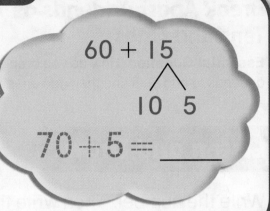

$$60 + 15$$
$$\bigwedge$$
$$10 \quad 5$$

$$70 + 5 = \underline{}$$

Share and Show

Break apart the addends to find the sum.

1.
$$35 \longrightarrow \underline{} + \underline{}$$
$$+54 \longrightarrow \underline{} + \underline{}$$

$$\underline{} + \underline{} = \underline{}$$

2.
$$43 \longrightarrow \underline{} + \underline{}$$
$$+29 \longrightarrow \underline{} + \underline{}$$

$$\underline{} + \underline{} = \underline{}$$

3.
$$56 \longrightarrow \underline{} + \underline{}$$
$$+38 \longrightarrow \underline{} + \underline{}$$

$$\underline{} + \underline{} = \underline{}$$

Name _____

On Your Own

Break apart the addends to find the sum.

4.   14 $\longrightarrow$ _____ + _____

  +23 $\longrightarrow$ _____ + _____

  _____ + _____ = _____

5.   37 $\longrightarrow$ _____ + _____

  +45 $\longrightarrow$ _____ + _____

  _____ + _____ = _____

6.   54 $\longrightarrow$ _____ + _____

  +16 $\longrightarrow$ _____ + _____

  _____ + _____ = _____

7.   **H.O.T.** Write the missing numbers in the problem.

  43 $\longrightarrow$ _____ + _____

  + _____ $\longrightarrow$ 30 + 7

  _____ + _____ = _____

Chapter 4 • Lesson 3   one hundred eighty-three **183**

PROBLEM SOLVING   REAL WORLD

Write Math

Choose a way to solve.
Write or draw to explain.

8. Julie read 18 pages of her book in the morning. She read 17 more pages in the afternoon. How many pages did she read?

    _____ pages

9. H.O.T. Christopher has 35 baseball cards. The rest of his cards are basketball cards. He has 58 cards in all. How many basketball cards does he have?

    _____ basketball cards

10. ⭐ **Test Prep** Tomás has 17 art pencils. He buys 26 more art pencils. How many art pencils does Tomás have now?

    ○ 31
    ○ 33
    ○ 41
    ○ 43

TAKE HOME ACTIVITY · Write 32 + 48 on a sheet of paper.
Have your child break apart the numbers and find the sum.

FOR MORE PRACTICE:
Standards Practice Book, pp. P83–P84

Model Regrouping for Addition

Essential Question When do you regroup in addition?

COMMON CORE STANDARDS CC.2.NBT.6, CC.2.NBT.9
Use place value understanding and properties of operations to add and subtract.

Listen and Draw REAL WORLD

Use ▭▭▭▭ ▭ to model the problem.
Draw quick pictures to show what you did.

Tens	Ones

Math Talk

Describe how you made a ten in your model.

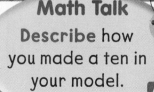

MATHEMATICAL PRACTICES

FOR THE TEACHER • Read the following problem. Brandon has 24 action figures. His friend Mario has 8 action figures. How many action figures do they have?

Chapter 4

one hundred eighty-five **185**

Model and Draw

Add 37 and 25.

Step 1 Look at the ones. Can you make a ten?

Tens	Ones

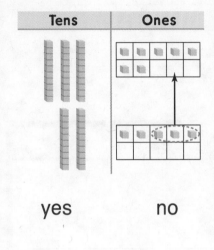

yes   no

Step 2 If you can make a ten, **regroup**.

Tens	Ones

Trade 10 ones for 1 ten to regroup.

Step 3 Write how many tens and ones. Write the sum.

Tens	Ones

_____ tens _____ ones

_____

Share and Show

Draw to show the regrouping. Write how many tens and ones in the sum. Write the sum.

1. Add 47 and 15.

Tens	Ones

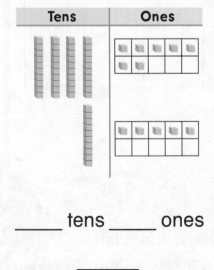

_____ tens _____ ones

_____

✓2. Add 48 and 8.

Tens	Ones

_____ tens _____ ones

_____

✓3. Add 26 and 38.

Tens	Ones

_____ tens _____ ones

_____

186 one hundred eighty-six

On Your Own

Draw to show if you regroup. Write how many tens and ones in the sum. Write the sum.

4. Add 79 and 6.

Tens	Ones

_____ tens _____ ones

_____

5. Add 18 and 64.

Tens	Ones

_____ tens _____ ones

_____

6. Add 23 and 39.

Tens	Ones

_____ tens _____ ones

_____

7. Add 54 and 25.

Tens	Ones

_____ tens _____ ones

_____

8. Add 33 and 7.

Tens	Ones

_____ tens _____ ones

_____

9. Add 27 and 68.

Tens	Ones

_____ tens _____ ones

_____

10. **H.O.T.** Draw a quick picture for the missing addend.

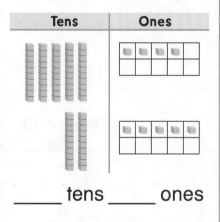

__8__ tens __0__ ones

__80__

Tens	Ones

PROBLEM SOLVING REAL WORLD

Write Math

Choose a way to solve.
Write or draw to explain.

11. Kara has 25 toy animals and 12 books. Jorge has 8 more toy animals than Kara has. How many toy animals does Jorge have?

_____ toy animals

12. **H.O.T.** Tim has 36 stickers. Margo has 44 stickers. How many more stickers would they need to have 100 stickers altogether?

_____ more stickers

13. ⭐ **Test Prep** Mrs. Sanders has two fish tanks. There are 14 fish in the small tank. There are 27 fish in the large tank. How many fish are in the two tanks?

- ○ 47
- ○ 41
- ○ 33
- ○ 31

TAKE HOME ACTIVITY • Ask your child to write a word problem with 2-digit numbers about adding two groups of stamps.

FOR MORE PRACTICE:
Standards Practice Book, pp. P85–P86

Name _____

Model and Record 2-Digit Addition

Essential Question How do you record
2-digit addition?

COMMON CORE STANDARD CC.2.NBT.6
Use place value understanding and
properties of operations to add
and subtract.

Listen and Draw

Use ▭▭▭▭▭ ▪ to model the problem.
Draw quick pictures to show what you did.

Tens	Ones

FOR THE TEACHER • Read the following problem.
Mr. Riley's class collected 54 cans for the food
drive. Miss Bright's class collected 35 cans. How
many cans did the two classes collect?

Math Talk
Did you trade blocks
in your model? **Explain**
why or why not.

Model and Draw

Trace over the quick pictures in the steps.

Step 1 Model 37 + 26. Are there 10 ones to regroup?

Tens	Ones

Tens	Ones
☐	
3	7
+ 2	6

Step 2 Write the regrouped ten. Write how many ones are in the ones place now.

Tens	Ones

Tens	Ones
1	
3	7
+ 2	6
	3

Step 3 How many tens are there? Write how many tens are in the tens place.

Tens	Ones

Tens	Ones
1	
3	7
+ 2	6
6	3

Share and Show

Draw quick pictures to help you solve. Write the sum.

☑ 1.

Tens	Ones
☐	
2	6
+ 3	2

Tens	Ones

☑ 2.

Tens	Ones
☐	
5	8
+ 2	4

Tens	Ones

On Your Own

Draw quick pictures to help you solve. Write the sum.

3.

Tens	Ones
□	
3	4
+	9

Tens	Ones

4.

Tens	Ones
□	
2	7
+ 2	4

Tens	Ones

5.

Tens	Ones
□	
3	5
+ 2	3

Tens	Ones

6.

Tens	Ones
□	
5	9
+	6

Tens	Ones

7.

Tens	Ones
□	
2	8
+ 6	2

Tens	Ones

8.

Tens	Ones
□	
4	9
+ 4	8

Tens	Ones

PROBLEM SOLVING REAL WORLD

Write Math

Choose a way to solve.
Write or draw to explain.

9. Edna has 35 color pencils. Manny gives her 18 more color pencils. How many color pencils does Edna have now?

_____ color pencils

10. **H.O.T.** Chris and Bianca got 80 points in all in the spelling contest. Each child got more than 20 points. How many points could each child have gotten?

Chris: _____ points

Bianca: _____ points

11. ⭐ **Test Prep** Ms. Green's students painted 19 pictures. Mr. Lee's students painted 23 pictures. How many pictures did the students paint?

○ 32
○ 36
○ 40
○ 42

TAKE HOME ACTIVITY · Write two 2-digit numbers and ask your child if he or she would regroup to find the sum.

FOR MORE PRACTICE:
Standards Practice Book, pp. P87–P88

Name _____

2-Digit Addition

Essential Question How do you record the steps
when adding 2-digit numbers?

COMMON CORE STANDARD CC.2.NBT.5
Use place value understanding and
properties of operations to add
and subtract.

Listen and Draw REAL WORLD

Draw quick pictures to model each problem.

Tens	Ones

Tens	Ones

FOR THE TEACHER • Read the following problem
and have children draw quick pictures to solve.
The animal shelter has 35 dogs and 47 cats for
adoption. How many pets are at the shelter?
Repeat the activity with this problem. After a pet
fair, there are only 18 dogs and 21 cats at the
shelter. How many pets are at the shelter now?

Math Talk
Explain when
you need to
regroup ones.
MATHEMATICAL
PRACTICES

© Houghton Mifflin Harcourt Publishing Company

Chapter 4

Model and Draw

Add 59 and 24.

Step 1 Add the ones.

$9 + 4 = 13$

Tens	Ones

Tens	Ones
5	9
+ 2	4

Step 2 Regroup.
13 ones is the same as 1 ten 3 ones.

Tens	Ones

Tens	Ones
1	
5	9
+ 2	4
	3

Step 3 Add the tens.

$1 + 5 + 2 = 8$

Tens	Ones

Tens	Ones
1	
5	9
+ 2	4
8	3

Share and Show

Regroup if you need to. Write the sum.

1.

Tens	Ones
4	2
+ 2	9

2.

Tens	Ones
3	1
+ 1	4

3.

Tens	Ones
2	7
+ 4	5

194 one hundred ninety-four

Name _____

On Your Own

Regroup if you need to. Write the sum.

4.

Tens	Ones
☐	
4	8
+	7

5.

Tens	Ones
☐	
3	5
+ 4	2

6.

Tens	Ones
☐	
7	3
+ 2	0

7.

3	3
+ 2	7

8.

5	2
+	5

9.

3	6
+ 5	8

10.

6	4
+ 2	5

11.

3	5
+ 3	8

12.

3	8
+ 5	2

 Write the missing digits.

13.

5	3
+ ☐	☐
7	8

14.

☐	☐
+ 4	7
9	3

15.

3	☐
+ 1	9
☐	0

PROBLEM SOLVING  REAL WORLD

16. **H.O.T.** Abby used a different way to add.

$$
\begin{array}{r}
35 \\
+\ 48 \\
\hline
13 \\
+\ 70 \\
\hline
83
\end{array}
$$

Find the sum, using Abby's way.

$$
\begin{array}{r}
5\ 7 \\
+\ 2\ 9 \\
\hline
\end{array}
$$

17. Describe Abby's way of adding 2-digit numbers.

_____

_____

_____

_____

18. ⭐ **Test Prep** Carlos had 68 stamps in his collection. He bought 14 more stamps. How many stamps does he have now?

○ 82

○ 74

○ 72

○ 56

TAKE HOME ACTIVITY · Ask your child to show you two ways to add 45 and 38.

FOR MORE PRACTICE:
Standards Practice Book, pp. P89–P90

Name _____

Practice 2-Digit Addition

Essential Question How do you record the steps when adding 2-digit numbers?

COMMON CORE STANDARD CC.2.NBT.5
Use place value understanding and properties of operations to add and subtract.

Listen and Draw REAL WORLD

Choose one way to solve the problem.
Draw or write to show what you did.

FOR THE TEACHER • Read the following problem. There were 45 boys and 63 girls who ran in the race. How many children ran in the race?

Math Talk
Explain why you chose your way of solving the problem.

MATHEMATICAL PRACTICES

Mrs. Meyers sold 47 snacks before the game. Then she sold 85 snacks during the game. How many snacks did she sell?

Step 1 Add the ones.

$7 + 5 = 12$

Regroup 12 ones as 1 ten 2 ones.

```
  1
  4 7
+ 8 5
-----
    2
```

Step 2 Add the tens.

$1 + 4 + 8 = 13$

```
  1
  4 7
+ 8 5
-----
    2
```

Step 3 13 tens can be regrouped as 1 hundred 3 tens. Write the hundreds digit and the tens digit in the sum.

```
  1
  4 7
+ 8 5
-----
13 2
```

Share and Show

Write the sum.

1.
```
  3 8
+ 9 4
-----
```

2.
```
  4 5
+ 5 2
-----
```

3.
```
  8 3
+ 7 6
-----
```

4.
```
  5 6
+ 3 5
-----
```

☑5.
```
  6 3
+ 5 1
-----
```

☑6.
```
  7 4
+ 4 9
-----
```

Name _____

On Your Own

Write the sum.

7.
```
    5 2
+   3 7
```

8.
```
    8 8
+   2 1
```

9.
```
    7 4
+   6 7
```

10.
```
    9 3
+   5 4
```

11.
```
    2 5
+   4 9
```

12.
```
    9 2
+   7 8
```

13.
```
    5 6
+   1 6
```

14.
```
    3 1
+   4 5
```

15.
```
    4 3
+   7 2
```

16. **H.O.T.** Without finding the sums, circle the pairs of addends for which the sum will be greater than 100.

Explain how you decided which pairs to circle.

73
18

54
71

47
62

36
59

_____

_____

_____

TAKE HOME ACTIVITY · Tell your child two 2-digit numbers. Have him or her write the numbers and find the sum.

Name _____

 # Mid-Chapter Checkpoint

Concepts and Skills

Break apart ones to make a ten.
Then add and write the sum. (CC.2.NBT.6)

1. $37 + 8 =$ _____

2. $55 + 7 =$ _____

Break apart the addends to find the sum. (CC.2.NBT.6)

3. $27 \longrightarrow$ _____ $+$ _____

   $+36 \longrightarrow$ _____ $+$ _____

   _____ $+$ _____ $=$ _____

Write the sum. (CC.2.NBT.5)

4.
```
   2 8
 + 5 7
```

5.
```
   6 7
 + 3 1
```

6.
```
   7 1
 + 1 9
```

⭐ Test Prep

7. Julia collected 25 cans to recycle.
Dan collected 14 cans. How many
cans did they collect? (CC.2.NBT.5)

   ○ 39
   ○ 29
   ○ 15
   ○ 11

Name _____

Rewrite 2-Digit Addition

Essential Question What are two different ways to write addition problems?

COMMON CORE STANDARD CC.2.NBT.5
Use place value understanding and properties of operations to add and subtract.

Listen and Draw REAL WORLD

Write the numbers for each addition problem.

$$+ \quad \underline{\hspace{3cm}}$$

$$+ \quad \underline{\hspace{3cm}}$$

$$+ \quad \underline{\hspace{3cm}}$$

$$+ \quad \underline{\hspace{3cm}}$$

FOR THE TEACHER • Read the following problem and have children write the addends in vertical format. Juan's family drove 32 miles to his grandmother's house. Then they drove 14 miles to his aunt's house. How many miles did they drive? Repeat for three more problems.

Math Talk
Explain why it is important to line up the digits of these addends in columns.
MATHEMATICAL PRACTICES

Model and Draw

Add. 28 + 45 = ?

Step 1 For 28, write the tens digit in the tens column.

Write the ones digit in the ones column.

Repeat for 45.

$$\begin{array}{r} 2\ 8 \\ +\ 4\ 5 \\ \hline \end{array}$$

Step 2 Add the ones.

Regroup if you need to.

Add the tens.

$$\begin{array}{r} 2\ 8 \\ +\ 4\ 5 \\ \hline \end{array}$$

Share and Show

Rewrite the addition problem. Then add.

1. 25 + 8

   _____ + _____

2. 37 + 10

   _____ + _____

3. 25 + 45

   _____ + _____

4. 38 + 29

   _____ + _____

5. 20 + 45

   _____ + _____

6. 63 + 9

   _____ + _____

✓ 7. 15 + 36

   _____ + _____

✓ 8. 74 + 18

   _____ + _____

Name _____

On Your Own

Rewrite the addition problem. Then add.

9. 27 + 54

\+ _____

10. 34 + 30

\+ _____

11. 26 + 17

\+ _____

12. 48 + 38

\+ _____

13. 50 + 32

\+ _____

14. 61 + 38

\+ _____

15. 37 + 43

\+ _____

16. 79 + 17

\+ _____

17. 45 + 40

\+ _____

18. 21 + 52

\+ _____

19. 17 + 76

\+ _____

20. 68 + 29

\+ _____

21. **Explain** how you can solve one of the exercises above without rewriting it.

_____

_____

_____

PROBLEM SOLVING REAL WORLD

Write Math

Use the table. Write or draw to show how you solved the problems.

Points Scored This Season	
Player	**Number of Points**
Anna	26
Lou	37
Becky	23
Kevin	19

22. How many points did Lou and Becky score?

_____ points

23. **H.O.T.** Which two players scored 56 points in all? Add to check your answer.

_____ and _____

24. ⭐ **Test Prep** John has 29 markers. Claire has 36 markers. How many markers do the two children have?

○ 53
○ 56
○ 65
○ 68

TAKE HOME ACTIVITY • Have your child write and solve another problem, using the table above.

FOR MORE PRACTICE:
Standards Practice Book, pp. P93–P94

Name _____

Problem Solving • Addition

Essential Question How can drawing a diagram
help when solving addition problems?

COMMON CORE STANDARD CC.2.OA.1
Represent and solve problems involving
addition and subtraction.

Kendra had 13 crayons. Her dad gave her
some more crayons. Then she had 19 crayons.
How many crayons did Kendra's dad give her?

🔑 Unlock the Problem

What do I need to find?

how many crayons
_____

Kendra's dad gave her

What information do I need to use?

She had _____ crayons.
After he gave her some
more crayons, she had
_____ crayons.

Show how to solve the problem.

13	

19

> There are
> 19 crayons
> in all.

13 + ■ = 19

_____ crayons

HOME CONNECTION • Your child used a bar model and a
number sentence to represent the problem. These help show
what the missing amount is in order to solve the problem.

© Houghton Mifflin Harcourt Publishing Company

Try Another Problem

Label the bar model. Write a number sentence with a   for the missing number. Solve.

> • What do I need to find?
> • What information do I need to use?

1. Mr. Kane has 24 red pens. He buys 19 blue pens. How many pens does he have now?

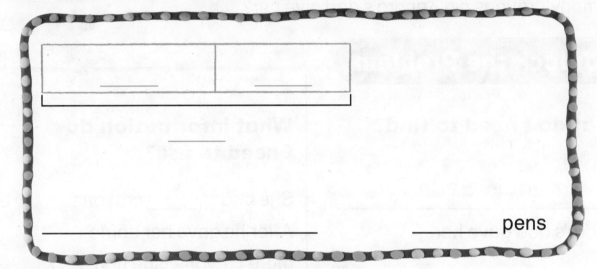

_____   _____ pens

2. Hannah has 10 pencils. Jim and Hannah have 17 pencils altogether. How many pencils does Jim have?

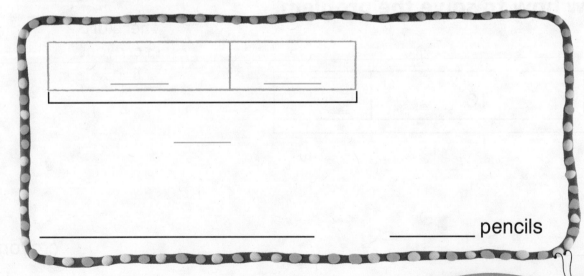

_____   _____ pencils

Math Talk

Explain how you know if an amount is a part or the whole in a problem.

MATHEMATICAL PRACTICES

Share and Show

Label the bar model. Write a number sentence with a ▪ for the missing number. Solve.

✅ **3.** There are 8 owls flying in the forest. There are 15 owls resting in trees. How many owls are there?

_____ owls

✅ **4.** Aimee and Matthew catch 17 crickets in all. Aimee catches 9 crickets. How many crickets does Matthew catch?

_____ crickets

---

5. Percy sees a grasshopper jumping in the grass. He counts 16 jumps. Then he counts 15 more jumps. How many jumps does he count?

_____ jumps

On Your Own

Choose a way to solve.
Write or draw to explain.

Write Math

6. Rita put 5 paper clips in each cup. There are 3 cups in all. How many paper clips are in the cups?

_____ paper clips

7. Jeff has 19 postcards and 2 pens. He buys 20 more postcards. How many postcards does he have now?

_____ postcards

8. **H.O.T.** Alicia drew 15 flowers. Marie drew 4 more flowers than Alicia drew. How many flowers did they draw?

_____ flowers

9. ⭐ **Test Prep** There are 23 books in a box. There are 29 books on a shelf. How many books are there?

○ 42
○ 52
○ 56
○ 61

TAKE HOME ACTIVITY · Ask your child to explain how to solve one of the problems above.

FOR MORE PRACTICE:
Standards Practice Book, pp. P95–P96

Algebra • Write Equations to Represent Addition

Essential Question How do you write a number sentence to represent a problem?

COMMON CORE STANDARD CC.2.OA.1
Represent and solve problems involving addition and subtraction.

Listen and Draw REAL WORLD

Draw to show how you found the answer.

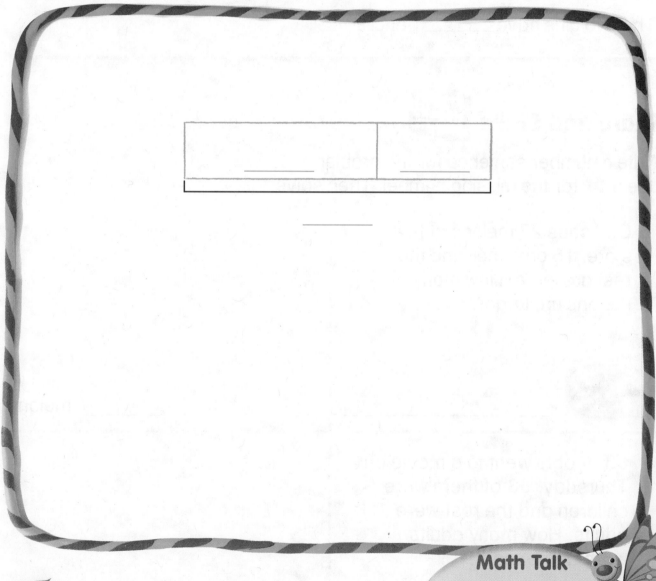

 FOR THE TEACHER • Read the following problem and have children choose their own methods for solving. There are 15 children on the bus. Then 9 more children get on the bus. How many children are on the bus now?

Math Talk
Explain how you found the number of children on the bus.

 MATHEMATICAL PRACTICES

Model and Draw

You can write a number sentence to show
a problem.

Sandy has 16 pencils. Nancy has
13 pencils. How many pencils do
the two girls have?

$$16 + 13 = \blacksquare$$

THINK:
16 pencils
+ 13 pencils
29 pencils

The two girls have _____ pencils.

Share and Show

Write a number sentence for the problem.
Use a ■ for the missing number. Then solve.

1. Carl sees 25 melons at the
store. 15 are small and the
rest are large. How many
melons are large?

_____

_____ melons

2. 83 people went to a movie on
Thursday. 53 of them were
children and the rest were
adults. How many adults
were at the movie?

_____

_____ adults

On Your Own

Write a number sentence for the problem.
Use a ▮ for the missing number. Then solve.

3. Chris and his friends went to the zoo. In the Reptile House, they saw 9 snakes and 14 lizards. How many reptiles did they see?

_____

_____ reptiles

4. Jake had some stamps. Then he bought 20 more stamps. Now he has 56 stamps. How many stamps did Jake have to start?

_____

_____ stamps

5. [H.O.T.] Amy has 19 daisies in a bunch. Keisha has 12 more daisies than Amy. How many daisies do Keisha and Amy have?

_____

_____ daisies

PROBLEM SOLVING

REAL WORLD

Write Math

Read about the field trip. Then solve the problems.

> Last week our class went to the park. We counted the plants and animals. We saw 26 oak trees and 14 maple trees. We also saw 13 cardinals and 35 blue jays.

6. How many birds did the class see at the park?

_____ birds

7.  Compare the number of trees and the number of birds that the class saw.

_____ ◯ _____

8. ⭐ **Test Prep** Mr. Walton baked 54 cookies last week. He baked 38 cookies this week. How many cookies did he bake in the two weeks?

- ◯ 92
- ◯ 82
- ◯ 26
- ◯ 16

TAKE HOME ACTIVITY · Have your child explain how he or she solved Exercise 8.

FOR MORE PRACTICE:
Standards Practice Book, pp. P97–P98

Name _____

Algebra • Find Sums for 3 Addends

Essential Question What are some ways to add 3 numbers?

COMMON CORE STANDARD CC.2.NBT.6
Use place value understanding and properties of operations to add and subtract.

Listen and Draw REAL WORLD

Draw to show each problem.

FOR THE TEACHER • Read the following problem and have children draw to show it. Mr. Kim bought 5 blue balloons, 4 red balloons, and 5 yellow balloons. How many balloons did Mr. Kim buy? Repeat for another problem.

Math Talk
Which numbers did you add first in the first problem? **Explain** why.

MATHEMATICAL PRACTICES

Chapter 4

two hundred thirteen **213**

There are different ways to add three numbers.

How can you add 23, 41, and 17?

Think of different ways to choose digits in the ones column to add first.

> You can make a ten first. Then add the other ones digit. Then add the tens.

> Add from top to bottom. First add the top two digits in the ones column, then add the next digit. Then add the tens.

```
  2 ⑶          3 + 7 = 10
  4 1          10 + 1 = 11
+ 1 ⑺
```

```
  2 ⑶          3 + 1 = 4
  4 ⑴          4 + 7 = 11
+ 1 7
```

Share and Show

Add.

1.	2.	3.	4.
33	47	65	58
34	21	13	27
+ 32	+ 7	+ 15	+ 22

5.	6.	✓7.	✓8.
12	10	31	30
22	42	21	29
+ 36	+ 36	+ 16	+ 48

On Your Own

Add.

9. 22 27 + 18	10. 26 31 + 19	11. 24 11 + 53	12. 33 43 + 4
13. 40 17 + 32	14. 25 25 + 25	15. 19 65 + 24	16. 73 4 + 16
17. 35 24 + 58	18. 32 18 + 28	19. 42 31 + 12	20. 70 18 + 17

21. **H.O.T.** Circle three numbers in the box that have a sum of 73. Use these clues.

- One number is the sum of 8 and 8.
- One number is between 20 and 30.

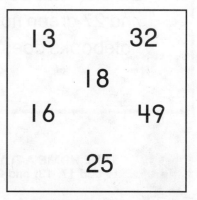

13	32
	18
16	49
	25

PROBLEM SOLVING REAL WORLD

Write Math

Solve. Write or draw to explain.

22. Sophia had 44 marbles. She bought 24 more marbles. Then John gave her 35 marbles. How many marbles does Sophia have now?

_____ marbles

23. H.O.T.   Write a story problem that could be solved using this number sentence.

$$28 + \blacksquare = 40$$

_____

_____

_____

24. ⭐ **Test Prep** Mrs. Shaw has 23 red notebooks, 15 blue notebooks, and 27 green notebooks. How many notebooks does she have?

- ○ 38
- ○ 42
- ○ 55
- ○ 65

TAKE HOME ACTIVITY • Ask your child to show you two ways to add 17, 13, and 24.

FOR MORE PRACTICE:
Standards Practice Book, pp. P99–P100

Name _____

Algebra • Find Sums for 4 Addends

Essential Question What are some ways to add 4 numbers?

COMMON CORE STANDARD CC.2.NBT.6
Use place value understanding and properties of operations to add and subtract.

Listen and Draw REAL WORLD

Show how you solved each problem.

FOR THE TEACHER • Read this problem and have children choose a way to solve it. Shelly counts 16 ants in her ant farm. Pedro counts 22 ants in his farm. Tara counts 14 ants in her farm. How many ants do the 3 children count? Repeat for another problem.

Math Talk
Describe how you found the answer to the first problem.

MATHEMATICAL PRACTICES

Chapter 4

Model and Draw

You can add digits in a column in more than one way. Add the ones first. Then add the tens.

Find a sum that you know. Then add to it.

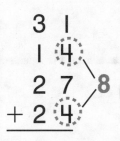

THINK:
8 + 1 = 9, then add on 7 more. The sum of the ones is 16 ones.

Add pairs of digits first. Then add these sums.

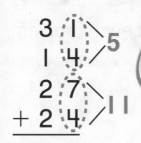

THINK:
5 + 11 = 16, so there are 16 ones in all.

Share and Show

Add.

1.
```
  23
  11
  22
+ 31
```

2.
```
  30
  15
   3
+ 25
```

3.
```
  13
  26
  54
+ 12
```

4.
```
  27
   2
  23
+ 13
```

☑ 5.
```
  45
  14
  35
+ 51
```

☑ 6.
```
  32
  21
  15
+ 30
```

Name _____

On Your Own

Add.

7. 36 12 21 + 26	**8.** 14 23 20 + 11	**9.** 22 13 15 + 27
10. 45 12 41 + 22	**11.** 59 31 51 + 73	**12.** 34 10 31 + 22
13. 14 40 51 + 32	**14.** 21 12 32 + 24	**15.** 16 61 25 + 44
16. 60 15 3 + 21	**17.** 22 43 33 + 30	**18.** 58 82 24 + 64

PROBLEM SOLVING REAL WORLD

Write Math

Use the table.
Write or draw to show how
you solved the problems.

Shells Collected at the Beach	
Child	Number of Shells
Katie	34
Paul	15
Noah	26
Laney	21

19. How many shells did the four children collect at the beach?

_____ shells

20. H.O.T. Which two children collected more shells at the beach, Katie and Paul, or Noah and Laney?

_____

21. ⭐ **Test Prep** There were 24 red beads, 31 blue beads, and 8 green beads in a jar. Then Sasha put 16 beads into the jar. How many beads are in the jar now?

○ 89
○ 79
○ 69
○ 63

TAKE HOME ACTIVITY • Have your child explain how he or she solved Exercise 19.

FOR MORE PRACTICE:
Standards Practice Book, pp. P101–P102

✓ Chapter 4 Review/Test

Vocabulary

Use a word in the box to complete each sentence.

| sum |
| regroup |
| addend |

1. When finding the sum for 37 + 14,

   _____ 10 ones to make 1 ten. (p. 186)

2. In 46 + 7 = 53, 53 is the _____ . (p. 174)

Concepts and Skills

Draw quick pictures to solve.
Write the sum. (CC.2.NBT.6)

3.

Tens	Ones
□	
2	6
+ 3	2

Tens	Ones

4.

Tens	Ones
□	
5	3
+ 2	7

Tens	Ones

Add. (CC.2.NBT.6)

5.
```
    44
    23
 + 16
```

6.
```
    24
    31
 + 23
```

7.
```
    15
    42
    30
 + 12
```

Fill in the bubble for the correct answer choice.

8. Lauren's family drove to the beach.
They saw 14 gulls the first day.
The next day they saw 7 more gulls.

How many gulls did they see
in the two days? (CC.2.NBT.6)

- ○ 7
- ○ 20
- ○ 21
- ○ 31

9. Mr. O'Brien visited a lighthouse. He climbed
26 stairs. Then he climbed 64 more stairs
to the top. How many stairs did he climb
at the lighthouse? (CC.2.NBT.6)

Tens	Ones

- ○ 90
- ○ 82
- ○ 80
- ○ 42

10. Nicole made a necklace. She used
13 red beads. She used 28 blue beads.
How many beads did she use? (CC.2.NBT.6)

- ○ 15
- ○ 31
- ○ 35
- ○ 41

Fill in the bubble for the correct answer choice.

11. Scott baked 24 muffins. He placed 15 muffins on the plate. How many muffins are not on the plate? (CC.2.OA.1)

- ○ 6
- ○ 8
- ○ 9
- ○ 19

12. Carlos is at the museum. There are 23 people in his group. There are 36 people in a second group. There are 44 people in a third group. How many people are in the three groups? (CC.2.NBT.6)

- ○ 913
- ○ 103
- ○ 80
- ○ 59

13. Amy picked 57 strawberries. Her mother picked 34 strawberries. How many strawberries did they pick? (CC.2.NBT.5)

- ○ 91
- ○ 90
- ○ 83
- ○ 81

Constructed Response

14. Mike saw 17 blue cars and 25 green cars at the toy store. How many cars did he see? Write a number sentence with a ■ for the missing number. Explain how the number sentence shows the problem. (CC.2.OA.1, CC.2.NBT.5)

_____

_____

_____

Performance Task (CC.2.OA.1, CC.2.NBT.5)

15. Ling saw these four signs at the theater.

Section A	Section B	Section C	Section D
35 seats	43 seats	17 seats	23 seats

Which two sections have 58 seats in all?

Draw or write to show how you solved the problem.

Explain how you found the numbers that have a sum of 58.

_____

_____

Chapter 5 2-Digit Subtraction

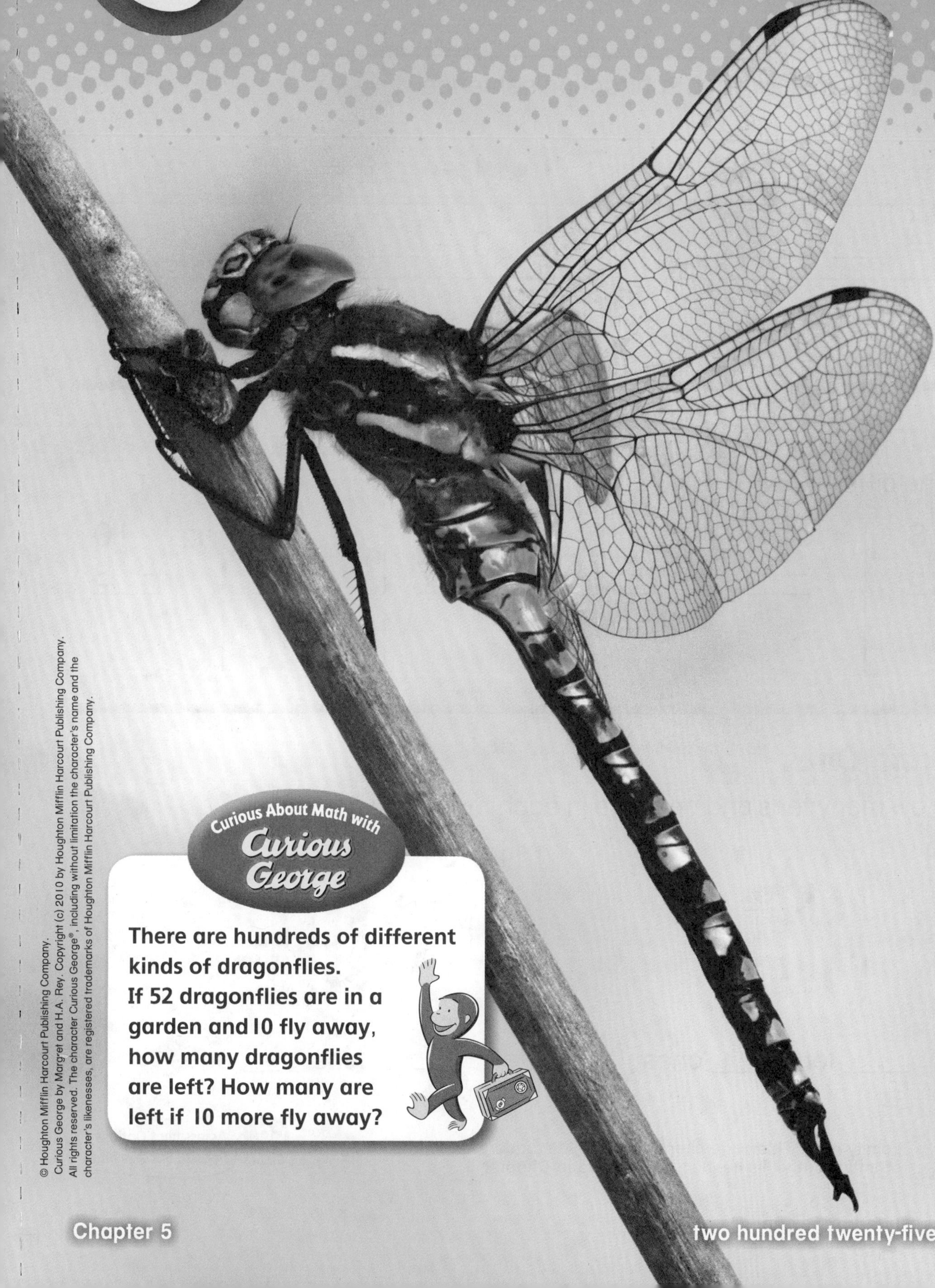

Curious About Math with Curious George

There are hundreds of different kinds of dragonflies.
If 52 dragonflies are in a garden and 10 fly away, how many dragonflies are left? How many are left if 10 more fly away?

Name _____

Show What You Know

Subtraction Patterns

Subtract 2. Complete each subtraction sentence.

1. 7 − _2_ = _5_

2. 6 − ___ = ___

3. 5 − ___ = ___

4. 4 − ___ = ___

5. 3 − ___ = ___

6. 2 − ___ = ___

Subtraction Facts

Write the difference.

7. 8
   − 5
   ___

8. 14
   − 6
   ___

9. 9
   − 6
   ___

10. 16
    − 7
    ___

11. 12
    − 6
    ___

12. 10
    − 8
    ___

Tens and Ones

Write how many tens and ones are in each model.

13. 54

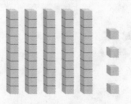

____ tens ____ ones

14. 45

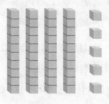

____ tens ____ ones

Family note: This page checks your child's understanding of important skills needed for success in Chapter 5.

Assessment Options
Soar to Success Math

© Houghton Mifflin Harcourt Publishing Company

Vocabulary Builder

Visualize It

Fill in the boxes of the graphic organizer.

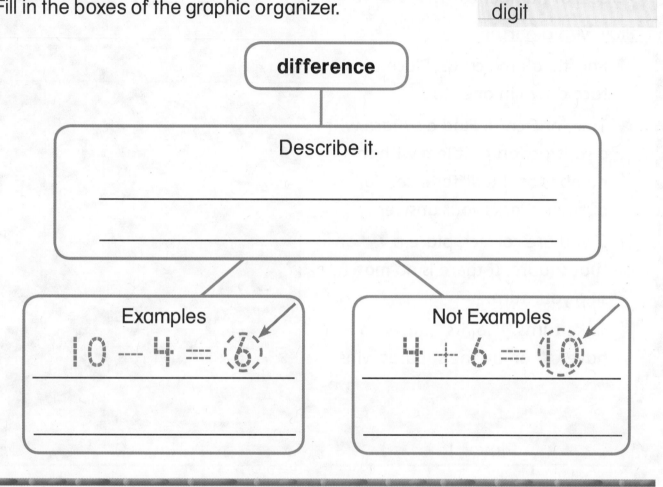

difference

Describe it.

_____

_____

Examples

$10 - 4 = 6$

_____

_____

Not Examples

$4 + 6 = 10$

_____

_____

Understand Vocabulary

Draw a line to complete the sentence.

1. A **digit** can be •   • as 2 **tens**.

2. You can **regroup** •   • 0, 1, 2, 3, 4, 5, 6, 7, 8, or 9.

3. 20 **ones** are the same •   • to trade 10 ones for 1 ten.

Game Subtraction Search

Materials

- 3 sets of number cards 4–9   • 18 ●

Play with a partner.

1. Shuffle all the cards. Place them face down in one stack.

2. Take one card. Find a square with a subtraction problem with this number as the difference. Your partner checks your answer.

3. If you are correct, place a ● on that square. If there is no match, skip your turn.

4. Take turns. The first player to have ● on all the squares wins.

Player 1

12 − 5	9 − 2	10 − 5
16 − 7	13 − 7	17 − 9
7 − 3	11 − 5	18 − 9

Player 2

8 − 3	15 − 7	11 − 6
17 − 8	9 − 3	16 − 8
13 − 9	6 − 2	14 − 7

Name _____

Algebra • Break Apart Ones to Subtract

Essential Question How does breaking apart a number make subtracting easier?

COMMON CORE STANDARD CC.2.NBT.5
Use place value understanding and properties of operations to add and subtract.

Listen and Draw

Write two addends for each sum.

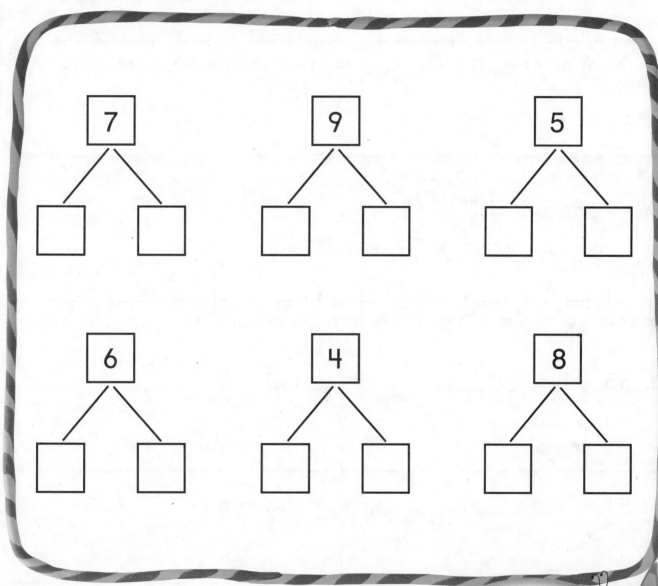

FOR THE TEACHER • After children have recorded addends for each sum, have a class discussion about the different facts that children represented on their papers.

Math Talk
Describe how you chose addends for each sum.

MATHEMATICAL PRACTICES

Break apart ones. Subtract in two steps.

$63 - 7 = \blacksquare$

3 4

> Start at 63.
> Subtract 3 to get
> to 60. Then subtract
> 4 more.

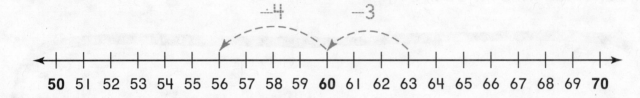

So, $63 - 7 = $ _____ .

Share and Show

Break apart ones to subtract. Write the difference.

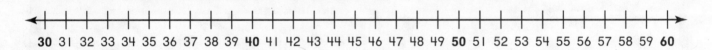

1. $55 - 8 = $ _____

    5 3

2. $42 - 5 = $ _____

    2 3

3. $41 - 9 = $ _____

4. $53 - 6 = $ _____

5. $44 - 7 = $ _____

6. $52 - 8 = $ _____

On Your Own

Break apart ones to subtract. Write the difference.

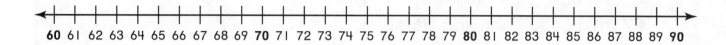

7. 75 − 7 = _____

8. 86 − 8 = _____

9. 82 − 5 = _____

10. 83 − 7 = _____

11. 72 − 7 = _____

12. 76 − 9 = _____

13. 85 − 8 = _____

14. 71 − 6 = _____

H.O.T. Write the differences. Then write the next fact in the pattern.

15. 54 − 5 = __49__

54 − 6 = _____

54 − 7 = _____

_____

16. 81 − 4 = __77__

71 − 4 = _____

61 − 4 = _____

_____

PROBLEM SOLVING REAL WORLD

Write Math

Choose a way to solve.
Write or draw to explain.

17. Cheryl built a toy train with 27 train cars. Then she added 18 more train cars to the train. How many train cars are on the toy train now?

_____ train cars

18. H.O.T. Samuel had 46 marbles. He gave some marbles to a friend and has 9 marbles left. How many marbles did Samuel give to his friend?

_____ marbles

19. ⭐ **Test Prep** Matthew had 73 blocks. He gave 8 blocks to his sister. How many blocks does Matthew have now?

- ○ 81
- ○ 70
- ○ 68
- ○ 65

TAKE HOME ACTIVITY • Ask your child to describe how to find 34 − 6.

FOR MORE PRACTICE:
Standards Practice Book, pp. P107–P108

Algebra • Break Apart Numbers to Subtract

Essential Question How does breaking apart a number make subtracting easier?

COMMON CORE STANDARD CC.2.NBT.5
Use place value understanding and properties of operations to add and subtract.

Listen and Draw  REAL WORLD

Draw jumps on the number line to show how to break apart the number to subtract.

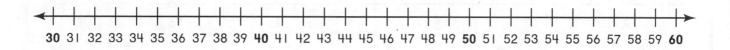

30 31 32 33 34 35 36 37 38 39 40 41 42 43 44 45 46 47 48 49 50 51 52 53 54 55 56 57 58 59 60

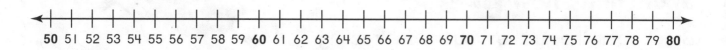

50 51 52 53 54 55 56 57 58 59 60 61 62 63 64 65 66 67 68 69 70 71 72 73 74 75 76 77 78 79 80

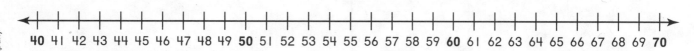

40 41 42 43 44 45 46 47 48 49 50 51 52 53 54 55 56 57 58 59 60 61 62 63 64 65 66 67 68 69 70

FOR THE TEACHER • Read the following problem. Have children draw jumps on the number line to solve. Mrs. Hill had 45 paintbrushes. She gave 9 paintbrushes to students in her art class. How many paintbrushes does Mrs. Hill have now? Repeat the same problem situation for 72 – 7 and 53 – 6.

Math Talk
For one of the problems, **describe** what you did.
MATHEMATICAL PRACTICES

Break apart the number you are subtracting
into tens and ones.

Subtract 10.
Next, subtract 2 to get to 60.
Then subtract 5 more.

$72 - 17 = $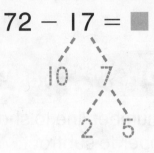

$10 + 2 + 5 = 17$

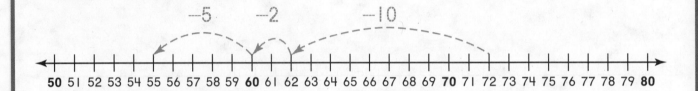

$$-5 \qquad -2 \qquad -10$$

50 51 52 53 54 55 56 57 58 59 **60** 61 62 63 64 65 66 67 68 69 **70** 71 72 73 74 75 76 77 78 79 **80**

So, $72 - 17 = $ _____.

Share and Show

Break apart the number you are subtracting.
Write the difference.

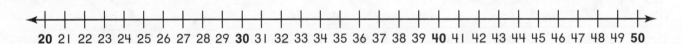

20 21 22 23 24 25 26 27 28 29 **30** 31 32 33 34 35 36 37 38 39 **40** 41 42 43 44 45 46 47 48 49 **50**

1. $43 - 18 = $ _____

  10   8

  3   5

2. $45 - 14 = $ _____

  10   4

☑ 3. $46 - 17 = $ _____

☑ 4. $44 - 16 = $ _____

Name _____

On Your Own

Break apart the number you are subtracting.
Write the difference.

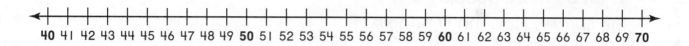

40 41 42 43 44 45 46 47 48 49 **50** 51 52 53 54 55 56 57 58 59 **60** 61 62 63 64 65 66 67 68 69 **70**

5. $57 - 15 = $ _____

6. $63 - 17 = $ _____

7. $68 - 19 = $ _____

8. $61 - 18 = $ _____

9. $65 - 13 = $ _____

10. $59 - 14 = $ _____

11. $62 - 11 = $ _____

12. $67 - 18 = $ _____

13. Look at Tom's steps to solve a problem.
Solve this problem in the same way.

$42 - 15 = ?$

Tom
$35 - 18 = ?$
$35 - 10 = 25$
$25 - 5 = 20$
$20 - 3 = $ ⑰

PROBLEM SOLVING REAL WORLD

Write Math

Solve. Write or draw to explain.

14. 38 people are in the library. Then 33 more people go into the library. How many people are in the library now?

_____ people

15. **H.O.T.** Jane has 53 toys in a box. She takes some toys out of the box. Then there are 36 toys in the box. How many toys did she take out of the box?

_____ toys

16. ⭐ **Test Prep** There are 32 papers in the first stack. There are 19 papers in the second stack. How many more papers are in the first stack than in the second stack?

- ○ 51
- ○ 27
- ○ 23
- ○ 13

TAKE HOME ACTIVITY · Ask your child to write a subtraction story that uses 2-digit numbers.

236 two hundred thirty-six

FOR MORE PRACTICE:
Standards Practice Book, pp. P109–P110

Model Regrouping for Subtraction

Essential Question When do you regroup in subtraction?

COMMON CORE STANDARDS CC.2.NBT.9, CC.2.NBT.5
Use place value understanding and properties of operations to add and subtract.

Listen and Draw REAL WORLD

Use ▭▭▭▭ ▫ to model the problem.
Draw quick pictures to show your model.

Tens	Ones

Math Talk
Describe why you traded a tens block for 10 ones blocks.

MATHEMATICAL PRACTICES

FOR THE TEACHER • Read the following problem. Michelle counted 21 butterflies in her garden. Then 7 butterflies flew away. How many butterflies were still in the garden?

Model and Draw

How do you subtract 26 from 53?

Step 1 Show 53. Are there enough ones to subtract 6?

Tens	Ones
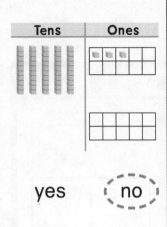	

yes   (no)

Step 2 If there are not enough ones, regroup 1 ten as 10 ones.

Tens	Ones
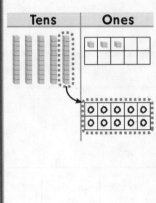	

Step 3 Subtract 6 ones from 13 ones.

Tens	Ones

Step 4 Subtract the tens. Write the tens and ones. Write the difference.

Tens	Ones

____ tens ____ ones

_____

Share and Show Math Board

Draw to show the regrouping. Write the difference two ways. Write the tens and ones. Write the number.

1. Subtract 13 from 41.

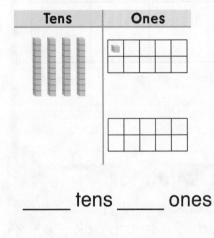

Tens	Ones

____ tens ____ ones

_____

☑ 2. Subtract 9 from 48.

Tens	Ones

____ tens ____ ones

_____

☑ 3. Subtract 28 from 52.

Tens	Ones

____ tens ____ ones

_____

238 two hundred thirty-eight

On Your Own

Draw to show the regrouping. Write the difference two ways. Write the tens and ones. Write the number.

4. Subtract 8 from 23.

Tens	Ones

_____ ten _____ ones

_____

5. Subtract 36 from 45.

Tens	Ones

_____ tens _____ ones

_____

6. Subtract 6 from 43.

Tens	Ones

_____ tens _____ ones

_____

7. Subtract 39 from 67.

Tens	Ones

_____ tens _____ ones

_____

8. Subtract 21 from 50.

Tens	Ones

_____ tens _____ ones

_____

9. Subtract 29 from 56.

Tens	Ones

_____ tens _____ ones

_____

10. **H.O.T.** Draw to find what number was subtracted from 53.

Subtract _____ from 53.

Tens	Ones

_____ 3 tens _____ 4 ones

_____ 34

PROBLEM SOLVING REAL WORLD

Write Math

Choose a way to solve.
Write or draw to explain.

11. Claire's puzzle has 85 pieces. She has used 46 pieces so far. How many puzzle pieces have not been used yet?

_____ puzzle pieces

12. **H.O.T.** Billy has 18 fewer marbles than Sara. Sara has 34 marbles. How many marbles does Billy have?

_____ marbles

13. ⭐ **Test Prep** There were 65 toy animals in the store. Then the clerk sold 17 toy animals. How many toy animals are in the store now?

- ○ 48
- ○ 52
- ○ 78
- ○ 82

TAKE HOME ACTIVITY · Ask your child to write a subtraction story and then explain how to solve it.

FOR MORE PRACTICE:
Standards Practice Book, pp. P111–P112

Model and Record 2-Digit Subtraction

Essential Question How do you record 2-digit subtraction?

COMMON CORE STANDARD CC.2.NBT.5
Use place value understanding and properties of operations to add and subtract.

Listen and Draw REAL WORLD

Use ▭▭▭▭ ▭ to model the problem.
Draw quick pictures to show your model.

Tens	Ones

FOR THE TEACHER • Read the following problem. Mr. Kelly made 47 muffins. His students ate 23 of the muffins. How many muffins were not eaten?

Math Talk
Did you trade blocks in your model? **Explain** why or why not.

MATHEMATICAL PRACTICES

Model and Draw

Trace over the quick pictures in the steps.

Subtract.　56
　　　　　−19

Step 1 Show 56. Are there enough ones to subtract 9?

Tens	Ones

Tens	Ones
5	6
− 1	9

Step 2 If there are not enough ones, regroup 1 ten as 10 ones.

Tens	Ones

Tens	Ones
4	16
5	6
− 1	9

Step 3 Subtract the ones.
$16 − 9 = 7$

Tens	Ones

Tens	Ones
4	16
5	6
− 1	9
	7

Step 4 Subtract the tens.
$4 − 1 = 3$

Tens	Ones

Tens	Ones
4	16
5	6
− 1	9
3	7

Share and Show

Draw a quick picture to solve. Write the difference.

✓1.

Tens	Ones
4	7
− 1	5

Tens	Ones

✓2.

Tens	Ones
3	2
− 1	8

Tens	Ones

On Your Own

Draw a quick picture to solve. Write the difference.

3.

Tens	Ones
□	□
3	5
− 2	9

Tens	Ones

4.

Tens	Ones
□	□
2	8
−	5

Tens	Ones

5.

Tens	Ones
□	□
5	3
− 2	6

Tens	Ones

6.

Tens	Ones
□	□
3	2
− 1	3

Tens	Ones

7.

Tens	Ones
□	□
4	4
− 1	7

Tens	Ones

8.

Tens	Ones
□	□
3	8
− 1	8

Tens	Ones

PROBLEM SOLVING REAL WORLD

 Write Math

Solve. Write or draw to explain.

9. Sophia got 63 points in the math contest. Dennis got 46 points. How many more points did Sophia get than Dennis?

_____ more points

10. **H.O.T.** There were some people at the park. 24 people went home. Then there were 19 people at the park. How many people were at the park before?

_____ people

11. ⭐ **Test Prep** Mr. Sims has a box of 44 erasers. He gives 18 erasers to his students. How many erasers does Mr. Sims have now?

- ○ 22
- ○ 26
- ○ 36
- ○ 62

 TAKE HOME ACTIVITY • Write 73 − 28 on a sheet of paper. Ask your child if he or she would regroup to find the difference.

FOR MORE PRACTICE:
Standards Practice Book, pp. P113–P114

2-Digit Subtraction

Essential Question How do you record the steps when subtracting 2-digit numbers?

COMMON CORE STANDARD CC.2.NBT.5
Use place value understanding and properties of operations to add and subtract.

Listen and Draw

Draw a quick picture to model each problem.

Tens	Ones

Tens	Ones

FOR THE TEACHER • Read the following problem. Devin had 36 toy robots on his shelf. He moved 12 of the robots to his closet. How many robots are on the shelf now? Repeat the activity with this problem: Devin had 54 toy cars. He gave 9 of them to his brother. How many cars does Devin have now?

Math Talk
Explain how you know when to regroup.
MATHEMATICAL PRACTICES

Subtract.   42
            − 15

Step 1 Are there enough ones to subtract 5?	**Step 2** Regroup 1 ten as 10 ones.	**Step 3** Subtract the ones. $12 - 5 = 7$	**Step 4** Subtract the tens. $3 - 1 = 2$

Tens	Ones
4	2
− 1	5

Tens	Ones
3	12
4̶	2̶
− 1	5

Tens	Ones
3	12
4̶	2̶
− 1	5
	7

Tens	Ones
3	12
4̶	2̶
− 1	5
2	7

Share and Show

Regroup if you need to. Write the difference.

1.

Tens	Ones
3	1
− 1	4

2.

Tens	Ones
5	6
− 2	1

3.

Tens	Ones
7	2
− 3	5

On Your Own

Regroup if you need to. Write the difference.

4.

Tens	Ones
□	□
2	3
− 1	4

5.

Tens	Ones
□	□
8	7
− 5	7

6.

Tens	Ones
□	□
3	4
− 1	8

7.

Tens	Ones
□	□
6	1
− 1	3

8.

4	5
− 1	8

9.

5	2
− 3	6

10.

3	2
− 1	3

11.

7	5
− 4	3

12.

5	6
− 2	7

13.

9	4
− 2	9

14.

8	7
− 3	9

15.

8	3
− 4	6

H.O.T. Write the missing numbers.

16.

6	14
□	□
− 2	6
4	8

17.

3	9
− □	□
2	7

18.

8	11
□	□
− 5	8
□	3

PROBLEM SOLVING REAL WORLD

Write Math

19. **H.O.T.** This is how Scott found the difference for 83 − 27.

```
   8 3
 − 2 0
 ─────
   6 3
 −   3
 ─────
   6 0
 −   4
 ─────
   5 6
```

Find the difference for 92 − 68 using Scott's way.

20. Describe Scott's way of subtracting 2-digit numbers.

_____

_____

_____

_____

21. ⭐ **Test Prep** There are 34 chickens in the barn. If 16 chickens go outside, into the yard, how many chickens will still be in the barn?

- ○ 18
- ○ 22
- ○ 42
- ○ 50

TAKE HOME ACTIVITY • Ask your child to write a 2-digit subtraction problem with no regrouping needed. Have your child explain why he or she chose those numbers.

FOR MORE PRACTICE:
Standards Practice Book, pp. P115–P116

Name _____

Practice 2-Digit Subtraction

Essential Question How do you record the steps when subtracting 2-digit numbers?

COMMON CORE STANDARD CC.2.NBT.5
Use place value understanding and properties of operations to add and subtract.

Listen and Draw  REAL WORLD

Choose one way to solve the problem.
Draw or write to show what you did.

Math Talk
Describe a different way that you could have solved the problem. MATHEMATICAL PRACTICES

FOR THE TEACHER • Read the following problem and have children choose their own methods for solving it. There are 74 books in Mr. Barron's classroom. 19 of the books are about computers. How many of the books are not about computers?

Chapter 5

Model and Draw

Carmen had 50 game cards. Then she gave 16 game cards to Theo. How many game cards does Carmen have now?

Step 1 Look at the ones. There are not enough ones to subtract 6 from 0. So, regroup.

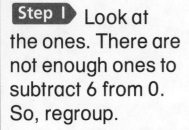

$$
\begin{array}{r}
^4\!\!\!\not5\ ^{10}\!\!\!\not0 \\
-\ 1\ 6 \\
\hline
\end{array}
$$

Step 2 Subtract the ones.

$10 - 6 = 4$

$$
\begin{array}{r}
^4\!\!\!\not5\ ^{10}\!\!\!\not0 \\
-\ 1\ 6 \\
\hline
4
\end{array}
$$

Step 3 Subtract the tens.

$4 - 1 = 3$

$$
\begin{array}{r}
^4\!\!\!\not5\ ^{10}\!\!\!\not0 \\
-\ 1\ 6 \\
\hline
3\ 4
\end{array}
$$

Share and Show

Write the difference.

1.
$$
\begin{array}{r}
3\ 8 \\
-\ 1\ 9 \\
\hline
\end{array}
$$

2.
$$
\begin{array}{r}
6\ 5 \\
-\ 3\ 2 \\
\hline
\end{array}
$$

3.
$$
\begin{array}{r}
5\ 0 \\
-\ 1\ 2 \\
\hline
\end{array}
$$

4.
$$
\begin{array}{r}
2\ 3 \\
-\ \ \ 4 \\
\hline
\end{array}
$$

✓5.
$$
\begin{array}{r}
7\ 0 \\
-\ 3\ 8 \\
\hline
\end{array}
$$

✓6.
$$
\begin{array}{r}
5\ 2 \\
-\ 1\ 7 \\
\hline
\end{array}
$$

250 two hundred fifty

Name _____

On Your Own

Write the difference.

7.	8.	9.
$\begin{array}{r} 4\ 1 \\ -\ 2\ 4 \\ \hline \end{array}$	$\begin{array}{r} 5\ 8 \\ -\ 1\ 6 \\ \hline \end{array}$	$\begin{array}{r} 6\ 0 \\ -\ 1\ 3 \\ \hline \end{array}$
10.	11.	12.
$\begin{array}{r} 5\ 2 \\ -\ 4\ 7 \\ \hline \end{array}$	$\begin{array}{r} 7\ 2 \\ -\ 4\ 6 \\ \hline \end{array}$	$\begin{array}{r} 3\ 7 \\ -\ \ \ 6 \\ \hline \end{array}$
13.	14.	15.
$\begin{array}{r} 7\ 4 \\ -\ 4\ 6 \\ \hline \end{array}$	$\begin{array}{r} 9\ 0 \\ -\ 1\ 8 \\ \hline \end{array}$	$\begin{array}{r} 4\ 0 \\ -\ \ \ 7 \\ \hline \end{array}$

16. Write the missing numbers in the subtraction problems. The regrouping for each problem is shown.

$$\begin{array}{r} 6\ \ 15 \\ \underline{} \\ - \\ \hline 4\ \ 7 \end{array} \qquad \begin{array}{r} 7\ \ 13 \\ \underline{} \\ - \\ \hline 2\ \ 5 \end{array}$$

TAKE HOME ACTIVITY • Ask your child to show you one way to find 80 − 34.

Chapter 5 • Lesson 6

FOR MORE PRACTICE:
Standards Practice Book, pp. P117–P118

two hundred fifty-one **251**

✔ Mid-Chapter Checkpoint

Concepts and Skills

Break apart the number you are subtracting. Use the number line to help. Write the difference. (CC.2.NBT.5)

20 21 22 23 24 25 26 27 28 29 **30** 31 32 33 34 35 36 37 38 39 **40** 41 42 43 44 45 46 47 48 49 **50**

1. $34 - 8 =$ _____

2. $45 - 17 =$ _____

Draw a quick picture to solve. Write the difference. (CC.2.NBT.5)

3.

Tens	Ones
☐	☐
4	2
− 2	9

Tens	Ones

4.

Tens	Ones
☐	☐
5	4
− 2	3

Tens	Ones

Write the difference. (CC.2.NBT.5)

5.
```
   7 8
 − 4 3
```

6.
```
   6 0
 − 2 6
```

7.
```
   8 5
 − 3 7
```

⭐ Test Prep (CC.2.NBT.5)

8. Marissa had 51 toy dinosaurs. She gave 14 toy dinosaurs to her brother. How many toy dinosaurs does she have now?

○ 33
○ 37
○ 47
○ 65

Name _____

Rewrite 2-Digit Subtraction

Essential Question What are two different ways to write subtraction problems?

COMMON CORE STANDARD CC.2.NBT.5
Use place value understanding and properties of operations to add and subtract.

Listen and Draw REAL WORLD

Write the numbers for each subtraction problem.

__ _____	__ _____
__ _____	__ _____

Math Talk
Explain why it is important to line up the digits of the numbers in columns.
MATHEMATICAL PRACTICES

FOR THE TEACHER • Read the following problem. Have children write the numbers in vertical format. There were 45 children at a party. Then 23 children left the party. How many children were still at the party? Repeat for three more problems.

two hundred fifty-three **253**

Model and Draw

What is 81 − 36?
Rewrite the subtraction problem.
Then find the difference.

Step 1 For 81, write the tens digit in the tens column.

Write the ones digit in the ones column.

Repeat for 36.

```
  8  1
- 3  6
```

Step 2 Look at the ones. Regroup if you need to.

Subtract the ones.
Subtract the tens.

```
  7  11
  8  1
- 3  6
```

Share and Show

Math Board

Rewrite the subtraction problem. Then find the difference.

1. 37 − 4

   ___
   _____

2. 48 − 24

   ___
   _____

3. 85 − 37

   ___
   _____

4. 63 − 19

   ___
   _____

5. 62 − 37

   ___
   _____

6. 51 − 27

   ___
   _____

7. 76 − 3

   ___
   _____

8. 95 − 48

   ___
   _____

On Your Own

Rewrite the subtraction problem. Then find the difference.

9. $49 - 8$

__ _____

10. $85 - 47$

__ _____

11. $63 - 23$

__ _____

12. $51 - 23$

__ _____

13. $60 - 15$

__ _____

14. $94 - 58$

__ _____

15. $47 - 20$

__ _____

16. $35 - 9$

__ _____

17. $78 - 10$

__ _____

18. $54 - 38$

__ _____

19. $92 - 39$

__ _____

20. $87 - 28$

__ _____

21. **Explain** how you can solve one of the exercises above without rewriting it.

_____

_____

_____

PROBLEM SOLVING REAL WORLD

Write Math

Read about the class trip. Then answer the questions.

> Pablo's class went to the art museum. They saw 26 paintings done by children. They saw 53 paintings done by adults. They also saw 18 sculptures and 31 photographs.

22. How many more paintings were done by adults than by children?

_____ more paintings

23. **H.O.T.** How many more paintings than sculptures did they see?

_____ more paintings

24. ⭐ **Test Prep** Tom drew 23 pictures last year. Beth drew 14 pictures. How many more pictures did Tom draw than Beth?

○ 37
○ 19
○ 11
○ 9

TAKE HOME ACTIVITY • Ask your child to write and solve a subtraction problem about a family trip.

FOR MORE PRACTICE:
Standards Practice Book, pp. P119–P120

Name _____

Add to Find Differences

Essential Question How can you use addition to solve subtraction problems?

COMMON CORE STANDARD CC.2.NBT.5
Use place value understanding and properties of operations to add and subtract.

Listen and Draw REAL WORLD

Draw pictures to show the problem.
Then write a number sentence for your drawing.

_____   _____ markers

Now draw pictures to show the next part of the problem.
Write a number sentence for your drawing.

_____   _____ markers

FOR THE TEACHER • Have children draw pictures to represent this problem. Sophie had 25 markers. She gave 3 markers to Josh. How many markers does Sophie have now? Then ask children: How many markers will Sophie have if Josh gives the 3 markers back to her?

Math Talk
Describe what happens when you add back the number that you had subtracted.

MATHEMATICAL PRACTICES

Chapter 5

Model and Draw

Count up from the number you are
subtracting to find the difference.

$$45 - 38 = \blacksquare$$

Start at 38. Count up to 40.

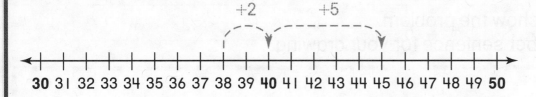

Then count up 5 more to 45.

So, $45 - 38 =$ _____ .

$$2 + 5 = 7$$

Share and Show

Use the number line. Count up to find the difference.

1. $36 - 27 =$ _____

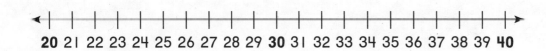

2. $56 - 49 =$ _____

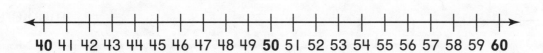

3. $64 - 58 =$ _____

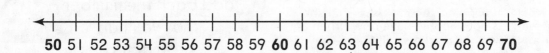

On Your Own

Use the number line. Count up to find the difference.

4. 33 − 28 = _____

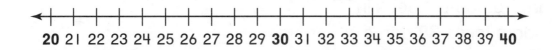

5. 45 − 37 = _____

6. 58 − 49 = _____

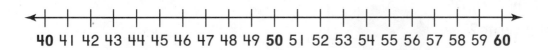

7. 65 − 59 = _____

8. 75 − 68 = _____

Chapter 5 · Lesson 8 two hundred fifty-nine **259**

PROBLEM SOLVING REAL WORLD

Write Math

Solve. You may wish to use the number line to help.

◄──┼──►
30 31 32 33 34 35 36 37 38 39 **40** 41 42 43 44 45 46 47 48 49 **50**

9. There are 46 game pieces in a box. Adam takes 38 game pieces out of the box. How many game pieces are still in the box?

_____ game pieces

10. **H.O.T.** Spencer wrote 5 fewer stories than Katie. Spencer wrote 18 stories. How many stories did Katie write?

_____ stories

11. ⭐ **Test Prep** Rachel had 27 craft sticks. Then she gave 19 craft sticks to Theo. How many craft sticks does Rachel have now?

○ 6
○ 7
○ 8
○ 9

◄──┼──►
10 11 12 13 14 15 16 17 18 19 **20** 21 22 23 24 25 26 27 28 29 **30**

TAKE HOME ACTIVITY · Have your child describe how he or she used a number line to solve one problem in this lesson.

FOR MORE PRACTICE:
Standards Practice Book, pp. P121–P122

Name _____

Problem Solving • Subtraction

Essential Question How can drawing a diagram help when solving subtraction problems?

COMMON CORE STANDARD CC.2.OA.1
Represent and solve problems involving addition and subtraction.

Jane and her mom made 33 puppets for the craft fair. They sold 14 puppets. How many puppets do they still have?

🔑 Unlock the Problem

What do I need to find?

how many puppets
_____
they still have

What information do I need to use?

They made _____ puppets.

They sold _____ puppets.

Show how to solve the problem.

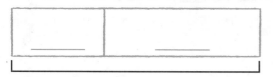

33 — 14 = ▪
_____

_____ puppets

HOME CONNECTION • Your child used a bar model and a number sentence to represent the problem. Using a bar model helps show what is known and what is needed to solve the problem.

© Houghton Mifflin Harcourt Publishing Company

Try Another Problem

Label the bar model. Write a number sentence with a ■ for the missing number. Solve.

- What do I need to find?
- What information do I need to use?

1. Carlette had a box of 46 craft sticks. She used 28 craft sticks to make a sailboat. How many craft sticks were not used?

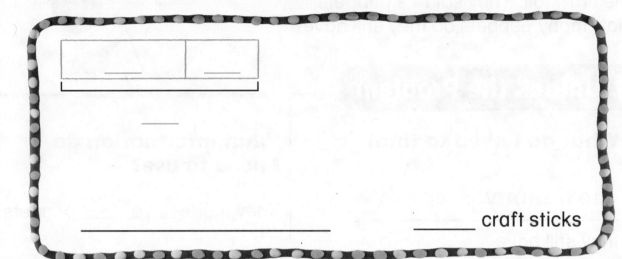

_____   _____ craft sticks

2. Rob's class made 31 clay bowls. Sarah's class made 15 clay bowls. How many more clay bowls did Rob's class make than Sarah's class?

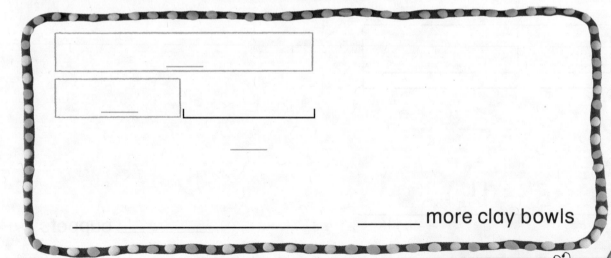

_____   _____ more clay bowls

Math Talk
Explain how you know that Exercise 1 is a take-away problem.

MATHEMATICAL PRACTICES

Share and Show

Label the bar model. Write a number sentence with a ▢ for the missing number. Solve.

☑ 3. Mr. Hayes makes 32 wooden frames. He gives away 15 frames as gifts. How many frames does he still have?

_____ frames

_____	_____

_____

_____

☑ 4. Wesley has 21 ribbons in a box. He has 15 ribbons on the wall. How many more ribbons does he have in the box than on the wall?

_____ more ribbons

_____

_____

_____

---

5. Jennifer wrote 22 poems. Some of her poems are in her notebook. 7 poems are not in her notebook. How many poems are in her notebook?

_____ poems

_____	_____

_____

_____

On Your Own

Choose a way to solve.
Write or draw to explain.

6. Fred had 34 rocks in his collection. Then he got 11 more rocks. How many rocks does Fred have now?

_____ rocks

7. Jean has 54 flowers in her garden. Nico has 19 fewer flowers in his garden. How many flowers does Nico have in his garden?

_____ flowers

8. **H.O.T.** There are 154 tulip plants, 162 daisy plants, and 147 rose plants at the store. Are there more tulip plants or more daisy plants?

more _____ plants

9. ⭐**Test Prep** There are 48 crackers in the bag. The children eat 25 crackers. How many crackers are still in the bag?

○ 13
○ 17
○ 23
○ 63

TAKE HOME ACTIVITY • Ask your child to explain how he or she solved one of the problems on this page.

FOR MORE PRACTICE:
Standards Practice Book, pp. P123–P124

Algebra • Write Equations to Represent Subtraction

Essential Question How do you write a number sentence to represent a problem?

COMMON CORE STANDARD CC.2.OA.1
Represent and solve problems involving addition and subtraction.

Listen and Draw REAL WORLD

Draw to show the problem. Write a number sentence. Then solve.

_____

FOR THE TEACHER • Read this problem to children. Riley has 53 crayons. He gives some crayons to Courtney. Now Riley has 38 crayons. How many crayons did Riley give to Courtney?

Math Talk
Describe how your drawing shows the problem.

MATHEMATICAL PRACTICES

You can write a number sentence to show a problem.

Liza has 65 postcards. She gives 24 postcards to Wesley. How many postcards does Liza have now?

$$65 - 24 = \blacksquare$$

THINK:
$$\begin{array}{r} 65 \text{ postcards} \\ -24 \text{ postcards} \\ \hline 41 \text{ postcards} \end{array}$$

Liza has _____ postcards now.

Share and Show

Write a number sentence for the problem.
Use a ▪ for the missing number. Then solve.

✓1. There were 32 birds in the trees. Then 18 birds flew away. How many birds are in the trees now?

_____   _____ birds

✓2. Carla read 43 pages in her book. Joe read 32 pages in his book. How many more pages did Carla read than Joe?

_____   _____ more pages

Name _____

On Your Own

Write a number sentence for the problem.
Use a ▮ for the missing number. Then solve.

3. There were 40 ants on a rock. Some ants moved to the grass. Now there are 26 ants on the rock. How many ants moved to the grass?

_____

_____ ants

4. Keisha had a box of ribbons. She took 29 ribbons out of the box. Then there were 17 ribbons still in the box. How many ribbons were in the box to start?

_____

_____ ribbons

5. H.O.T. There are 50 bees in a hive. Some bees fly out. If fewer than 20 bees are still in the hive, how many bees could have flown out?

_____ bees

Use subtraction to prove your answer.

PROBLEM SOLVING

REAL WORLD

Write Math

Solve. Write or draw to explain.

6. Haley had some stickers. John gave her 15 more stickers. Now Haley has 44 stickers. How many stickers did she have to start with?

_____ stickers

7. **H.O.T.** Brendan made this number line to find a difference. What was he subtracting from 100? Explain your answer.

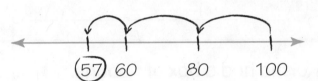

57 60   80   100

_____

_____

_____

8. ⭐ **Test Prep** There are 48 pictures on the zoo wall. Of these, 25 are wild cats and the rest are birds. How many of the pictures are birds?

○ 63
○ 37
○ 23
○ 13

TAKE HOME ACTIVITY • Have your child explain how he or she solved one problem in this lesson.

FOR MORE PRACTICE:
Standards Practice Book, pp. P125–P126

Name _____

Solve Multistep Problems

Essential Question How do you decide what steps to do to solve a problem?

COMMON CORE STANDARD CC.2.OA.1
Represent and solve problems involving addition and subtraction.

Listen and Draw REAL WORLD

Label the bar model to show each problem. Then solve.

FOR THE TEACHER • Read this 1st problem for children. Cassie has 32 sheets of paper. She gives Jeff 9 sheets of paper. How many sheets of paper does Cassie have now? After children solve, read this 2nd problem. Cassie draws 18 pictures. Jeff draws 16 pictures. How many pictures do they draw?

Math Talk

Describe how the two bar models are different.

MATHEMATICAL PRACTICES

Model and Draw

Bar models help you know what to do to solve a problem.

Ali has 27 stamps. Matt has 38 stamps. How many more stamps are needed so they will have 91 stamps?

27	38

‾‾‾‾

They have _____ stamps now.

___	___

91

> First, find how many stamps they have now.

> Next, find how many more stamps they need.

They need _____ more stamps.

Share and Show

Complete the bar models for the steps you do to solve the problem.

> **THINK:** What do you need to find first?

✓ 1. Jen has 93 beads. Ana has 46 red beads and 29 blue beads. How many more beads does Ana need to have 93 beads also?

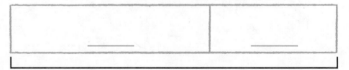

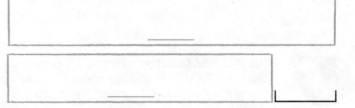

_____ more beads

270 two hundred seventy

© Houghton Mifflin Harcourt Publishing Company

Name _____

On Your Own

Complete the bar models for the steps you do
to solve the problem.

2. Max has 35 trading cards. He
buys 22 more cards. Then he
gives 14 cards to Rudy. How
many cards does Max have now?

_____ cards

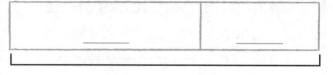

3. Drew has 32 toy cars. He
trades 7 of those cars for
11 other toy cars. How many
toy cars does Drew have now?

_____ toy cars

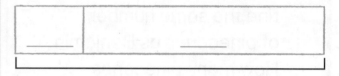

4. Marta and Debbie each have
17 ribbons. They buy 1 package
with 8 ribbons in it. How many
ribbons do they have now?

_____ ribbons

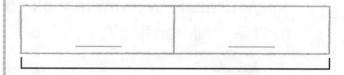

© Houghton Mifflin Harcourt Publishing Company

PROBLEM SOLVING REAL WORLD

Write Math

Solve. Write or draw to explain.

5. Shelby had 32 rocks. She finds 33 more rocks at the park and gives 28 rocks to George. How many rocks does she have now?

_____ rocks

6. **H.O.T.** Benjamin finds 31 pinecones at the park. Together, Jenna and Ellen find the same number of pinecones as Benjamin. How many pinecones could each girl have found?

Jenna: _____ pinecones

Ellen: _____ pinecones

7. ⭐ **Test Prep** Tanya finds 22 leaves. Maurice finds 5 more leaves than Tanya finds. How many leaves do the two children find?

- ○ 59
- ○ 49
- ○ 27
- ○ 17

 TAKE HOME ACTIVITY · Have your child explain how he or she would solve Exercise 6 if the number 31 was changed to 42.

FOR MORE PRACTICE:
Standards Practice Book, pp. P127–P128

✓ Chapter 5 Review/Test

Vocabulary

Use a word from the box to complete the sentence.

| ones |
| tens |
| regroup |

1. In 64 − 8, you could break apart _____ in the number 8 before you subtract. (p. 230)

2. You can trade 1 ten for 10 ones when you _____. (p. 238)

Concepts and Skills

Break apart the number you are subtracting. Use the number line to help. Write the difference. (CC.2.NBT.5)

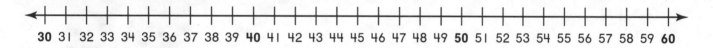

30 31 32 33 34 35 36 37 38 39 **40** 41 42 43 44 45 46 47 48 49 **50** 51 52 53 54 55 56 57 58 59 **60**

3. 43 − 7 = _____

4. 48 − 9 = _____

5. 51 − 16 = _____

6. 55 − 18 = _____

Draw a quick picture to solve. Write the difference. (CC.2.NBT.5)

7.

Tens	Ones
□	□
4	2
− 1	5

Tens	Ones

8.

Tens	Ones
□	□
5	4
− 3	1

Tens	Ones

Fill in the bubble for the correct answer choice.

9. Amanda bought 43 stickers. She gave 16 stickers to her sister. How many stickers does Amanda have now? (CC.2.OA.1)

- ○ 17
- ○ 27
- ○ 39
- ○ 59

10. This year there were 34 sailboats in a race. Last year there were 19 sailboats in a race. How many more sailboats were in the race this year than last year? (CC.2.NBT.5)

- ○ 15
- ○ 25
- ○ 33
- ○ 53

11. Jorge had 40 favorite games saved on his computer. He erased 12 of the games. How many favorite games does he have saved now? (CC.2.NBT.9, CC.2.NBT.5)

Tens	Ones

- ○ 28
- ○ 32
- ○ 48
- ○ 52

274 two hundred seventy-four

Name _____

Fill in the bubble for the correct answer choice.

12. Caleb baked 36 muffins. He brought them
    to school to share with his class. 29 muffins
    were eaten. How many muffins were not eaten? (CC.2.OA.1)

    ○ 65

    ○ 55

    ○ 17

    ○ 7

13. On Monday, 52 children played basketball.
    On Friday, 19 children played baseball and
    27 children played basketball.

    How many more children played games on
    Monday than on Friday? (CC.2.OA.1)

    ○ 25

    ○ 16

    ○ 11

    ○ 6

14. Lauren needs 30 objects for a treasure hunt.
    She has collected some objects, but still
    needs 11 more objects. How many objects
    has she collected so far? (CC.2.NBT.5)

    ○ 9

    ○ 19

    ○ 21

    ○ 41

Constructed Response

15. Linda had 63 shells. She gave 34 shells to Joe. How many shells does she have now? Write a number sentence with a ■ for the missing number. Explain how the number sentence shows the problem. (CC.2.OA.1, CC.2.NBT.5)

_____

_____

_____

Performance Task (CC.2.OA.1, CC.2.NBT.5)

16. At the bike store, there are 42 bikes in all. There are large bikes and small bikes. 18 bikes are small.

How many bikes are large?
Draw or write to show how you found your answer.

How many more large bikes than small bikes are there?
Draw or write to show how you found your answer.

3-Digit Addition and Subtraction

Curious About Math with
Curious George

Monarch butterflies roost together during migration.

If you count 83 butterflies on one tree and 72 on another, how many butterflies have you counted altogether?

Show What You Know ✓

Model Subtracting Tens

Write the difference.

1.

5 tens − 3 tens = _____ tens

50 − 30 = _____

2.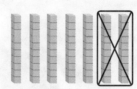

7 tens − 2 tens = _____ tens

70 − 20 = _____

2-Digit Addition

Write the sum.

3. 54
   + 25

4. 35
   + 18

5. 82
   + 67

6. 29
   + 81

Hundreds, Tens, and Ones

Write the hundreds, tens, and ones shown. Write the number.

7.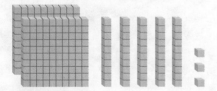

Hundreds	Tens	Ones

_____

8.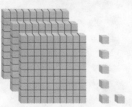

Hundreds	Tens	Ones

_____

 Family note: This page checks your child's understanding of important skills needed for success in Chapter 6.

 GO Online

Assessment Options
Soar to Success Math

© Houghton Mifflin Harcourt Publishing Company

Name _____

Vocabulary Builder

Review Words

regroup
sum
difference
hundreds

Visualize It

Fill in the graphic organizer by writing examples of ways to **regroup**.

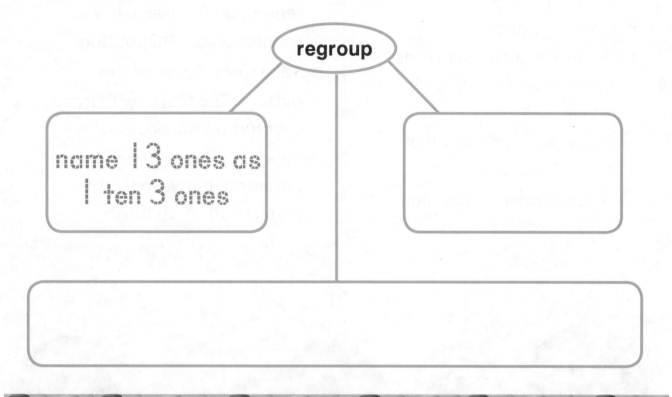

regroup

name 13 ones as 1 ten 3 ones

Understand Vocabulary

1. Write a number that has a **hundreds** digit that is greater than its tens digit. _____

_____

2. Write an addition sentence that has a **sum** of 20. _____

_____

3. Write a subtraction sentence that has a **difference** of 10. _____

© Houghton Mifflin Harcourt Publishing Company

GO Online
• eStudent Edition
• Multimedia eGlossary

Chapter 6

Game 2-Digit Shuffle

Materials

- number cards 10–50
- 15 🔴 • 15 🔵

Play with a partner.

① Shuffle the number cards. Place them face down in a pile.

② Take two cards. Say the sum of the two numbers.

③ Your partner checks your sum.

④ If your sum is correct, place a counter on a button. If you regrouped to solve, place a counter on another button.

⑤ Take turns. Cover all the buttons. The player with more counters on the board wins.

⑥ Repeat the game, saying the difference between the two numbers for each turn.

Name _____

Draw to Represent 3-Digit Addition

Essential Question How do you draw quick pictures to show adding 3-digit numbers?

COMMON CORE STANDARD CC.2.NBT.7
Use place value understanding and properties of operations to add and subtract.

Listen and Draw REAL WORLD

Draw quick pictures to model the problem.
Then solve.

Tens	Ones

_____ pages

Math Talk
Explain how your quick pictures show the problem.

MATHEMATICAL PRACTICES

FOR THE TEACHER • Read this problem to children. Manuel read 45 pages in a book. Then he read 31 more pages. How many pages did Manuel read? Have children draw quick pictures to solve the problem.

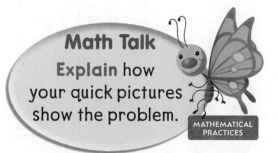

Model and Draw

Add 234 and 141.

Hundreds	Tens	Ones
	|||	:::
	||||	:

_____3_____ hundreds _____7_____ tens _____5_____ ones

_____375_____

Share and Show

Draw quick pictures. Write how many hundreds, tens, and ones in all. Write the number.

✓ 1. Add 125 and 344.

Hundreds	Tens	Ones
	||	::::

_____ hundreds _____ tens _____ ones

_____

✓ 2. Add 307 and 251.

Hundreds	Tens	Ones

_____ hundreds _____ tens _____ ones

_____

On Your Own

Name _____

Draw quick pictures. Write how many hundreds, tens, and ones in all. Write the number.

3. Add 231 and 218.

Hundreds	Tens	Ones

_____ hundreds _____ tens _____ ones

_____

4. Add 232 and 150.

Hundreds	Tens	Ones

_____ hundreds _____ tens _____ ones

_____

5. Add 173 and 205.

Hundreds	Tens	Ones

_____ hundreds _____ tens _____ ones

_____

PROBLEM SOLVING   REAL WORLD

Write Math

Solve. Write or draw to explain.

6. There are 125 poems in Carrie's book and 143 poems in Angie's book. How many poems are in these two books?

_____ poems

7. **H.O.T.** The baker made 85 bagels. He sold 47 bagels in the morning and 23 bagels in the afternoon. How many bagels were not sold?

_____ bagels

8. Describe how you solved Exercise 7.

_____

_____

_____

_____

9. ⭐ **Test Prep** There are 452 girls and 310 boys at the game. How many children are at the game?

- ○ 862
- ○ 772
- ○ 762
- ○ 742

TAKE HOME ACTIVITY • Write 145 + 122. Have your child explain how he or she can draw quick pictures to find the sum.

FOR MORE PRACTICE:
Standards Practice Book, pp. P133–P134

Name _____

Break Apart 3-Digit Addends

Essential Question How do you break apart addends to add hundreds, tens, and then ones?

COMMON CORE STANDARD CC.2.NBT.7
Use place value understanding and properties of operations to add and subtract.

Listen and Draw

Write the number. Draw a quick picture for the number. Then write the number in different ways.

_____

____ hundreds ____ tens ____ ones

_____ + _____ + _____

_____

____ hundreds ____ tens ____ ones

_____ + _____ + _____

FOR THE TEACHER • Have children write 258 on the blank in the left corner of the first box. Have children draw a quick picture for this number and then complete the other two forms for the number. Repeat the activity for 325.

Math Talk
What number can be written as 400 + 20 + 9?

MATHEMATICAL PRACTICES

Model and Draw

Break apart the addends into hundreds, tens, and ones.
Add the hundreds, the tens, and the ones.
Then find the total sum.

538 ⟶ 500 + 30 + 8

+216 ⟶ 200 + 10 + 6

700 + ___ + ___ = _____

Share and Show

Break apart the addends to find the sum.

1. 321 ⟶ _____ + _____ + _____

    +457 ⟶ _____ + _____ + _____

    _____ + _____ + _____ = _____

2. 744 ⟶ _____ + _____ + _____

    +162 ⟶ _____ + _____ + _____

    _____ + _____ + _____ = _____

3. 254 ⟶ _____ + _____ + _____

    +536 ⟶ _____ + _____ + _____

    _____ + _____ + _____ = _____

On Your Own

Break apart the addends to find the sum.

4.   374 ⟶ _____ + _____ + _____

    +518 ⟶ _____ + _____ + _____
    _____

        _____ + _____ + _____ = _____

---

5.   425 ⟶ _____ + _____ + _____

    +232 ⟶ _____ + _____ + _____
    _____

        _____ + _____ + _____ = _____

---

6.   849 ⟶ _____ + _____ + _____

    +123 ⟶ _____ + _____ + _____
    _____

        _____ + _____ + _____ = _____

7. **H.O.T.** Write the missing numbers in the problem.

    412 ⟶ _____ + _____ + _____

    + ____ ⟶ 500 + 60 + _____
    _____

        _____ + _____ + __10__ = _____

PROBLEM SOLVING · REAL WORLD

Write Math

Solve. Write or draw to explain.

8. Mr. Jones has 158 sheets of art paper and 231 sheets of plain paper. How many sheets of paper does he have?

_____ sheets of paper

9. **H.O.T.** Wesley added in a different way.

```
  327
+ 468
─────
  700     7 hundreds
   80     8 tens
+  15     15 ones
─────
  795
```

Use Wesley's way to find the sum.

```
  539
+ 247
─────
```

10. ⭐ **Test Prep** There are 324 children at Theo's school. There are 419 children at Latasha's school. How many children are at the two schools?

- ○ 733
- ○ 743
- ○ 745
- ○ 825

TAKE HOME ACTIVITY · Write 347 + 215. Have your child break apart the numbers and then find the sum.

FOR MORE PRACTICE:
Standards Practice Book, pp. P135–P136

3-Digit Addition: Regroup Ones

Essential Question When do you regroup ones in addition?

COMMON CORE STANDARD CC.2.NBT.7
Use place value understanding and properties of operations to add and subtract.

Listen and Draw REAL WORLD

Use [blocks image] to model the problem.
Draw quick pictures to show what you did.

Hundreds	Tens	Ones

FOR THE TEACHER • Read the following problem and have children model it with blocks. There were 213 people at the show on Friday and 156 people at the show on Saturday. How many people were at the show on the two nights? Have children draw quick pictures to show how they solved the problem.

Math Talk

Describe how you modeled the problem.

MATHEMATICAL PRACTICES

Model and Draw

Add the ones.

$6 + 7 = 13$

Regroup 13 ones as 1 ten 3 ones.

Hundreds	Tens	Ones
	[1]	
2	4	6
+ 1	1	7
		3

Hundreds	Tens	Ones

Add the tens.

$1 + 4 + 1 = 6$

Hundreds	Tens	Ones
	1	
2	4	6
+ 1	1	7
	6	3

Hundreds	Tens	Ones

Add the hundreds.

$2 + 1 = 3$

Hundreds	Tens	Ones
	1	
2	4	6
+ 1	1	7
3	6	3

Hundreds	Tens	Ones

Share and Show

Write the sum.

1.

Hundreds	Tens	Ones
	☐	
3	2	8
+ 1	3	4

2.

Hundreds	Tens	Ones
	☐	
4	4	5
+	2	3

On Your Own

Write the sum.

3.

Hundreds	Tens	Ones
	☐	
5	2	6
+ 1	0	3

4.

Hundreds	Tens	Ones
	☐	
3	4	8
+	1	9

5.

Hundreds	Tens	Ones
	☐	
6	2	8
+ 3	4	7

6.

Hundreds	Tens	Ones
	☐	
2	3	5
+ 2	5	7

7.

Hundreds	Tens	Ones
	☐	
5	6	2
+ 3	2	9

8.

Hundreds	Tens	Ones
	☐	
1	4	7
+ 1	2	5

9.

Hundreds	Tens	Ones
	☐	
4	3	5
+ 2	1	4

10.

Hundreds	Tens	Ones
	☐	
3	2	9
+ 2	4	8

PROBLEM SOLVING REAL WORLD

Write Math

Solve. Write or draw to explain.

11. The gift shop is 140 steps away from the zoo entrance. The train stop is 235 steps away from the gift shop. How many total steps is this?

_____ steps

12.  **H.O.T.** On Thursday, there were 326 visitors at the zoo. There were 200 more visitors at the zoo on Friday than on Thursday. How many visitors were at the zoo on both days?

_____ visitors

13. ⭐ **Test Prep** On Thursday, 175 drinks were sold at the zoo. On Friday, 219 drinks were sold. How many drinks were sold on both days?

- ○ 484
- ○ 464
- ○ 404
- ○ 394

TAKE HOME ACTIVITY · Ask your child to explain why he or she regrouped in only some of the problems in this lesson.

FOR MORE PRACTICE:
Standards Practice Book, pp. P137–P138

3-Digit Addition: Regroup Tens

Essential Question When do you regroup tens in addition?

COMMON CORE STANDARD CC.2.NBT.7
Use place value understanding and properties of operations to add and subtract.

Listen and Draw REAL WORLD

Use [blocks] to model the problem.
Draw quick pictures to show what you did.

Hundreds	Tens	Ones

 FOR THE TEACHER • Read the following problem and have children model it with blocks. On Monday, 253 children visited the aquarium. On Tuesday, 324 children visited the aquarium. How many children visited the aquarium those two days? Have children draw quick pictures to show how they solved the problem.

Math Talk
Explain how your quick pictures show what happened in the problem.

MATHEMATICAL PRACTICES

Model and Draw

Add the ones.

$2 + 5 = 7$

Hundreds	Tens	Ones
☐	☐	
1	4	2
+ 2	8	5
		7

Hundreds	Tens	Ones
☐	||||	∘∘
☐ ☐	||||||||	∘∘∘∘∘

Add the tens.

$4 + 8 = 12$

Regroup 12 tens as
1 hundred 2 tens.

Hundreds	Tens	Ones
☐1	☐	
1	4	2
+ 2	8	5
	2	7

Hundreds	Tens	Ones
☐ ☐	||||	∘∘
☐ ☐	|||||||| |	∘∘∘∘∘

Add the hundreds.

$1 + 1 + 2 = 4$

Hundreds	Tens	Ones
1	☐	
1	4	2
+ 2	8	5
4	2	7

Hundreds	Tens	Ones
☐ ☐		∘∘
☐ ☐	||	∘∘∘∘∘

Share and Show

Write the sum.

1.

Hundreds	Tens	Ones
☐	☐	
3	4	7
+ 2	9	1

☑2.

Hundreds	Tens	Ones
☐	☐	
1	6	5
+ 3	5	4

☑3.

Hundreds	Tens	Ones
☐	☐	
5	3	8
+ 1	4	0

Name _____

On Your Own

Write the sum.

4.

Hundreds	Tens	Ones
□	□	
1	5	6
+	4	2

5.

Hundreds	Tens	Ones
□	□	
7	6	4
+ 1	5	3

6.

Hundreds	Tens	Ones
□	□	
3	7	2
+ 1	8	5

7.

$$\begin{array}{r} 2\ 2\ 4 \\ +\ 1\ 5\ 7 \\ \hline \end{array}$$

8.

$$\begin{array}{r} 2\ 5\ 4 \\ +\ 4\ 0\ 5 \\ \hline \end{array}$$

9.

$$\begin{array}{r} 6\ 4\ 4 \\ +\ \ 9\ 2 \\ \hline \end{array}$$

10.

$$\begin{array}{r} 1\ 3\ 2 \\ +\ 2\ 5\ 8 \\ \hline \end{array}$$

11.

$$\begin{array}{r} 3\ 1\ 4 \\ +\ 4\ 3\ 5 \\ \hline \end{array}$$

12.

$$\begin{array}{r} 7\ 5\ 3 \\ +\ 1\ 5\ 2 \\ \hline \end{array}$$

Rewrite the numbers. Then add.

13. $760 + 178$

$$\begin{array}{r} \\ + \\ \hline \end{array}$$

14. $216 + 346$

$$\begin{array}{r} \\ + \\ \hline \end{array}$$

15. $423 + 285$

$$\begin{array}{r} \\ + \\ \hline \end{array}$$

PROBLEM SOLVING · REAL WORLD

Write Math

These lists show the pieces of fruit that Mr. Olson and Mr. Lee sold at the market.

Mr. Olson	**Mr. Lee**
257 apples	314 pears
281 plums	229 peaches

Write or draw to explain.

16. How many pieces of fruit did Mr. Olson sell?

_____ pieces of fruit

17. **H.O.T.** Who sold more pieces of fruit? How many more?

_____

_____ more pieces of fruit

18. ⭐ **Test Prep** There are 465 oranges packed in boxes. There are 253 oranges in baskets. How many oranges are there?

- ○ 718
- ○ 708
- ○ 698
- ○ 612

TAKE HOME ACTIVITY · Have your child choose a new combination of two fruits on this page and find the total number of pieces of the two types of fruit.

FOR MORE PRACTICE:
Standards Practice Book, pp. P139–P140

Addition: Regroup Ones and Tens

Essential Question How do you know when to regroup in addition?

COMMON CORE STANDARD CC.2.NBT.7
Use place value understanding and properties of operations to add and subtract.

Listen and Draw REAL WORLD

Write an addition problem to find each answer. Draw quick pictures to prove that each sum is correct.

FOR THE TEACHER • Read the following problem and have children solve it. There are 259 girls and 304 boys at Elm Street School. How many children are at Elm Street School? Repeat the activity for 462 + 374.

Math Talk
Did you regroup in the same way for both problems? Explain.

MATHEMATICAL PRACTICES

Sometimes you will regroup more than once in addition problems.

$$
\begin{array}{r}
\overset{1\ 1}{2\ 5\ 9} \\
+\ 4\ 7\ 6 \\
\hline
7\ 3\ 5
\end{array}
$$

> 9 ones + 6 ones = 15 ones, or 1 ten 5 ones

> 1 ten + 5 tens + 7 tens = 13 tens, or 1 hundred 3 tens

> 1 hundred + 2 hundreds + 4 hundreds = 7 hundreds

THINK:
Are there 10 or more ones?
Are there 10 or more tens?

Share and Show

Write the sum.

1.
$$
\begin{array}{r}
1\ 8\ 4 \\
+\ 3\ 2\ 9 \\
\hline
\end{array}
$$

2.
$$
\begin{array}{r}
5\ 4\ 6 \\
+\ 2\ 7\ 8 \\
\hline
\end{array}
$$

3.
$$
\begin{array}{r}
3\ 2\ 7 \\
+\ 3\ 5\ 3 \\
\hline
\end{array}
$$

4.
$$
\begin{array}{r}
2\ 3\ 4 \\
+\ 1\ 5\ 2 \\
\hline
\end{array}
$$

☑ 5.
$$
\begin{array}{r}
3\ 7\ 5 \\
+\ 2\ 7\ 2 \\
\hline
\end{array}
$$

☑ 6.
$$
\begin{array}{r}
1\ 8\ 9 \\
+\ 6\ 2\ 3 \\
\hline
\end{array}
$$

Name _____

On Your Own

Write the sum.

7.
```
   5 7 4
 + 2 8 1
 _____
```

8.
```
   4 1 6
 + 4 8 3
 _____
```

9.
```
   3 4 6
 + 5 9 7
 _____
```

10.
```
   3 6 5
 + 2 8 3
 _____
```

11.
```
   6 4 7
 + 1 0 9
 _____
```

12.
```
   5 4 6
 + 3 5 6
 _____
```

13.
```
   3 4 8
 + 6 3 1
 _____
```

14.
```
   4 5 5
 + 1 3 9
 _____
```

15.
```
   5 6 3
 + 2 4 5
 _____
```

 H.O.T. Write the missing digits.

16.
```
   ▢ ▢ 6
 + 4 5 ▢
 _____
   6 9 0
```

17.
```
   6 ▢ 7
 + 2 3 ▢
 _____
   ▢ 6 2
```

18.
```
   1 3 4
 + ▢ 7 ▢
 _____
   5 ▢ 3
```

 TAKE HOME ACTIVITY · Have your child write a 3-digit addition problem and then solve it.

Mid-Chapter Checkpoint

Concepts and Skills

Break apart the addends to find the sum. (CC.2.NBT.7)

1. 567 ⟶ _____ + _____ + _____

    +324 ⟶ _____ + _____ + _____
    _____

    _____ + _____ + _____ = _____

Write the sum. (CC.2.NBT.7)

2.
```
   2 4 8
 + 3 4 6
 _____
```

3.
```
   6 1 0
 + 2 6 4
 _____
```

4.
```
   3 9 1
 + 5 3 7
 _____
```

 **Test Prep**

5. There are 148 small sand dollars and 119 large sand dollars at the store. How many sand dollars are at the store? (CC.2.NBT.7)

    ○ 257
    ○ 267
    ○ 357
    ○ 367

Problem Solving • 3-Digit Subtraction

Essential Question How can making a model help when solving subtraction problems?

COMMON CORE STANDARD CC.2.NBT.7
Use place value understanding and properties of operations to add and subtract.

There were 436 people at the art show. 219 people left the art show early. How many people stayed at the art show?

🔑 Unlock the Problem

What do I need to find?	**What information do I need to use?**
how many people stayed at the art show	_____ people were at the art show. Then, _____ people left the show.

Show how to solve the problem.

Make a model. Then draw a quick picture of your model.

_____ people

HOME CONNECTION · Your child used a model and a quick picture to represent and solve a subtraction problem.

Try Another Problem

Make a model to solve. Then draw a quick picture of your model.

- What do I need to find?
- What information do I need to use?

1. There are 532 pieces of art at the show. 319 pieces of art are paintings. How many pieces of art are not paintings?

_____ pieces of art

2. 245 children go to the face-painting event. 114 of the children are boys. How many of the children are girls?

_____ girls

Math Talk
Explain how you solved the first problem on this page.

MATHEMATICAL PRACTICES

Name _____

Share and Show

Make a model to solve. Then draw
a quick picture of your model.

☑ **3.** There were 237 books on the
shelves. Miss Lane took
126 books off the shelves.
How many books were still
on the shelves?

_____ books

☑ **4.** 164 children and 31 adults
saw the movie in the morning.
125 children saw the movie in
the afternoon. How many fewer
children saw the movie in the
afternoon than in the morning?

_____ fewer children

---

5. There were 232 postcards
on the table. Janet used
118 postcards to cover the
bulletin board. How many
postcards were not used?

_____ postcards

On Your Own

Choose a way to solve. Write or draw to explain.

6. There were some grapes in a bowl. Clancy's friends ate 24 of the grapes. Then there were 38 grapes in the bowl. How many grapes were in the bowl before?

_____ grapes

7. **H.O.T.** Maria has 127 animal cards. Ellen has twice that number of cards. How many animal cards do the girls have?

_____ animal cards

8. ⭐ **Test Prep** Mr. Grant had 350 balloons. He sold 133 balloons at the park. How many balloons does he have now?

○ 217
○ 223
○ 423
○ 483

TAKE HOME ACTIVITY · Ask your child to choose one of the problems in this lesson and solve it in a different way.

© Houghton Mifflin Harcourt Publishing Company

FOR MORE PRACTICE:
Standards Practice Book, pp. P143–P144

Name _____

3-Digit Subtraction: Regroup Tens

Essential Question When do you regroup tens in subtraction?

COMMON CORE STANDARD CC.2.NBT.7
Use place value understanding and properties of operations to add and subtract.

Listen and Draw REAL WORLD

Use [blocks] to model the problem.
Draw a quick picture to show what you did.

Hundreds	Tens	Ones

FOR THE TEACHER • Read the following problem and have children model it with blocks. 473 people went to the football game. 146 people were still there at the end of the game. How many people left before the end of the game? Have children draw quick pictures of their models.

Math Talk
Describe what to do when there are not enough ones to subtract from.

MATHEMATICAL PRACTICES

$354 - 137 = ?$

Are there enough ones to subtract 7?

yes   (no)

Regroup 1 ten as 10 ones.

Hundreds	Tens	Ones
	4	14
3	5	4
− 1	3	7

Hundreds	Tens	Ones

Now there are enough ones.

Subtract the ones.

$14 - 7 = 7$

Hundreds	Tens	Ones
	4	14
3	5	4
− 1	3	7
		7

Hundreds	Tens	Ones

Subtract the tens.

$4 - 3 = 1$

Subtract the hundreds.

$3 - 1 = 2$

Hundreds	Tens	Ones
	4	14
3	5	4
− 1	3	7
2	1	7

Hundreds	Tens	Ones

Share and Show

Solve. Write the difference.

✓ 1.

Hundreds	Tens	Ones
	□	□
4	3	1
− 3	2	6

✓ 2.

Hundreds	Tens	Ones
	□	□
6	5	8
− 2	3	7

On Your Own

Solve. Write the difference.

3.

Hundreds	Tens	Ones
	☐	☐
7	2	8
− 1	0	7

4.

Hundreds	Tens	Ones
	☐	☐
4	5	2
− 2	1	6

5.

Hundreds	Tens	Ones
	☐	☐
9	6	5
− 2	3	8

6.

Hundreds	Tens	Ones
	☐	☐
4	8	9
− 1	4	9

7.

Hundreds	Tens	Ones
	☐	☐
6	4	5
− 2	2	7

8.

Hundreds	Tens	Ones
	☐	☐
6	7	0
− 1	3	8

9.

Hundreds	Tens	Ones
	☐	☐
8	7	4
− 4	3	8

10.

Hundreds	Tens	Ones
	☐	☐
9	8	4
− 7	1	5

PROBLEM SOLVING REAL WORLD

Write Math

Solve. Write or draw to explain.

11. There are 235 whistles and 42 bells in the store. Ryan counts 128 whistles on the shelf. How many whistles are not on the shelf?

_____ whistles

12. **H.O.T.** There were 287 music books in the store. After some of the music books were sold, there are 159 music books left. How many music books were sold?

_____ music books

13. ⭐ **Test Prep** Ms. Watson has 254 stickers. She gives 123 stickers to her students. How many stickers does she still have?

○ 121
○ 127
○ 131
○ 137

TAKE HOME ACTIVITY • Ask your child to explain why he or she regrouped in only some of the problems in this lesson.

308 three hundred eight

FOR MORE PRACTICE:
Standards Practice Book, pp. P145–P146

3-Digit Subtraction: Regroup Hundreds

Essential Question When do you regroup hundreds in subtraction?

COMMON CORE STANDARD CC.2.NBT.7
Use place value understanding and properties of operations to add and subtract.

Listen and Draw REAL WORLD

Draw quick pictures to show the problem.

Hundreds	Tens	Ones

FOR THE TEACHER • Read the following problem and have children model it with quick pictures. The Reading Club collected 349 books. 173 books were fiction books. The other books were nonfiction books. How many nonfiction books were there?

Math Talk

Describe what to do when there are not enough tens to subtract from.

MATHEMATICAL PRACTICES

Model and Draw

$428 - 153 = ?$

Subtract the ones.

$8 - 3 = 5$

Hundreds	Tens	Ones
☐	☐	☐
4	2	8
− 1	5	3
		5

Hundreds	Tens	Ones

There are not enough tens to subtract from.

Regroup 1 hundred. 4 hundreds 2 tens is now 3 hundreds 12 tens.

Hundreds	Tens	Ones
3	12	☐
4	2	8
− 1	5	3
		5

Hundreds	Tens	Ones

Subtract the tens.

$12 - 5 = 7$

Subtract the hundreds.

$3 - 1 = 2$

Hundreds	Tens	Ones
3	12	☐
4	2	8
− 1	5	3
2	7	5

Hundreds	Tens	Ones

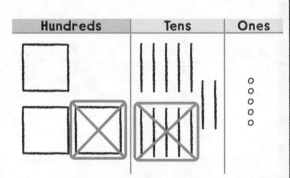

Share and Show

Solve. Write the difference.

☑ 1.

Hundreds	Tens	Ones
☐	☐	☐
4	7	8
− 3	5	6

☑ 2.

Hundreds	Tens	Ones
☐	☐	☐
8	1	4
− 2	6	3

On Your Own

Solve. Write the difference.

3.

Hundreds	Tens	Ones
☐	☐	☐
6	2	9
− 4	8	2

4.

Hundreds	Tens	Ones
☐	☐	☐
9	3	6
− 1	7	3

5.

4	3	5
− 1	9	2

6.

3	8	7
−	4	7

7.

```
  5 8 8
− 4 5 0
```

8.

```
  3 4 5
− 2 6 3
```

Rewrite the numbers. Then subtract.

9. 567 − 183

```
  _____
−
  _____
```

10. 718 − 467

```
  _____
−
  _____
```

PROBLEM SOLVING

REAL WORLD

 Write Math

Solve. Write or draw to explain.

11. There were 375 puzzle pieces in the box. Liz took 190 pieces out of the box. How many puzzles pieces are still in the box?

_____ puzzle pieces

12. **H.O.T.** Sam built two towers. He used 139 blocks for the first tower. He used 276 blocks in all. For which tower did he use more blocks?

_____

Explain how you solved the problem.

_____

_____

_____

13. ⭐ **Test Prep** Mr. Simms has 315 paper hats. He gives 140 paper hats to students in the parade. How many paper hats does he have now?

- ○ 255
- ○ 235
- ○ 215
- ○ 175

TAKE HOME ACTIVITY • Have your child explain how to find the difference for 745 – 341.

FOR MORE PRACTICE:
Standards Practice Book, pp. P147–P148

Name _____

Subtraction: Regroup Hundreds and Tens

Essential Question How do you know when to regroup in subtraction?

COMMON CORE STANDARD CC.2.NBT.7
Use place value understanding and properties of operations to add and subtract.

Listen and Draw  REAL WORLD

Write a subtraction problem to find each answer.
Draw a quick picture to prove that each difference is correct.

FOR THE TEACHER • Read the following problem and have children solve. There are 128 adults and 431 children at the museum. How many more children than adults are there? Repeat the activity for 738 – 275.

Math Talk
Did you regroup in the same way for each problem? **Explain.**

MATHEMATICAL PRACTICES

Sometimes you will regroup more than once in subtraction problems.

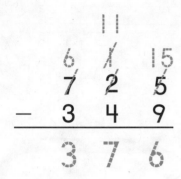

Regroup 2 tens 5 ones as 1 ten 15 ones. Subtract the ones.

Regroup 7 hundreds 1 ten as 6 hundreds 11 tens. Subtract the tens.

Subtract the hundreds.

Share and Show

Solve. Write the difference.

1.	2.	3.
4 2 1 − 1 3 8	2 7 4 − 1 8 2	5 4 6 − 2 6 7

4.	☑ 5.	☑ 6.
8 5 9 − 5 7	7 4 7 − 1 5 9	9 3 8 − 3 7 0

Name _____

On Your Own

Solve. Write the difference.

7.
```
  3 4 2
-   1 3 8
```

8.
```
  4 6 3
-   2 8 1
```

9.
```
  8 5 5
-   4 9 7
```

10.
```
  6 5 7
-   3 8 4
```

11.
```
  5 2 1
-   1 4 6
```

12.
```
  7 5 8
-   5 3 7
```

13.
```
  5 4 2
-   1 6 8
```

14.
```
  8 2 3
-   6 7 3
```

15.
```
  9 4 7
-   5 7 9
```

 Write the missing digits.

16.
```
    ▢ 5 8
-   2 ▢ 2
    5 1 ▢
```

17.
```
      4  15
  9   ▢   ▢
-   6 2 8
    3 2 7
```

18.
```
      7  13
  ▢   ▢   7
-   1 5 ▢
    6 8 1
```

PROBLEM SOLVING REAL WORLD

Write Math

Solve.

19. **H.O.T.** This is how Walter found the difference for 617 − 350.

$$
\begin{aligned}
350 \\
400 \quad &+ 50 \\
600 \quad &+ 200 \\
617 \quad &+ 17
\end{aligned}
$$

267

Find the difference for 843 − 270 using Walter's way.

20. ⭐ **Test Prep** There are 471 children at Caleb's school. 256 children ride buses to get to school.

How many children do not ride buses to get to school?

- ○ 127
- ○ 215
- ○ 225
- ○ 227

TAKE HOME ACTIVITY · Ask your child to find the difference when subtracting 182 from 477.

FOR MORE PRACTICE:
Standards Practice Book, pp. P149–P150

Name _____

Regrouping with Zeros

Essential Question How do you regroup when there are zeros in the number you start with?

COMMON CORE STANDARD CC.2.NBT.7
Use place value understanding and properties of operations to add and subtract.

Listen and Draw  REAL WORLD

Draw or write to show how you solved the problem.

FOR THE TEACHER • Read the following problem and have children solve. There were 403 cookies in the bakery. 159 of the cookies are sold. How many cookies were not sold? Encourage children to discuss and show different ways to solve the problem.

Math Talk
Describe another way that you could solve the problem.

MATHEMATICAL PRACTICES

Model and Draw

Ms. Dean has a book with 504 pages in it. She has read 178 pages so far. How many more pages does she still have to read?

$$\begin{array}{r} 5\ 0\ 4 \\ -\ 1\ 7\ 8 \\ \hline \end{array}$$

Step 1 There are not enough ones to subtract from.

Since there are 0 tens, regroup 5 hundreds as 4 hundreds 10 tens.

$$\begin{array}{r} {\scriptstyle 4\ \ 10} \\ 5\!\!\!/\ 0\!\!\!/\ 4 \\ -\ 1\ 7\ 8 \\ \hline \end{array}$$

Step 2 Next, regroup 10 tens 4 ones as 9 tens 14 ones.

Now there are enough ones to subtract from.

$$14 - 8 = 6$$

$$\begin{array}{r} {\scriptstyle\ \ 9} \\ {\scriptstyle 4\ \ \cancel{10}\ \ 14} \\ \cancel{5}\ \cancel{0}\ 4 \\ -\ 1\ 7\ 8 \\ \hline 6 \end{array}$$

Step 3 Subtract the tens.

$$9 - 7 = 2$$

Subtract the hundreds.

$$4 - 1 = 3$$

$$\begin{array}{r} {\scriptstyle\ \ 9} \\ {\scriptstyle 4\ \ \cancel{10}\ \ 14} \\ \cancel{5}\ \cancel{0}\ \cancel{4} \\ -\ 1\ 7\ 8 \\ \hline 3\ 2\ 6 \end{array}$$

Share and Show

Solve. Write the difference.

1.
$$\begin{array}{r} 3\ 0\ 8 \\ -\ 2\ 5\ 9 \\ \hline \end{array}$$

2.
$$\begin{array}{r} 7\ 5\ 5 \\ -\ 4\ 3\ 8 \\ \hline \end{array}$$

3.
$$\begin{array}{r} 8\ 0\ 1 \\ -\ 3\ 7\ 5 \\ \hline \end{array}$$

On Your Own

Solve. Write the difference.

4.

$$
\begin{array}{r}
5\ 6\ 3 \\
-\ 1\ 8\ 2 \\
\hline
\end{array}
$$

5.

$$
\begin{array}{r}
9\ 0\ 4 \\
-\ 5\ 6\ 8 \\
\hline
\end{array}
$$

6.

$$
\begin{array}{r}
7\ 0\ 5 \\
-\ 2\ 3\ 1 \\
\hline
\end{array}
$$

7.

$$
\begin{array}{r}
6\ 0\ 3 \\
-\ 3\ 2\ 8 \\
\hline
\end{array}
$$

8.

$$
\begin{array}{r}
4\ 4\ 2 \\
-\ 2\ 3\ 8 \\
\hline
\end{array}
$$

9.

$$
\begin{array}{r}
9\ 0\ 1 \\
-\ 6\ 7\ 5 \\
\hline
\end{array}
$$

10.

$$
\begin{array}{r}
7\ 0\ 2 \\
-\ 4\ 2\ 6 \\
\hline
\end{array}
$$

11.

$$
\begin{array}{r}
6\ 8\ 4 \\
-\ 2\ 1\ 9 \\
\hline
\end{array}
$$

12.

$$
\begin{array}{r}
4\ 7\ 9 \\
-\ 1\ 3\ 7 \\
\hline
\end{array}
$$

 H.O.T. First, solve for the difference.
Then use addition to check your work.

13.

$$
\begin{array}{r}
3\ 0\ 4 \\
-\ 1\ 3\ 8 \\
\hline
\end{array}
\quad + \underline{\hspace{2cm}}
$$

14.

$$
\begin{array}{r}
9\ 0\ 5 \\
-\ 7\ 5\ 6 \\
\hline
\end{array}
\quad + \underline{\hspace{2cm}}
$$

PROBLEM SOLVING REAL WORLD

15. Miguel has 125 more baseball cards than Chad. Miguel has 435 baseball cards. How many baseball cards does Chad have?

_____ baseball cards

16. H.O.T. Claire has 250 pennies. Some pennies are in a box and some are in her bank. There are more than 100 pennies in each place. How many pennies could be in each place?

_____ pennies in a box

_____ pennies in her bank

Explain how you solved the problem.

_____

_____

_____

_____

17. ⭐ **Test Prep** There are 403 cats and dogs at the Pet Fair. There are 227 dogs. How many cats are there?

- ○ 186
- ○ 184
- ○ 176
- ○ 164

TAKE HOME ACTIVITY • Ask your child to explain how he or she solved one of the problems in this lesson.

FOR MORE PRACTICE:
Standards Practice Book, pp. P151–P152

Name _____

 **Chapter 6 Review/Test**

Vocabulary

Use a word in the box to complete each sentence.

| sum |
| regroup |
| difference |

1. You can _____ 7 hundreds 1 ten as 6 hundreds 11 tens. (p. 310)

2. In 235 − 108 = 127, 127 is the _____. (p. 306)

Concepts and Skills

Draw quick pictures. Write how many hundreds, tens, and ones in all. Write the number. (CC.2.NBT.7)

3. Add 246 and 132.

Hundreds	Tens	Ones

_____ hundreds _____ tens _____ ones

_____

Break apart the addends to find the sum. (CC.2.NBT.7)

4.   413 ⟶ _____ + _____ + _____

   +278 ⟶ _____ + _____ + _____

   _____ + _____ + _____ = _____

Fill in the bubble for the correct answer choice.

5. Mr. Kent's art class used 234 craft sticks.
   Ms. Reed's art class used 358 craft sticks.
   How many craft sticks were used by the
   two classes? (CC.2.NBT.7)

   ○ 524
   ○ 582
   ○ 592
   ○ 692

6. At the marine park, 563 people were at
   the dolphin show. 281 people were at
   the otter show.

   How many people were at the two shows? (CC.2.NBT.7)

   ○ 844
   ○ 854
   ○ 944
   ○ 954

7. 116 girls and 122 boys saw the school play.
   How many children saw the school play? (CC.2.NBT.7)

   ○ 338
   ○ 238
   ○ 234
   ○ 226

Fill in the bubble for the correct answer choice.

8. Mr. Brown had 542 baseball cards in his collection. He sold 128 of the cards. How many cards does he have now? (CC.2.NBT.7)

- ○ 676
- ○ 670
- ○ 426
- ○ 414

9. At the library, there are 668 books and magazines. There are 565 books at the library. How many magazines are there? (CC.2.NBT.7)

- ○ 13
- ○ 103
- ○ 403
- ○ 1,233

10. Mrs. Preston had 509 leaves. She gave 274 leaves to her students.

How many leaves does she still have? (CC.2.NBT.7)

- ○ 225
- ○ 235
- ○ 335
- ○ 375

Constructed Response

11. Find the sum for each problem.

$$
\begin{array}{r} 1\,5\,6 \\ +\ 4\,0\,8 \\ \hline \end{array}
\qquad\qquad
\begin{array}{r} 5\,7\,2 \\ +\ 1\,3\,5 \\ \hline \end{array}
$$

Describe how these problems are different. (CC.2.NBT.7)

_____

_____

Performance Task (CC.2.NBT.7)

12. This is how many blocks each child used.

Anna
118 blocks

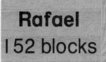
Rafael
152 blocks

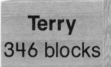
Terry
346 blocks

How many blocks did Anna and Terry use?
Draw or write to show how you found your answer.

How many more blocks did Terry use than Rafael?
Draw or write to show how you found your answer.

Making a Kite

by Kathryn Krieger and Christine Ruiz

COMMON CORE

CRITICAL AREA Using standard units of measure

Ellie and Mike get the materials to make a kite. Then they make the body of the kite.

Materials

paper kite pattern
tape
straw
10 small paper clips
scissors
hole punch
string
3 sheets of paper
streamer paper

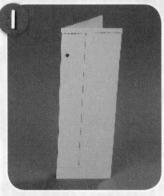

1

Fold the pattern in half.

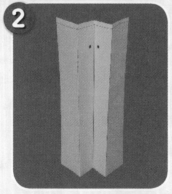

2

Fold along both dashed lines.

3

Tape on each end.

Science

What are the parts of a kite?

Mike does not want the front of the kite to bend too much. He uses a straw to make the kite stronger.

Measure 3 paper clips long. Cut.

Tape the straw on the line.

Why is a straw used as part of the kite?

327

The kite must have a string for Ellie or Mike to hold. If the kite does not have a string, it will blow away. Ellie will tie the string onto the kite.

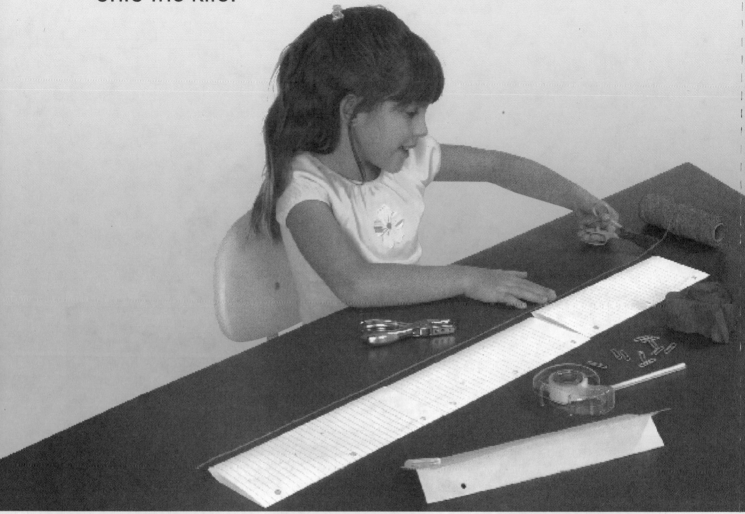

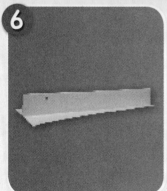

6 Punch one hole.

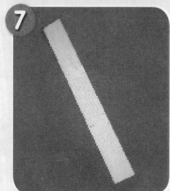

7 Measure 3 paper-lengths of string. Cut.

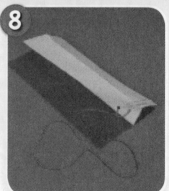

8 Put the string through the hole and tie it.

328

Why is a string needed on a kite?

A tail will help the kite fly straight. Mike measures streamer paper and will tape it to the kite. Then the kite will be finished!

Measure 10 paper-clip-lengths of streamer paper. Cut.

Tape the streamer to the kite as a tail.

Why is a tail needed on a kite?

You can make a kite too.
Start at the beginning of
this story. Follow the steps.

© Houghton Mifflin Harcourt Publishing Company

Science

How do all of the parts help the kite fly?

Write About the Story

Draw and write a story about making a kite. Explain how to measure the parts of the kite in your story.

Vocabulary Review

measure

length

_____

_____

_____

_____

What is the length?

Estimate the length of each straw.
Then measure the length of each
straw using small paper clips.

1. Estimate: about _____ paper clips long

   Measure: about _____ paper clips long

2. Estimate: about _____ paper clips long

   Measure: about _____ paper clips long

3. Estimate: about _____ paper clips long

   Measure: about _____ paper clips long

Look around the classroom. Find other
objects to measure. Measure the length
of each object using small paper clips.

Chapter 7
Money and Time

Curious About Math with
Curious George

A sundial shows the time using the position of the sun. It has numbers around it, like a clock face. What numbers are on a clock face?

Name _____

Show What You Know ✓

Order Numbers to 100 on a Number Line

Write the number that is just before, between, or just after.

1. 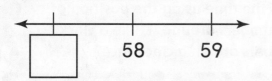 58 59

2. 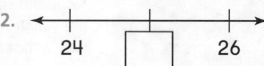 24 26

Skip Count by Fives and Tens

3. Count by fives. Write how many in all.

_____   _____ paints in all

4. Count by tens. Write how many in all.

_____   _____ paints in all

Time to the Hour

Write the time shown on the clock.

5.

6.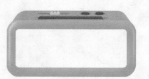

 Family note: This page checks your child's understanding of important skills needed for success in Chapter 7.

© Houghton Mifflin Harcourt Publishing Company

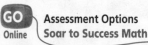 Assessment Options
Soar to Success Math

Review Words
count
pattern
count on

Vocabulary Builder

Visualize It

Fill in the graphic organizer.
Show ways to **count on**.

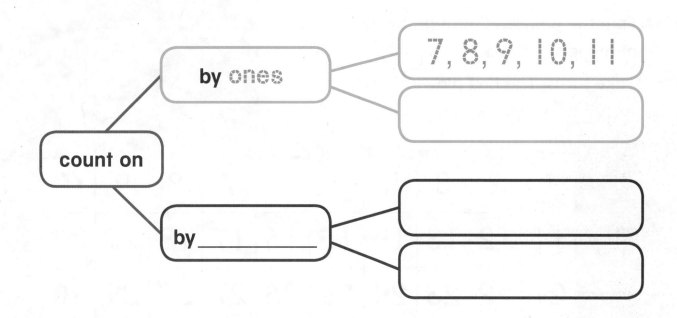

by ones   7, 8, 9, 10, 11

count on

by _____

Understand Vocabulary

Write the missing numbers in each counting **pattern.**

1. **Count** by ones.   40, ____, ____, ____, 44, ____, 46, ____

2. **Count** by fives.   10, 15, ____, ____, ____, 35, ____, ____

3. **Count** by tens.   20, ____, ____, 50, ____, ____, 80, ____

Game

5 and 10 Count

Materials • 1 🎲 • 1 🎲 • 🔄

Play with a partner.

1. Spin the pointer on 🔄 for your starting number. Put your cube on that number.

2. Spin the pointer. Count on by that number two times.

3. Take turns. The first player to get to 100 wins. Play again.

Spinner: 10 | 5 | 5 | 10

1	2	3	4	**5**	6	7	8	9	**10**
11	12	13	14	**15**	16	17	18	19	**20**
21	22	23	24	**25**	26	27	28	29	**30**
31	32	33	34	**35**	36	37	38	39	**40**
41	42	43	44	**45**	46	47	48	49	**50**
51	52	53	54	**55**	56	57	58	59	**60**
61	62	63	64	**65**	66	67	68	69	**70**
71	72	73	74	**75**	76	77	78	79	**80**
81	82	83	84	**85**	86	87	88	89	**90**
91	92	93	94	**95**	96	97	98	99	**100**

Name _____

Dimes, Nickels, and Pennies

Essential Question How do you find the total value of a group of dimes, nickels, and pennies?

COMMON CORE STANDARD CC.2.MD.8
Work with time and money.

Listen and Draw REAL WORLD

Sort the coins. Then draw the coins.

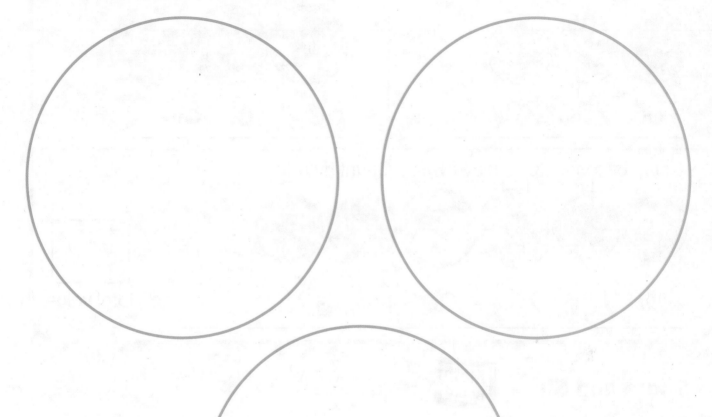

FOR THE TEACHER • Distribute play coins of dimes, nickels, and pennies and discuss their values. Have children sort the coins and draw them inside the three circles. Have children label the drawings with the numbers *1, 5,* or *10* to indicate the cent value of each coin drawn.

Chapter 7

Math Talk
A nickel has the same value as how many pennies? **Explain.**

MATHEMATICAL PRACTICES

Model and Draw

 10 cents
10¢

 5 cents
5¢

 I cent
I¢

dime

¢ is the **cent sign**.

nickel

penny

Count dimes by tens.	Count nickels by fives.

10¢, 20¢, 30¢	5¢, 10¢, 15¢

Count by tens.   Count by fives.   Count by ones.

10¢, 20¢, 25¢, 30¢, 31¢, 32¢

32¢

total value

Share and Show

Count on to find the total value.

1.

_____

total value

2.

_____

total value

Name _____

On Your Own

Count on to find the total value.

3.

_____

total value

4.

_____

total value

5.

total value

6.

total value

7.

total value

8.

total value

Chapter 7 • Lesson 1

PROBLEM SOLVING REAL WORLD

 Write Math

Solve. Write or draw to explain.

9. Maggie had 5 nickels. She gave 2 nickels to her sister. What is the total value of the nickels that Maggie has now?

_____

10. Jackson has 4 pennies and 3 dimes. How much money does Jackson have?

_____

11. **H.O.T.** Draw two ways to show 25¢. You can use dimes, nickels, and pennies.

12. ⭐ **Test Prep** Sue has these coins. How much money is this?

○ 4¢
○ 20¢
○ 40¢
○ 80¢

TAKE HOME ACTIVITY • Draw pictures of five coins, using dimes, nickels, and pennies. Ask your child to find the total value.

FOR MORE PRACTICE:
Standards Practice Book, pp. P157–P158

Name _____

Quarters

Essential Question How do you find the
total value of a group of coins?

COMMON CORE STANDARD CC.2.MD.8
Work with time and money.

Listen and Draw

Sort the coins. Then draw the coins.

FOR THE TEACHER • Distribute play coins of
quarters, dimes, and nickels and discuss their
values. Have children sort the coins and draw
them inside the three boxes. Have them label
the drawings with 5¢, 10¢, or 25¢.

Math Talk
Describe how the
value of a quarter is
greater than the
value of a dime.

MATHEMATICAL
PRACTICES

Chapter 7

three hundred forty-one **341**

Model and Draw

A **quarter** has a value of 25 cents.

25¢

Count by twenty-fives.   Count by tens.   Count by ones.

25¢, 50¢, 60¢, 70¢, 71¢, 72¢

72¢

total value

Share and Show

Count on to find the total value.

1.

_____

total value

2.

_____

total value

3.

_____

total value

On Your Own

Count on to find the total value.

4.

    _____

    ☐

    total value

5.

    _____

    ☐

    total value

6.

    ☐

    total value

7.

    ☐

    total value

8.

    ☐

    total value

PROBLEM SOLVING

 REAL WORLD

Write Math

Read the clue. Choose the name of a coin from the box to answer the question.

nickel	dime
quarter	penny

9. I have the same value as 5 pennies.

What coin am I?

_____

10. I have the same value as 25 pennies.

What coin am I?

_____

11. I have the same value as 2 nickels.

What coin am I?

12. **H.O.T.** I have the same value as a group of 4 nickels and 5 pennies.

What coin am I?

_____

13. ⭐ **Test Prep** Tom gives these coins to his brother.

How much money does Tom give to his brother?

○ 80¢

○ 65¢

○ 50¢

○ 25¢

TAKE HOME ACTIVITY · Have your child draw two quarters, two dimes, and two nickels, and then find the total value.

FOR MORE PRACTICE:
Standards Practice Book, pp. P159–P160

Count Collections

Essential Question How do you order coins to help find the total value of a group of coins?

COMMON CORE STANDARD CC.2.MD.8
Work with time and money.

Listen and Draw REAL WORLD

Line up the coins from greatest value to least value. Then draw the coins in that order.

greatest	least

greatest	least

FOR THE TEACHER • Give each child a mixture of four play coins. Have children order their coins and then draw them. Have children trade sets of coins and repeat.

Math Talk
Describe how the values of the different kinds of coins compare.
MATHEMATICAL PRACTICES

Model and Draw

Order the coins from greatest value to least value.
Then find the total value.

(25¢) (25¢) (10¢) (1¢) (1¢)

> Count the cents.
> 25, 50, 60, 61, 62

_____
total value

Share and Show

Draw and label the coins from greatest
to least value. Find the total value.

> Remember: Write
> the cent sign.

1.

_____

☑ 2.

_____

☑ 3.

_____

346 three hundred forty-six

© Houghton Mifflin Harcourt Publishing Company

On Your Own

Draw and label the coins from greatest to least value. Find the total value.

4.

_____

5.

_____

6.

_____

7.

_____

8.

_____

Chapter 7 • Lesson 3

PROBLEM SOLVING REAL WORLD

Write Math

Solve. Write or draw to explain.

9. Paulo had these coins.

He spent 1 quarter. How much
money does he have now?

_____

10. Rachel has 2 quarters, 3 dimes,
and 1 nickel in her bank. How
much money is in Rachel's bank?

_____

11. **H.O.T.** Blake has only nickels and dimes.
He has twice as many nickels as dimes.
The total value of his coins is 60¢.
What coins does Blake have?

_____ nickels   _____ dimes

12. ⭐ **Test Prep** Tyler has these coins in his
pocket. What is the total value of these coins?

○ 65¢
○ 60¢
○ 55¢
○ 50¢

TAKE HOME ACTIVITY • Have your child draw and label
coins with a total value of 32¢.

348 three hundred forty-eight

FOR MORE PRACTICE:
Standards Practice Book, pp. P161–P162

Name _____

Show Amounts in Two Ways

Essential Question How do you choose coins to show a money amount in different ways?

COMMON CORE STANDARD CC.2.MD.8
Work with time and money.

Listen and Draw REAL WORLD

Show the amount with coins. Draw the coins.
Write the amount.

FOR THE TEACHER • Distribute play coins. Tell children to use coins to show 27 cents. Then have them draw the coins and write the amount. Repeat the activity for 51 cents.

Math Talk
Can you show 10¢ with 3 coins? **Explain** how you know.

MATHEMATICAL PRACTICES

Chapter 7

Model and Draw

Here are two ways to show 30¢.

Look at Matthew's way. If you trade 2 dimes and 1 nickel for 1 quarter, the coins will show Alicia's way.

Count the cents. Start with the dimes.

Count the cents. Start with the quarter.

Matthew

30¢

Alicia

30¢

Share and Show

Use coins. Show the amount in two ways. Draw and label the coins.

✓ 1.

61¢

✓ 2.

36¢

On Your Own

Use coins. Show the amount in two ways.
Draw and label the coins.

3.

55¢

4.

90¢

5.

75¢

6.

42¢

PROBLEM SOLVING REAL WORLD

Write Math

Use coins to solve.

7. Lee buys a pen for 50¢. Draw coins to
   show two different ways to pay 50¢.

8. **H.O.T.** Delia used 4 coins to buy
   a book for 40¢. Draw coins to show
   two ways to pay 40¢ with 4 coins.

9. ⭐**Test Prep** Rex buys an eraser that costs 20¢.
   Which group of coins has a total value of 20¢?

   ○ 2 nickels and 10 pennies

   ○ 1 dime and 1 nickel

   ○ 3 nickels and 1 dime

   ○ 1 quarter and 5 pennies

TAKE HOME ACTIVITY • With your child, take turns drawing
different collections of coins to show 57¢.

FOR MORE PRACTICE:
Standards Practice Book, pp. P163–P164

Name _____

One Dollar

Essential Question How can you show the value of one dollar with coins?

COMMON CORE STANDARD CC.2.MD.8
Work with time and money.

Listen and Draw REAL WORLD

Draw the coins. Write the total value.

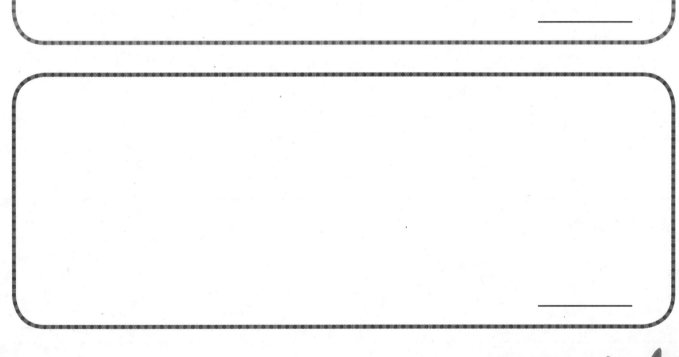

_____

_____

FOR THE TEACHER • In the first box, have children draw eight nickels and then count to find the total value. In the second box, have children draw eight dimes and then count to find the total value.

Math Talk
How many pennies have the same value as 80¢? **Explain.**

MATHEMATICAL PRACTICES

Chapter 7

One **dollar** has the same value as 100 cents.

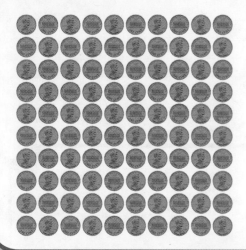

$$\$1.00 = 100¢$$

dollar sign ⟶   ⟵ **decimal point**

The decimal point separates the dollars from the cents.

Share and Show

Draw the coins to show $1.00. Write the total value.

Count 100 cents for one dollar.

1. nickels

$1.00
_____

2. quarters

_____

3. dimes

_____

Name _____

On Your Own

Circle coins to make $1.00.
Cross out the coins you do not use.

4.

5.

6.

7. **H.O.T.** Draw more coins to show $1.00.

TAKE HOME ACTIVITY • Have your child draw a group of
coins to show $1.00.

Name _____

Mid-Chapter Checkpoint

Concepts and Skills

Count on to find the total value. (CC.2.MD.8)

1.

☐

total value

2.

☐

total value

Use coins. Show the amount in two ways.
Draw and label the coins. (CC.2.MD.8)

3.

31¢

4. ⭐ **Test Prep** Mary used
these coins to buy a folder.
What is the total value of
these coins? (CC.2.MD.8)

○ 30¢
○ 35¢
○ 60¢
○ 70¢

Amounts Greater Than $1

Essential Question How do you show money amounts greater than one dollar?

COMMON CORE STANDARD CC.2.MD.8
Work with time and money.

Listen and Draw REAL WORLD

Draw and label the coins.
Write the total value.

_____
total value

Math Talk

Explain how you found the total value of the coins in the coin bank.

MATHEMATICAL PRACTICES

FOR THE TEACHER • Read the following problem: Dominic has 1 quarter, 2 dimes, 3 nickels, and 1 penny in his coin bank. How much money is in Dominic's bank? Have children draw and label coins to help them solve the problem.

Model and Draw

When you write amounts greater than one dollar,
use a dollar sign and a decimal point.

$1.00

$1.27
_____
total value

$1.50
_____
total value

Share and Show

Circle the money that makes $1.00. Then
write the total value of the money shown.

1.

_____

2.

_____

Name _____

On Your Own

Circle the money that makes $1.00. Then write the total value of the money shown.

3.

_____

4.

_____

5.

_____

6.

_____

PROBLEM SOLVING REAL WORLD

Write Math

Solve. Write or draw to explain.

7. Martin used 3 quarters and 7 dimes to pay for a kite. How much money did he use?

_____

8. **H.O.T.** Pam has fewer than 9 coins. The coins have a total value of $1.15. What coins could she have?

Draw the coins. Then write a list of her coins.

_____

_____

9. ⭐ **Test Prep** Jason put this money in his bank. What is the total value of this money?

○ $1.10
○ $1.25
○ $1.30
○ $1.35

TAKE HOME ACTIVITY • With your child, take turns drawing coins or a $1 bill and coins with a total value of $1.23.

FOR MORE PRACTICE:
Standards Practice Book, pp. P167–P168

Problem Solving • Money

Essential Question How does acting it out help when solving problems about money?

COMMON CORE STANDARD CC.2.MD.8
Work with time and money.

Kendra gave 2 dimes, 2 nickels, 1 quarter, and two $1 bills to the clerk for a puzzle. How much money did Kendra give the clerk?

🔑 Unlock the Problem

What do I need to find?	**What information do I need to use?**
how much money Kendra gave the clerk	Kendra gave the clerk 2 dimes,

Show how to solve the problem.
Draw to show the money that Kendra used.

Kendra gave the clerk _____.

HOME CONNECTION • Your child used play money to act out the problem. Representing problems with materials can be a useful strategy for children to use to solve problems.

© Houghton Mifflin Harcourt Publishing Company

Try Another Problem

Use play coins and bills to solve.
Draw to show what you did.

- What do I need to find?
- What information do I need to use?

1. Jacob has two $1 bills, 2 dimes, and 3 pennies in his pocket. How much money does Jacob have in his pocket?

_____

2. Amber used 2 quarters, 1 nickel, 1 dime, and three $1 bills to buy a toy. How much money did Amber use to buy the toy?

_____

Math Talk
Explain how you found the amount of money in Jacob's pocket.

MATHEMATICAL PRACTICES

Name _____

Share and Show

Use play coins and bills to solve.
Draw to show what you did.

✓ **3.** Val used 3 quarters, 2 nickels, 2 pennies, and one $1 bill to buy a book. How much money did Val use to buy the book?

_____

✓ **4.** Derek has two $1 bills, 2 quarters, and 6 dimes. How much money does he have?

_____

---

5. Katy gave the clerk 3 quarters, 2 nickels, 2 dimes, and 3 pennies. How much money did she give to the clerk?

_____

On Your Own

Solve. Write or draw to explain.

Write Math

6. Mr. Murphy has 120 fewer stickers than Miss Chen. Mr. Murphy has 364 stickers. How many stickers does Miss Chen have?

_____ stickers

7. H.O.T. Mia found 38 shells at the beach on Monday and 45 shells on Tuesday. She gave 26 shells to her sister. How many shells does Mia have now?

_____ shells

Describe how you solved the problem.

_____

_____

_____

_____

8. ⭐ **Test Prep** Ross has 2 quarters, 1 dime, and two $1 bills. How much money does Ross have?

- ○ $2.60
- ○ $2.55
- ○ $2.35
- ○ $1.60

TAKE HOME ACTIVITY • Ask your child to explain how he or she solved the problem in Exercise 8.

FOR MORE PRACTICE:
Standards Practice Book, pp. P169–P170

Name _____

Time to the Hour and Half Hour

Essential Question How do you tell time to the hour and half hour on a clock?

COMMON CORE STANDARD CC.2.MD.7
Work with time and money.

Listen and Draw REAL WORLD

Draw the hour hand to show each time.

FOR THE TEACHER • Call out times to the hour and to the half hour. Begin with 3:00. Have children draw the hour hand to show the time. Repeat the activity for half past 5:00, 11:00, and half past 8:00.

Math Talk
Describe where the hour hand points to show half past 4:00.

MATHEMATICAL PRACTICES

Chapter 7

Model and Draw

It takes 5 **minutes** for the minute hand to move from one number to the next number on a clock face.

The clock hands on these clocks show 4:00 and 4:30. Write the times below the clocks.

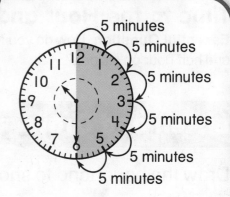

4:00

4:30

The 30 tells you that the time is 30 minutes after the hour.

Share and Show

Look at the clock hands. Write the time.

1.

 2.

3.

On Your Own

Look at the clock hands. Write the time.

4.

5.

6.

7.

8.

9.

H.O.T. Look at the time. Draw the hour hand and the minute hand to show the same time.

10.

11.

12.

PROBLEM SOLVING REAL WORLD

Write Math

13. **H.O.T.** Allie eats lunch when the hour hand points halfway between the 11 and the 12, and the minute hand points to the 6. When does Allie eat lunch? Show the time on both clocks.

How do you know what time to write in the digital clock? Explain.

_____

_____

_____

14. ⭐ **Test Prep** Reggie's guitar lesson starts at 10:30. Which clock shows this time?

○

○

○

○

TAKE HOME ACTIVITY · Have your child explain how he or she completed the exercises on this page.

FOR MORE PRACTICE:
Standards Practice Book, pp. P171–P172

Name _____

Time to 5 Minutes

Essential Question How do you tell and show time to five minutes?

COMMON CORE STANDARD CC.2.MD.7
Work with time and money.

Listen and Draw REAL WORLD

Draw the hour hand and the minute hand to show the time.

 FOR THE TEACHER • Read the following story and have children draw the hour and minute hands to show each time. Sofia goes to music at 10:30. She goes to the playground at 11:00. She eats lunch at 11:30. Show the times Sofia does these things.

Math Talk
Describe where the minute hand points to show half past the hour.

MATHEMATICAL PRACTICES

Model and Draw

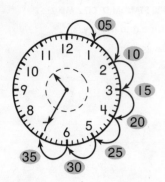

What does it mean when the minute hand points to the 7?

Count by fives until you reach the 7.

Remember:
The minute hand moves from one number to the next in 5 minutes.

The hour hand points between the 10 and the 11. The minute hand points to the 7.

The time is ___10:35___.

Share and Show

Look at the clock hands. Write the time.

1.

2.

3.

4.

✓ 5.

✓ 6.

Name _____

On Your Own

Look at the clock hands. Write the time.

7.

8.

9.

10.

11.

12.

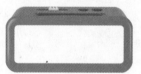 Look at the time. Draw the minute hand to show the same time.

13.

14.

15.

PROBLEM SOLVING

REAL WORLD

Write Math

Draw the minute hand to show the time.
Then write the time.

16. My hour hand points between
the 8 and the 9. My minute hand
points to the 5. What time do
I show?

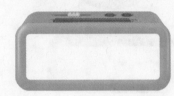

17. H.O.T. How many minutes does it take for the minute
hand to travel around the clock from the 12 to the 12?

_____

18. ⭐ **Test Prep** What time is shown
on this clock?

○ 1:45

○ 12:45

○ 12:09

○ 9:05

TAKE HOME ACTIVITY • Have your child draw a large blank clock face
and use two pencils as clock hands to show some different times.

FOR MORE PRACTICE:
Standards Practice Book, pp. P173–P174

Practice Telling Time

Essential Question What are the different ways you can read the time on a clock?

COMMON CORE STANDARD CC.2.MD.7
Work with time and money.

Listen and Draw REAL WORLD

Write the times on the digital clocks.
Then label the clocks with the children's names.

 FOR THE TEACHER • First have children write the time for each analog clock. Then write *Luke, Beth, Kelly,* and *Mike* on the board. Tell children to listen for each name to label the different times with. Luke plays football at 3:25. Beth eats lunch at 11:45. Kelly reads a book at 6:10. Mike eats breakfast at 7:15.

Math Talk

Where would the minute hand point to show 15 minutes after the hour? **Explain.**

MATHEMATICAL PRACTICES

Model and Draw

These are different ways to write and say the time.

15 minutes after 8
quarter past 8

30 minutes after 8
half past 8

Share and Show

Draw the minute hand to show the time. Write the time.

1. 15 minutes after 1

2. half past 9

3. quarter past 5

4. quarter past 10

☑5. 40 minutes after 3

☑6. half past 7

On Your Own

Draw the minute hand to show the time.
Write the time.

7. 15 minutes after 11

8. quarter past 4

9. 25 minutes after 8

10. 10 minutes after 6

11. half past 2

12. 45 minutes after 3

13. 5 minutes after 7

14. 30 minutes after 12

15. quarter past 10

PROBLEM SOLVING REAL WORLD

Write Math

16. Lily eats lunch at quarter past 12. Meg eats lunch at 12:30. Katie eats lunch at 12:15. Which girls eat lunch at the same time?

_____ and _____

17. Austin arrives at school at half past 8. Draw clock hands to show half past 8. Then write the time.

18. **H.O.T.** Soccer practice starts at 4:30. Gabe arrives at soccer practice at 4:15. Does he arrive before or after practice starts? Explain.

_____

_____

_____

19. ⭐ **Test Prep** What time is shown on this clock?

- ○ half past 4
- ○ half past 5
- ○ 6 minutes after 4
- ○ quarter past 5

TAKE HOME ACTIVITY • Name a time to 5 minutes. Ask your child to describe where the clock hands point at this time.

FOR MORE PRACTICE:
Standards Practice Book, pp. P175–P176

Name _____

A.M. and P.M.

Essential Question How do you use A.M. and P.M. to describe times?

COMMON CORE STANDARD CC.2.MD.7
Work with time and money.

Listen and Draw REAL WORLD

Draw the clock hands to show each time.
Then write each time.

Morning	Evening

FOR THE TEACHER • Have children draw a picture and write a label for the picture for an activity they do in the morning and for an activity they do in the evening. Then have them show the time they do each activity on the clocks.

Math Talk
Describe some activities that you do in both the morning and in the evening.

MATHEMATICAL PRACTICES

Model and Draw

Noon is 12:00 in the daytime.
Midnight is 12:00 at night.

Times after midnight and before noon are written with **A.M.**

11:00 A.M. is in the morning.

Times after noon and before midnight are written with **P.M.**

11:00 P.M. is in the evening.

Share and Show

Write the time. Then circle **A.M.** or **P.M.**

1. eat breakfast

(A.M.)

P.M.

2. go to art class

A.M.

P.M.

☑ 3. do homework

A.M.

P.M.

☑ 4. arrive at school

A.M.

P.M.

On Your Own

Write the time. Then circle A.M. or P.M.

5. go to the library

A.M.

P.M.

6. wake up

A.M.

P.M.

7. eat lunch

A.M.

P.M.

8. leave school

A.M.

P.M.

9. go to science class

A.M.

P.M.

10. look at the moon

A.M.

P.M.

PROBLEM SOLVING

REAL WORLD

Write Math

11. Use the times in the list. Complete the story.

Don got to school at _____.

His class went to the library

at _____. After school,

Don read a book at _____.

| 10:15 A.M. |
| 3:20 P.M. |
| 8:30 A.M. |

12. **H.O.T.** Some times are shown on this time line. Write a label for each dot that names something you do at school during that part of the day.

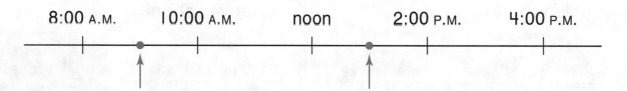

8:00 A.M.   10:00 A.M.   noon   2:00 P.M.   4:00 P.M.

_____   _____

At what times would you say the dots are placed on the time line?

_____ and _____

13. ⭐ **Test Prep** The clock shows the time that Jane went to recess. At what time did she go to recess?

○ 6:00 A.M.
○ 11:30 A.M.
○ 6:30 P.M.
○ 11:30 P.M.

TAKE HOME ACTIVITY • Name some activities and times. Have your child say A.M. or P.M. for the times.

FOR MORE PRACTICE:
Standards Practice Book, pp. P177–P178

✓ Chapter 7 Review/Test

Vocabulary

Use a word in the box to complete each sentence.

dime
dollar
A.M.
P.M.

1. One _____ has the same value as 100 cents. (p. 354)

2. The value of one _____ is 10 cents. (p. 338)

3. Times after noon and before midnight are written with _____. (p. 378)

Concepts and Skills

Count on to find the total value. (CC.2.MD.8)

4.

total value

Use coins. Show the amount in two ways.
Draw and label the coins. (CC.2.MD.8)

5.

42¢

Fill in the bubble for the correct answer choice.

6. The clock shows the time that the museum opens.
What time is shown? (CC.2.MD.7)

- ○ 8:00
- ○ 9:00
- ○ 10:00
- ○ 12:00

7. The play begins at 8:30. Which clock shows 8:30? (CC.2.MD.7)

○

○

○

○

8. The clock shows the time that music class starts.
At what time does music class start? (CC.2.MD.7)

- ○ 7:25 A.M.
- ○ 7:25 P.M.
- ○ 4:35 A.M.
- ○ 4:35 P.M.

Fill in the bubble for the correct answer choice.

9. Lindsey wants to buy lemonade that costs one dollar. Which coins could she use to buy the lemonade? (CC.2.MD.8)

○ 4 quarters

○ 4 dimes

○ 4 nickels

○ 4 pennies

10. Pete uses these coins to buy a marker. How much money is this? (CC.2.MD.8)

○ 45¢

○ 50¢

○ 55¢

○ 65¢

11. Chris used this money to buy a book. How much money is this? (CC.2.MD.8)

○ $1.50

○ $1.65

○ $1.75

○ $1.80

Constructed Response

12. Wes has 4 nickels and 10 pennies. Draw to show this amount using a different group of coins.

Explain how you decided what coins to draw. (CC.2.MD.8)

_____

_____

_____

Performance Task (CC.2.MD.7)

13. The clocks show when Rachel started each activity. Write the time for each activity.

ate a snack   played soccer   read a book

Do you think these are A.M. times or P.M. times? Explain.

_____

_____

Length in Customary Units

Curious About Math with

Curious George

The Missouri River is the longest river in the United States.

What is the longest piece of furniture in your classroom? How would you find out?

Name _____

Compare Lengths

1. Order the pencils from shortest to longest.
   Write 1, 2, 3.

_____

_____

_____

Use Nonstandard Units to Measure Length

Use real objects and ■ to measure.

2.

about _____ ■

3.

about _____ ■

Measure Length Twice: Nonstandard Units

Use ⊂⊃ first. Then use ⬛.
Measure the length of the pencil.

4. about _____ ⊂⊃

5. about _____ ⬛

Family note: This page checks your child's understanding
of important skills needed for success in Chapter 8.

© Houghton Mifflin Harcourt Publishing Company

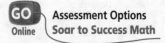

GO
Online

Assessment Options
Soar to Success Math

Vocabulary Builder

Review Words
length
longer
shorter
longest
shortest

Visualize It

Fill in the graphic organizer to describe the lengths of different objects.

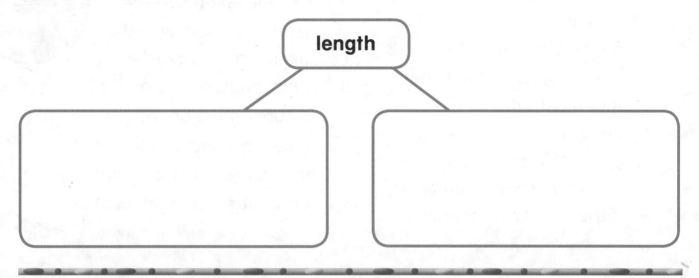

Understand Vocabulary

Use review words. Complete the sentences.

1. The blue pencil is the _____ pencil.

_____

2. The red pencil is the _____ pencil.

_____

3. The red pencil is _____ than the yellow pencil.

_____

4. The blue pencil is _____ than the yellow pencil.

Chapter **8**

 **Game**

Longer or Shorter?

Materials

- 9
- 9
-

Play with a partner.

1 Each player chooses a picture on the board and then finds a real object that matches that picture.

2 Place the objects next to each other to find which is longer and which is shorter. If the objects are the same length, choose another object.

3 Spin the pointer on the spinner. The player with the object that matches the spinner puts a cube on that picture on the board.

4 Take turns until all the pictures have cubes. The player with more cubes on the board wins.

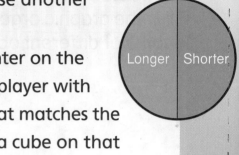

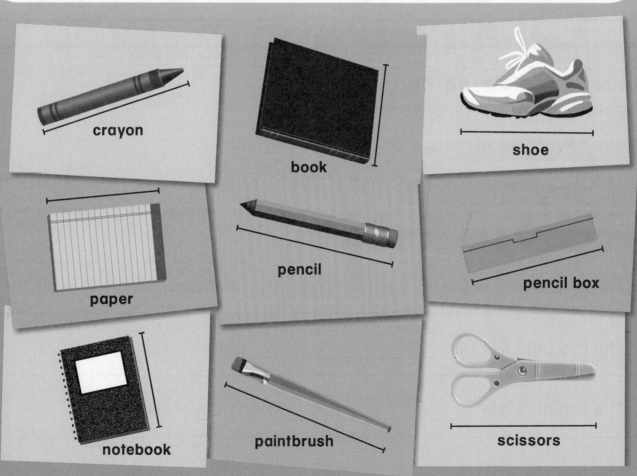

crayon

book

shoe

paper

pencil

pencil box

notebook

paintbrush

scissors

Name _____

Measure with Inch Models

Essential Question How can you use inch models to measure length?

COMMON CORE STANDARD CC.2.MD.1
Measure and estimate lengths in standard units.

Listen and Draw  REAL WORLD

Use color tiles to measure the length.

_____ color tiles

_____ color tiles

_____ color tiles

HOME CONNECTION • Your child used color tiles as an introduction to measurement of length before using standard measurement tools.

Math Talk

Describe how to use color tiles to measure the length of an object.

MATHEMATICAL PRACTICES

A color tile is about 1 **inch** long.

About how many inches long is this string?

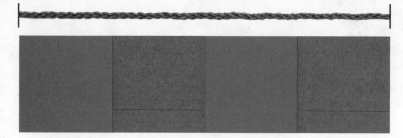

The string is 4 color tiles long.

So, the string is about _____4_____ inches long.

> Count the color tiles to find how many inches long the string is.

Share and Show

Use color tiles. Measure the length of the object in inches.

1.

about _____ inches

2.

about _____ inches

✓ 3.

about _____ inches

✓ 4.

about _____ inches

On Your Own

Use color tiles. Measure the length of the object in inches.

5.

about _____ inches

6.

about _____ inches

7.

about _____ inches

8.

about _____ inches

9.

about _____ inches

10.

about _____ inches

© Houghton Mifflin Harcourt Publishing Company

PROBLEM SOLVING REAL WORLD

Look in your classroom. Find two objects that are about 2 inches long. Draw and label the objects.

11.

12.

_____

_____

13. **H.O.T.** Liza has a piece of ribbon that is 12 inches long. She needs to cut it into pieces that are each 4 inches long. How many pieces can she make?

_____ pieces

14. ⭐ **Test Prep** Jeremy used color tiles to measure a string.

Which is the best choice for the length of the string?

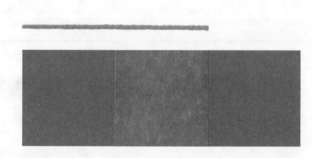

○ about 1 inch

○ about 2 inches

○ about 3 inches

○ about 4 inches

TAKE HOME ACTIVITY • Have your child use several of the same small item (such as paper clips) to measure the lengths of some objects at home.

FOR MORE PRACTICE:
Standards Practice Book, pp. P183–P184

Name _____

Make and Use a Ruler

Essential Question Why is using a ruler similar to using a row of color tiles to measure length?

COMMON CORE STANDARD CC.2.MD.1
Measure and estimate lengths in standard units.

Listen and Draw REAL WORLD

Use color tiles. Make the given length. Trace along the edge to show the length.

4 inches

2 inches

3 inches

Math Talk

Describe how you knew how many color tiles to use for each length.

MATHEMATICAL PRACTICES

HOME CONNECTION · Your child used color tiles as 1-inch models to show different lengths. This activity helps to make inch units a more familiar concept.

Model and Draw

Use a color tile to make a ruler on a paper strip.
Color 6 parts that are each about 1 inch long.

How to use your ruler:
Line up the left edge of an object with the first mark.

Share and Show

Measure the length with your ruler.
Count the inches.

1.

about _____ inches

☑ 2.

about _____ inches

☑ 3.

about _____ inches

On Your Own

Measure the length with your ruler.
Count the inches.

4.

about _____ inches

5.

about _____ inches

6.

about _____ inches

7.

about _____ inches

8.

about _____ inches

PROBLEM SOLVING REAL WORLD

Write Math

Work with a classmate.

9. **H.O.T.** Together, use both of your rulers to measure the length of a bulletin board or a window. What is the length?

about _____ inches

10. Describe what you did in Exercise 9. How did you measure a length that is longer than your rulers?

_____

_____

_____

_____

11. ⭐ **Test Prep** Use your ruler. What is the best choice for the length of this piece of yarn?

○ about 6 inches

○ about 5 inches

○ about 4 inches

○ about 3 inches

TAKE HOME ACTIVITY • Choose one object in this lesson. Have your child find objects that are longer, about the same length, and shorter.

FOR MORE PRACTICE:
Standards Practice Book, pp. P185–P186

Estimate Lengths in Inches

Essential Question How do you estimate the lengths of objects in inches?

COMMON CORE STANDARD CC.2.MD.3
Measure and estimate lengths in standard units.

Listen and Draw REAL WORLD

Choose three objects. Measure their lengths with your ruler. Draw the objects and write their lengths.

about _____ inches

about _____ inches

about _____ inches

FOR THE TEACHER • Provide a collection of small objects, 2 to 6 inches in length, for children to measure. Have them select one object, measure it, and return it before selecting another object.

Math Talk

Describe how the three lengths compare. Which is the longest object?

MATHEMATICAL PRACTICES

Model and Draw

The bead is 1 inch long. Use this bead to help find how many beads will fit on the string. Which is the best estimate for the length of the string?

2 inches   (5 inches)   8 inches

2 inches is too short.   5 inches is about right.   8 inches is too long.

Share and Show

Circle the best estimate for the length of the string.

1.

1 inch   3 inches   5 inches

☑ 2.

2 inches   4 inches   6 inches

☑ 3.

4 inches   6 inches   8 inches

On Your Own

Circle the best estimate for the length of the string.

4.

4 inches   7 inches   10 inches

5.

3 inches   6 inches   9 inches

6.

1 inch   3 inches   5 inches

7. Use the 1-inch mark. Estimate the length of each ribbon.

|← 1 inch →|

Estimates:

red ribbon: about _____ inches

blue ribbon: about _____ inches

PROBLEM SOLVING REAL WORLD

Write Math

Solve. Write or draw to explain.

8. Sasha has a string that is the length of 5 beads. Each bead is 2 inches long. What is the length of the string?

_____ inches

9. **H.O.T.** Maurice has a string that is 15 inches long. He has beads that are each 3 inches long. How many beads will fit on the string?

_____ beads

10. ⭐ **Test Prep** Tameka has this string. She has many beads that are 1 inch long, like this blue bead.

Which is the best estimate for the length of the string?

- ○ 10 inches
- ○ 5 inches
- ○ 2 inches
- ○ 1 inch

TAKE HOME ACTIVITY • With your child, estimate the lengths in inches of some small objects, such as books.

FOR MORE PRACTICE:
Standards Practice Book, pp. P187–P188

Name _____

Measure with an Inch Ruler

Essential Question How do you use an inch ruler to measure lengths?

COMMON CORE STANDARD CC.2.MD.1
Measure and estimate lengths in standard units.

Listen and Draw *REAL WORLD*

Draw each caterpillar to match the given length.

FOR THE TEACHER • Have children use the rulers that they made in Lesson 8.2 to draw a caterpillar that is 1 inch long. Have children use the 1-inch-long caterpillar as a guide to draw a caterpillar that is 2 inches long and a caterpillar that is 3 inches long, without using their rulers.

Math Talk
Describe how you decided how long to draw the 2-inch and 3-inch caterpillars.

MATHEMATICAL PRACTICES

Model and Draw

What is the length of the string to the nearest inch?

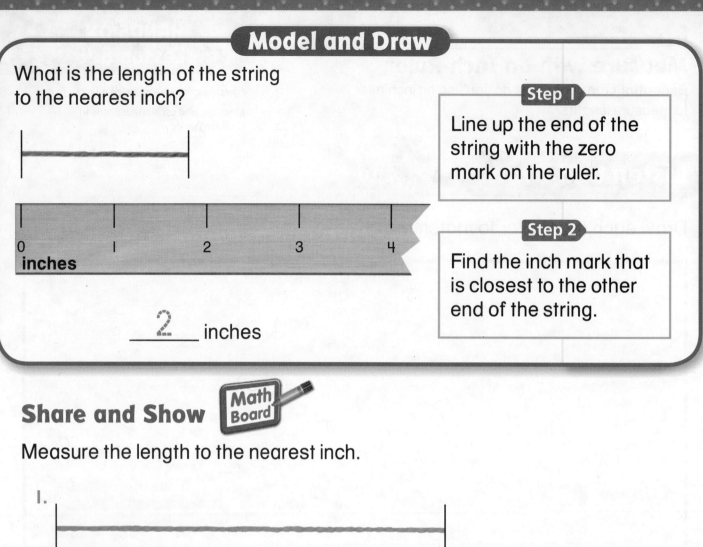

___2___ inches

Step 1

Line up the end of the string with the zero mark on the ruler.

Step 2

Find the inch mark that is closest to the other end of the string.

Share and Show

Measure the length to the nearest inch.

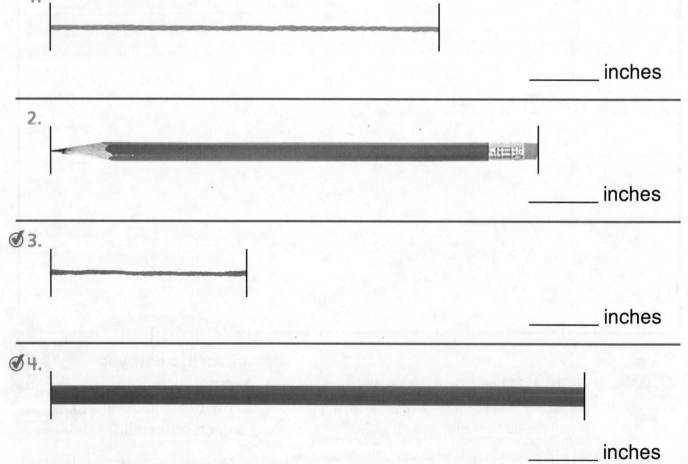

1. _____ inches

2. _____ inches

☑ 3. _____ inches

☑ 4. _____ inches

On Your Own

Measure the length to the nearest inch.

5.

_____ inches

6.

_____ inches

7.

_____ inches

8.

_____ inches

9.

_____ inches

10.

_____ inches

PROBLEM SOLVING REAL WORLD

Write Math

Solve.

11. Measure. What is the total length?

_____ inches

12. Measure. What is the total length?

_____ inches

13. **H.O.T.** How much longer is the red string than the blue string?

_____ inches longer

14. **H.O.T.** If the red and blue strings were straight and placed end to end, what would the total length be?

_____ inches

15. ⭐ **Test Prep** Use an inch ruler. What is the length of the pencil to the nearest inch?

○ 1 inch

○ 2 inches

○ 3 inches

○ 5 inches

TAKE HOME ACTIVITY • Have your child measure the lengths of some objects to the nearest inch using a ruler or a similar measuring tool.

FOR MORE PRACTICE:
Standards Practice Book, pp. P189–P190

Name _____

Problem Solving • Add and Subtract in Inches

Essential Question How can drawing a diagram help when solving problems about length?

COMMON CORE STANDARDS CC.2.MD.5, CC.2.MD.6
Relate addition and subtraction to length.

There is a paper clip chain that is 16 inches long.
Ann removes 9 inches of paper clips from the chain.
How long is the paper clip chain now?

Unlock the Problem REAL WORLD

What do I need to find?

how long the paper

clip chain is now

What information do I need to use?

The chain is _____ inches long.

_____ inches of paper clips are

removed from the chain.

Show how to solve the problem.

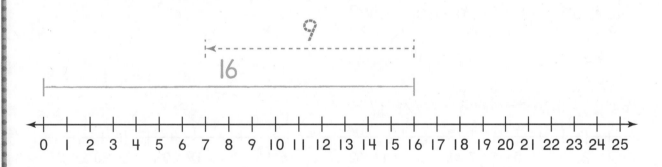

_____

The paper clip chain is _____ inches long now.

HOME CONNECTION • Your child drew a diagram to represent a problem about lengths. The diagram can be used to choose the operation for solving the problem.

Try Another Problem

Draw a diagram. Write a number sentence using a ▮ for the missing number. Solve.

1. Carmen has a string that is 13 inches long and a string that is 8 inches long. How many inches of string does she have?

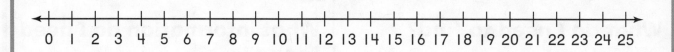

_____

Carmen has _____ inches of string.

2. Eli has a cube train that is 24 inches long.
He removes 9 inches of cubes from the train.
How long is Eli's cube train now?

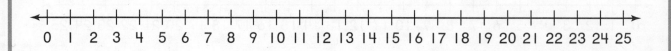

_____

Eli's cube train is _____ inches long now.

Math Talk
Describe how your diagram shows what happened in the second problem.

MATHEMATICAL PRACTICES

© Houghton Mifflin Harcourt Publishing Company

Share and Show

Draw a diagram. Write a number sentence using
a ⬜ for the missing number. Solve.

☑**3.** Lee has a paper strip chain that is 25 inches
long. He unhooks 13 inches from the chain.
How long is Lee's paper strip chain now?

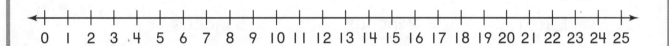

0 1 2 3 4 5 6 7 8 9 10 11 12 13 14 15 16 17 18 19 20 21 22 23 24 25

_____

Lee's paper strip chain is _____ inches long now.

---

4. **H.O.T.** Sue has two ribbons that have the
same length. She has 18 inches of ribbon in all.
How long is each ribbon?

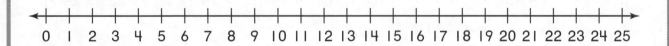

0 1 2 3 4 5 6 7 8 9 10 11 12 13 14 15 16 17 18 19 20 21 22 23 24 25

_____

Each ribbon is _____ inches long.

TAKE HOME ACTIVITY · Have your child explain how
he or she used a diagram to solve Exercise 4.

✓ Mid-Chapter Checkpoint

Concepts and Skills

Use color tiles. Measure the length of the object in inches. (CC.2.MD.1)

1.

about _____ inches

The bead is one inch long. Circle the best estimate for the length of the string. (CC.2.MD.3)

2.

      1 inch   2 inches   5 inches

Draw a diagram. Write a number sentence using a ▇ for the missing number. Solve.

3. A mark is 17 inches long. Katy erases 9 inches from the mark. How long is the mark now? (CC.2.MD.5, CC.2.MD.6)

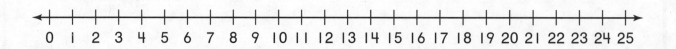

_____

The mark is _____ inches long now.

4. ⭐ **Test Prep** Use an inch ruler. What is the length of the string to the nearest inch? (CC.2.MD.1)

   ○ 1 inch

   ○ 2 inches

   ○ 3 inches

   ○ 5 inches

Name _____

Measure in Inches and Feet

Essential Question Why is measuring in feet different from measuring in inches?

COMMON CORE STANDARD CC.2.MD.2
Measure and estimate lengths in standard units.

Listen and Draw  REAL WORLD

Draw or write to describe how you did each measurement.

First measurement

Second measurement

FOR THE TEACHER • Have pairs of children stand apart and measure the distance between them with sheets of paper folded in half lengthwise. Then have them measure the same distance using large paper clips.

Math Talk
Describe how the length of a sheet of paper and the length of a paper clip are different.

MATHEMATICAL PRACTICES

Chapter 8

four hundred nine **409**

Model and Draw

12 inches is the same as 1 **foot.**
A 12-inch ruler is about 1 foot long.
You can measure lengths in inches
and also in feet.

The real table is about 60 inches long.
The real table is also about 5 feet long.

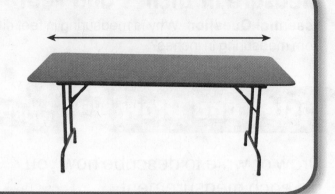

Share and Show

Measure to the nearest inch.
Then measure to the nearest foot.

Find the real object.	Measure.
desk 1.	_____ inches _____ feet
window ☑ 2.	_____ inches _____ feet
door MR. MARTIN'S CLASS ☑ 3.	_____ inches _____ feet

410 four hundred ten

© Houghton Mifflin Harcourt Publishing Company

On Your Own

Measure to the nearest inch.
Then measure to the nearest foot.

Find the real object.	Measure.
chalkboard 	_____ inches _____ feet
poster 	_____ inches _____ feet
teacher's desk 	_____ inches _____ feet
easel 	_____ inches _____ feet
bulletin board 	_____ inches _____ feet

4.

5.

6.

7.

8.

PROBLEM SOLVING REAL WORLD

Write Math

9. Use a ruler to measure the length of a real shelf in inches and in feet.

Measurements: _____ inches

_____ feet

10. **H.O.T.** Look at your measurements for the shelf. Why is the number of inches different from the number of feet?

_____

_____

_____

11. ⭐ **Test Prep** Stephen is telling his brother about using a ruler. Which sentence is true?

○ 1 inch is the same length as 1 foot.

○ 1 foot is a greater length than 1 inch.

○ 1 inch is a greater length than 1 foot.

○ Inches are not used to measure length.

TAKE HOME ACTIVITY · Have your child measure the distance of a few footsteps in inches and then in feet.

FOR MORE PRACTICE:
Standards Practice Book, pp. P193–P194

Name _____

Estimate Lengths in Feet

Essential Question How do you estimate the lengths of objects in feet?

COMMON CORE STANDARD CC.2.MD.3
Measure and estimate lengths in standard units.

Listen and Draw

Look for 3 classroom objects that are about the same length as an inch ruler. Draw and label the objects.

FOR THE TEACHER • Provide a collection of objects for children to choose from. Set a 12-inch ruler on the table with the objects for children to use as a visual comparison.

Math Talk
Which objects have a greater length than the ruler? **Explain.**

MATHEMATICAL PRACTICES

Chapter 8

Model and Draw

Estimate how many 12-inch rulers will be about the same length as this bulletin board.

Think about how many rulers will fit end-to-end.

_____ rulers, or _____ feet

Share and Show

Find each object. Estimate how many 12-inch rulers will be about the same length as the object.

☑ 1. bookshelf

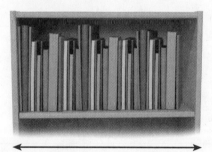

Estimate: _____ rulers, or _____ feet

☑ 2. chair

Estimate: _____ rulers, or _____ feet

On Your Own

Find each object. Estimate how many 12-inch rulers
will be about the same length as the object.

3. desktop

Estimate: _____ rulers, or _____ feet

4. wall map

Estimate: _____ rulers, or _____ feet

5. window

Estimate: _____ rulers, or _____ feet

6. teacher's desk

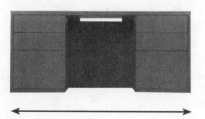

Estimate: _____ rulers, or _____ feet

PROBLEM SOLVING REAL WORLD

Write Math

Solve. Write or draw to explain.

7. Jorge and Nina place 12-inch rulers end-to-end along the entire length of a window. They each use 2 rulers. About how many feet long is the window?

about _____ feet

8. **H.O.T.** Estimate the distance from your desk to the door in feet. Then estimate the same distance in inches.

_____ feet

_____ inches

Explain how you made your estimates for the number of feet and for the number of inches.

_____

_____

_____

_____

9. ⭐ **Test Prep** Which is the best estimate for the length of a real bat?

○ 1 foot

○ 3 feet

○ 6 feet

○ 10 feet

TAKE HOME ACTIVITY • With your child, estimate the lengths of some objects in feet.

FOR MORE PRACTICE:
Standards Practice Book, pp. P195–P196

Name _____

Choose a Tool

Essential Question How do you choose a measuring tool to use when measuring lengths?

COMMON CORE STANDARD CC.2.MD.1
Measure and estimate lengths in standard units.

Listen and Draw  REAL WORLD

Draw or write to describe how you measured the distances with the yarn.

Distance 1

Distance 2

FOR THE TEACHER • Have each small group use a 1-yard piece of yarn to measure a distance marked on the floor with masking tape. Have groups repeat the activity to measure another distance that is different from the first one.

Math Talk
Which distance was longer? **Explain** how you know.

MATHEMATICAL PRACTICES

Model and Draw

You can use different tools to measure lengths and distances.

inch ruler

An inch ruler can be used to measure shorter lengths.

yardstick

A **yardstick** shows 3 feet. It can be used to measure greater lengths and distances.

measuring tape

A **measuring tape** can be used to measure lengths and distances that are not flat or straight.

Share and Show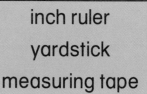

Choose the best tool for measuring the real object. Then measure and record the length or distance.

inch ruler
yardstick
measuring tape

☑ 1. the length of a book

Tool: _____

Length: _____

☑ 2. the distance around a cup

Tool: _____

Distance: _____

418 four hundred eighteen

© Houghton Mifflin Harcourt Publishing Company

Name _____

On Your Own

Choose the best tool for measuring the real object.
Then measure and record the length or distance.

| inch ruler |
| yardstick |
| measuring tape |

3. the length of a chalkboard

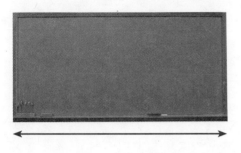

Tool: _____

Length: _____

4. the length of a marker

Tool: _____

Length: _____

5. the distance around a globe

Tool: _____

Distance: _____

6. the length of a classroom wall

Tool: _____

Length: _____

PROBLEM SOLVING

REAL WORLD

 Write Math

Choose the better tool for measuring.
Explain your choice.

7. Rachel wants to measure the length of
a sidewalk. Should she use an inch ruler
or a yardstick? Explain.

Rachel should use _____ because

_____

_____

_____

8. **H.O.T.** What is an object that you would
measure with a measuring tape? Explain
why you would use this tool.

_____

_____

_____

9. ⭐ **Test Prep** Jim wants to measure some
books to find a book that is 9 inches long.
Which is the best tool for Jim to use?

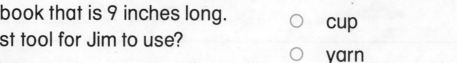

○ large paper clip

○ cup

○ yarn

○ inch ruler

TAKE HOME ACTIVITY · Have your child name some objects
that he or she would measure using a yardstick.

FOR MORE PRACTICE:
Standards Practice Book, pp. P197–P198

Display Measurement Data

Essential Question How can a line plot be used to show measurement data?

COMMON CORE STANDARD CC.2.MD.9
Represent and interpret data.

Listen and Draw REAL WORLD

Use an inch ruler. Measure and record each length.

_____ inches

_____ inches

_____ inches

Math Talk
Describe how the lengths of the three strings are different.

MATHEMATICAL PRACTICES

HOME CONNECTION · Your child practiced measuring different lengths in inches in preparation for collecting measurement data in this lesson.

A **line plot** is a way to show data.
On this line plot, each **X** stands for
the length of one paintbrush in inches.

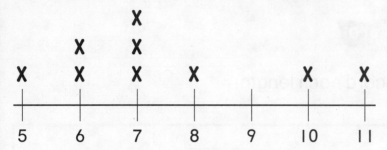

Lengths of Paintbrushes in Inches

How many paintbrushes
are just 6 inches long?
How many different
paintbrushes are shown
in this data?

Share and Show

✓ 1. Use an inch ruler. Measure and
record the lengths of 5 books
in inches.

1st book: _____ inches	
2nd book: _____ inches	
3rd book: _____ inches	
4th book: _____ inches	
5th book: _____ inches	

✓ 2. Write a title for the line plot. Then write
the numbers and draw the **X**s.

Name _____

On Your Own

3. Use an inch ruler. Measure and record the lengths of 5 pencils in inches.

| 1st pencil: _____ inches |
| 2nd pencil: _____ inches |
| 3rd pencil: _____ inches |
| 4th pencil: _____ inches |
| 5th pencil: _____ inches |

4. Write a title for the line plot. Then write the numbers and draw the **X**s.

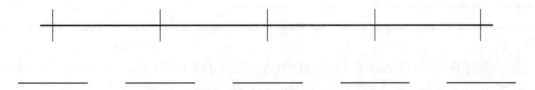

_____

5. Use an inch ruler. Measure and record the lengths of 4 crayons in inches. Then complete the line plot.

| 1st crayon: _____ inches |
| 2nd crayon: _____ inches |
| 3rd crayon: _____ inches |
| 4th crayon: _____ inches |

PROBLEM SOLVING REAL WORLD

Write Math

6. Use the data in the list to complete the line plot.

Lengths of Ribbons
6 inches
5 inches
8 inches
7 inches
6 inches

7. **H.O.T.** Suppose there were two more ribbons that were each 7 inches long. How would you change the line plot above to include this data?

_____

_____

8. ⭐ **Test Prep** Use the line plot.
How many leaves are 4 inches long?

- ○ 2
- ○ 3
- ○ 5
- ○ 8

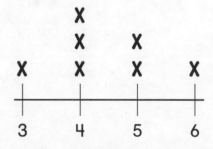

Lengths of Leaves in Inches

TAKE HOME ACTIVITY · Have your child describe the information found in the line plot in Exercise 8.

424 four hundred twenty-four

FOR MORE PRACTICE:
Standards Practice Book, pp. P199–P200

Chapter 8 Review/Test

Vocabulary

Use a word in the box to complete each sentence.

| foot |
| yardstick |
| inch |

1. A _____ is the same length

   as 12 inches. (p. 410)

2. An _____ is shorter than a foot. (p. 410)

Concepts and Skills

Use color tiles. Measure the length of the object in inches. (CC.2.MD.1)

3.

about _____ inches

Draw a diagram. Write a number sentence using

a ▨ for the missing number. Solve. (CC.2.MD.5, CC.2.MD.6)

4. Paula has two ribbons. One ribbon is 11 inches long and the other ribbon is 9 inches long. How many inches of ribbon does Paula have?

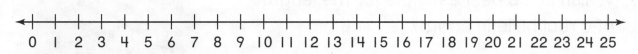

_____

Paula has _____ inches of ribbon.

Fill in the bubble for the correct answer choice.

5. Use an inch ruler. Measure the length of the pen to the nearest inch.

Which is the best choice for the length of the pen? (CC.2.MD.1)

○ 10 inches

○ 6 inches

○ 3 inches

○ 1 inch

6. The bead is one inch long. Which is the best estimate for the length of the string? (CC.2.MD.3)

○ 4 inches

○ 7 inches

○ 9 inches

○ 10 inches

7. Which is the best estimate for the length of a real bulletin board? (CC.2.MD.3)

○ 300 feet

○ 30 feet

○ 3 feet

○ 1 foot

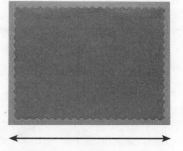

Name _____

Fill in the bubble for the correct answer choice.

8. Use an inch ruler to measure. What is the length of the ribbon to the nearest inch? (CC.2.MD.1)

- ○ 2 inches
- ○ 5 inches
- ○ 8 inches
- ○ 12 inches

9. The bead is one inch long. Which is the best estimate for the length of the string? (CC.2.MD.3)

- ○ 9 inches
- ○ 6 inches
- ○ 3 inches
- ○ 1 inch

10. Use the line plot. How many books are 8 inches long? (CC.2.MD.9)

- ○ 3
- ○ 4
- ○ 6
- ○ 10

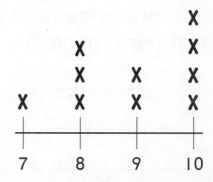

Lengths of Books in Inches

Constructed Response

11. Janet wants to measure the length of a wall in inches and in feet. Describe how these two measurements will be different. (CC.2.MD.2)

_____

_____

_____

Performance Task (CC.2.MD.5, CC.2.MD.1)

12. Dustin will use the red string and the blue string for a project. How many inches of string will he use?

| blue string: 15 inches |
| red string: 8 inches |
| green string: 6 inches |

Draw or write to show how you found your answer.

_____

Suppose Dustin has some yellow string for his project. Should he use an inch ruler, a measuring tape, or a yardstick to measure the length of the string? Explain your choice.

_____

_____

_____

_____

Length in Metric Units

Curious About Math with

Curious George

A wind farm is a group of wind turbines used to make electricity. One way to measure the distance between two wind turbines is by counting footsteps. What is another way?

Name _____

Show What You Know ✓

Compare Lengths

1. Order the strings from shortest to longest.
   Write 1, 2, 3.

 _____

 _____

_____

Use Nonstandard Units to Measure Length

Use real objects and ■ to measure.

2.

about _____ ■

3.

about _____ ■

Measure Length Twice: Nonstandard Units

Use ▪ first. Then use ▱ .
Measure the length of the ribbon.

4. about _____ ▪   5. about _____ ▱

© Houghton Mifflin Harcourt Publishing Company

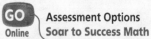 GO Online   Assessment Options   Soar to Success Math

Vocabulary Builder

Review Words
measure
length
estimate

Visualize It

Fill in the graphic organizer. Think of an object and write about how you can **measure** the **length** of that object.

length

Understand Vocabulary

Use the color tiles to **estimate** the length of each straw.

1. _____

about _____ tiles

2. _____

about _____ tiles

Game

Estimating Length

Materials

- 12 ●
- 12 ○
- 15 ▣
- 15 ▣

Play with a partner.

① Take turns choosing a picture. Find the real object.

② Each player estimates the length of the object in cubes and then makes a cube train for his or her estimate.

③ Compare the cube trains to the length of the object. The player with the closer estimate puts a counter on the picture. If there is a tie, both players put a counter on the picture.

④ Repeat until all pictures are covered. The player with more counters on the board wins.

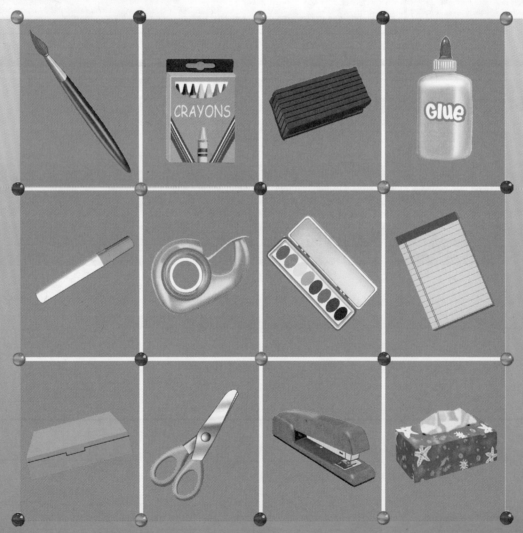

Name _____

Measure with a Centimeter Model

Essential Question How do you use a centimeter model to measure the lengths of objects?

COMMON CORE STANDARD CC.2.MD.1
Measure and estimate lengths in standard units.

Listen and Draw REAL WORLD

Use ▨ to measure the length.

_____ unit cubes

_____ unit cubes

_____ unit cubes

Math Talk
Describe how to use unit cubes to measure an object's length.
MATHEMATICAL PRACTICES

HOME CONNECTION · Your child used unit cubes as an introduction to measurement of length before using metric measurement tools.

Model and Draw

A unit cube is about 1 **centimeter** long.

About how many centimeters long is this string?

The string is about ___11___ centimeters long.

> You can make a mark for each centimeter to keep track and to count.

Share and Show

Use a unit cube. Measure the length in centimeters.

1.

about _____ centimeters

✓ 2.

about _____ centimeters

✓ 3.

about _____ centimeters

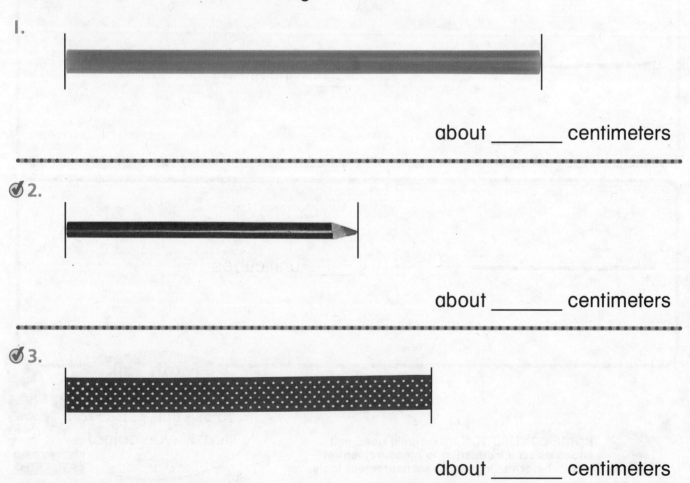

On Your Own

Use a unit cube. Measure the length in centimeters.

4.

about _____ centimeters

5.

about _____ centimeters

6.

about _____ centimeters

7.

about _____ centimeters

8.

about _____ centimeters

PROBLEM SOLVING

Solve. Write or draw to explain.

9. **H.O.T.** Mrs. Duncan measured the
lengths of a crayon and a pencil.
The pencil is twice as long as the crayon.
The sum of their lengths is 24 centimeters.
What are their lengths?

crayon: _____

pencil: _____

10. ⭐ **Test Prep** Marita used unit cubes to
measure the length of a straw.

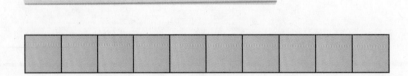

Which is the best choice for the length
of the straw?

○   I centimeter

○   3 centimeters

○   7 centimeters

○   I0 centimeters

 TAKE HOME ACTIVITY • Have your child compare the lengths
of other objects to those in this lesson.

FOR MORE PRACTICE:
Standards Practice Book, pp. P205–P206

Name _____

Estimate Lengths in Centimeters

Essential Question How do you use known lengths to estimate unknown lengths?

COMMON CORE STANDARD CC.2.MD.3
Measure and estimate lengths in standard units.

Listen and Draw REAL WORLD

Find three classroom objects that are shorter than your 10-centimeter strip. Draw the objects. Write estimates for their lengths.

about _____ centimeters

about _____ centimeters

about _____ centimeters

Math Talk
Which object has a length closest to 10 centimeters? **Explain.**

MATHEMATICAL PRACTICES

HOME CONNECTION · Your child used a 10-centimeter strip of paper to practice estimating the lengths of some classroom objects.

Model and Draw

This pencil is about 10 centimeters long.
Which is the most reasonable estimate
for the length of the ribbon?

7 centimeters

13 centimeters

20 centimeters

The ribbon is longer than the pencil. 7 centimeters is not reasonable.

The ribbon is not twice as long as the pencil. 20 centimeters is not reasonable.

The ribbon is a little longer than the pencil.
So, 13 centimeters is the most reasonable estimate.

Share and Show

✓1. The yarn is about 5 centimeters long. Circle the
   best estimate for the length of the crayon.

10 centimeters

15 centimeters

20 centimeters

✓2. The string is about 12 centimeters long.
   Circle the best estimate for the length of the straw.

3 centimeters

7 centimeters

11 centimeters

On Your Own

3. The rope is about 8 centimeters long. Circle the
best estimate for the length of the paper clip.

2 centimeters

4 centimeters

8 centimeters

4. The pencil is about 11 centimeters long.
Circle the best estimate for the length of the chain.

6 centimeters

10 centimeters

13 centimeters

5. The hair clip is about 7 centimeters long.
Circle the best estimate for the length of the yarn.

10 centimeters

17 centimeters

22 centimeters

6. The ribbon is about 13 centimeters long.
Circle the best estimate for the length of the string.

5 centimeters

11 centimeters

17 centimeters

PROBLEM SOLVING REAL WORLD

Write Math

Circle the best estimate.

7. About how long is a new crayon?

5 centimeters

10 centimeters

20 centimeters

8. About how long is a new pencil?

20 centimeters

40 centimeters

50 centimeters

9. **H.O.T.** Mr. Lott has 250 more centimeters of tape than Mrs. Simon. Mr. Lott has 775 centimeters of tape. How many centimeters of tape does Mrs. Simon have?

_____ centimeters

10. ⭐ **Test Prep** The length of the feather is about 7 centimeters.

Which is the best estimate for the length of the yarn?

○ 5 centimeters

○ 7 centimeters

○ 14 centimeters

○ 70 centimeters

TAKE HOME ACTIVITY · Give your child an object that is about 5 centimeters long. Have him or her use it to estimate the lengths of some other objects.

FOR MORE PRACTICE:
Standards Practice Book, pp. P207–P208

Name _____

Measure with a Centimeter Ruler

Essential Question How do you use a centimeter ruler to measure lengths?

COMMON CORE STANDARD CC.2.MD.1
Measure and estimate lengths in standard units.

Listen and Draw REAL WORLD

Find three small objects in the classroom.
Use unit cubes to measure their lengths.
Draw the objects and write their lengths.

_____ centimeters

_____ centimeters

_____ centimeters

HOME CONNECTION • Your child used unit cubes to measure the lengths of some classroom objects as an introduction to measuring lengths in centimeters.

Math Talk

Describe how the three lengths compare. Which object is shortest?

MATHEMATICAL PRACTICES

What is the length of the crayon to the nearest centimeter?

Remember: Line up the left edge of the object with the zero mark on the ruler.

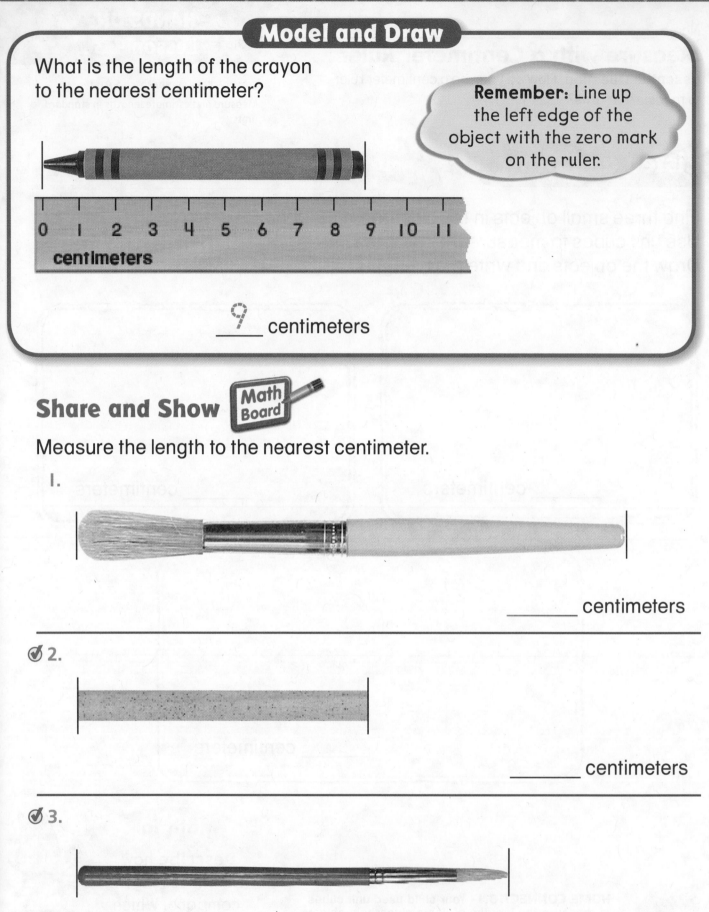

_9_ centimeters

Share and Show

Measure the length to the nearest centimeter.

1.

_____ centimeters

2.

_____ centimeters

3.

_____ centimeters

On Your Own

Measure the length to the nearest centimeter.

4.

_____ centimeters

5.

_____ centimeters

6.

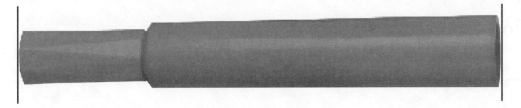

_____ centimeters

7.

_____ centimeters

8.

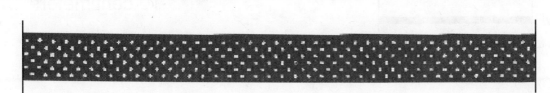

_____ centimeters

PROBLEM SOLVING REAL WORLD

9. **H.O.T.** The crayon was on the table next to the centimeter ruler. The left edge of the crayon was not lined up with the zero mark on the ruler.

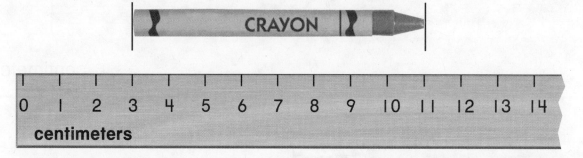

What is the length of the crayon?

about _____

Explain how you found your answer.

_____

_____

_____

10. ⭐ **Test Prep** Use a centimeter ruler. Which is the best choice for the length of this string?

○ 1 centimeter
○ 4 centimeters
○ 7 centimeters
○ 10 centimeters

TAKE HOME ACTIVITY • Have your child measure the lengths of some objects using a centimeter ruler.

FOR MORE PRACTICE:
Standards Practice Book, pp. P209–P210

Problem Solving • Add and Subtract Lengths

COMMON CORE STANDARDS CC.2.MD.6, CC.2.MD.5
Relate addition and subtraction to length.

Essential Question How can drawing a diagram help when solving problems about lengths?

Nate had 23 centimeters of string.
He gave 9 centimeters of string to Myra.
How much string does Nate have now?

? Unlock the Problem REAL WORLD

What do I need to find?

how much string
Nate has now

What information do I need to use?

Nate had _____ centimeters of string.

He gave _____ centimeters of string to Myra.

Show how to solve the problem.

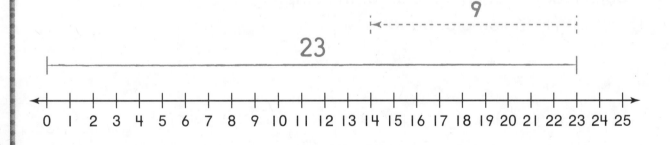

_____

Nate has _____ centimeters of string now.

HOME CONNECTION · Your child drew a diagram to represent a problem about lengths. The diagram can be used to choose the operation for solving the problem.

Try Another Problem

Draw a diagram. Write a number sentence using a ■ for the missing number. Then solve.

- What do I need to find?
- What information do I need to use?

1. Ellie has a ribbon that is 12 centimeters long. Gwen has a ribbon that is 9 centimeters long. How many centimeters of ribbon do they have?

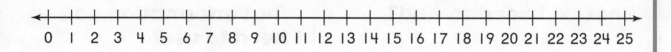

They have _____ centimeters of ribbon.

- -

2. A strip of paper is 24 centimeters long. Justin tears 8 centimeters off of the strip. How long is the strip of paper now?

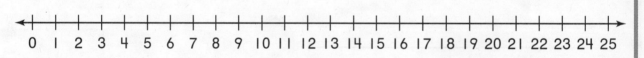

Now the strip of paper is _____ centimeters long.

Math Talk

Explain how your diagram shows what happened in the first problem.

MATHEMATICAL PRACTICES

Name _____

Share and Show

Draw a diagram. Write a number sentence using
a ▓ for the missing number. Then solve.

✓3. A chain of paper clips is 18 centimeters long.
Sondra adds 6 centimeters of paper clips to
the chain. How long is the chain now?

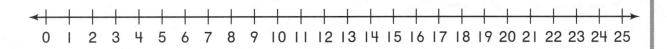

_____

The chain is _____ centimeters long now.

---

4. **H.O.T.** A chalk mark was 22 centimeters long. Then
Greg erased part of the mark and it was 5 centimeters
long. How many centimeters of the mark did
Greg erase?

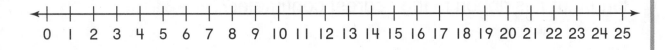

_____

Greg erased _____ centimeters of the mark.

TAKE HOME ACTIVITY · Have your child explain how
he or she used a diagram to solve Exercise 3.

FOR MORE PRACTICE:
Standards Practice Book, pp. P211–P212

✓ Mid-Chapter Checkpoint

Concepts and Skills

Use a unit cube. Measure the length in centimeters. (CC.2.MD.1)

1.

about _____ centimeters

2.

about _____ centimeters

3. The pencil is about 11 centimeters long. Circle
the best estimate for the length of the string. (CC.2.MD.3)

7 centimeters

10 centimeters

16 centimeters

4. ⭐ **Test Prep** Use a centimeter ruler. What is the
length of this ribbon to the nearest centimeter? (CC.2.MD.1)

○ 18 centimeters

○ 13 centimeters

○ 9 centimeters

○ 5 centimeters

Name _____

Centimeters and Meters

Essential Question How is measuring in meters different from measuring in centimeters?

COMMON CORE STANDARD CC.2.MD.2
Measure and estimate lengths in standard units.

Listen and Draw  REAL WORLD

Draw or write to describe how you did each measurement.

> 1st measurement

> 2nd measurement

FOR THE TEACHER • Have each small group use a 1-meter piece of yarn to measure a distance marked on the floor with masking tape. Then have them measure the same distance using a sheet of paper folded in half lengthwise.

Math Talk

Describe how the lengths of the yarn and the sheet of paper are different.

MATHEMATICAL PRACTICES

I **meter** is the same as 100 centimeters.

The real door is about 200 centimeters tall.
The real door is also about 2 meters tall.

Share and Show

Measure to the nearest centimeter.
Then measure to the nearest meter.

Find the real object.	Measure.
chair 1.	_____ centimeters _____ meters
teacher's desk 2.	_____ centimeters _____ meters
wall 3.	_____ centimeters _____ meters

On Your Own

Measure to the nearest centimeter.
Then measure to the nearest meter.

Find the real object.	Measure.
chalkboard 4.	_____ centimeters _____ meters
bookshelf 5.	_____ centimeters _____ meters
table 6.	_____ centimeters _____ meters
bulletin board 7.	_____ centimeters _____ meters

PROBLEM SOLVING REAL WORLD

Write Math

8. **H.O.T.** Jason and his dad are walking next to a barn. They want to measure the length of the barn. Would the length be a greater number of centimeters or a greater number of meters?

_____

Explain your answer.

_____

_____

_____

_____

9. **Test Prep** Use a centimeter ruler to measure.

Which is the best choice for the length of the pencil?

○ 30 centimeters

⊙ 25 centimeters

○ 20 centimeters

○ 15 centimeters

TAKE HOME ACTIVITY • Have your child describe how centimeters and meters are different.

FOR MORE PRACTICE:
Standards Practice Book, pp. P213–P214

Estimate Lengths in Meters

Essential Question How do you estimate the lengths of objects in meters?

Lesson 9.6

COMMON CORE STANDARD CC.2.MD.3
Measure and estimate lengths in standard units.

Listen and Draw REAL WORLD

Find a writing tool that is about 10 centimeters long. Draw and label it.

Is there a classroom object that is about 50 centimeters long? Draw and label it.

FOR THE TEACHER • Provide a collection of objects for children to choose from. Above the table of displayed objects, draw and label a 10-centimeter line segment and a 50-centimeter line segment.

Math Talk
Describe how the lengths of the two real objects compare.

MATHEMATICAL PRACTICES

Model and Draw

Estimate. About how many meter sticks will match the width of a door?

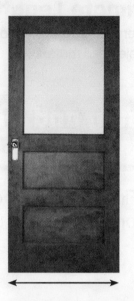

A 1-meter measuring stick is about 100 centimeters long.

about _____ meters

Share and Show

Find the real object.
Estimate its length in meters.

☑ 1. bookshelf

about _____ meters

☑ 2. bulletin board

about _____ meters

Name _____

On Your Own

Find the real object.
Estimate its length in meters.

3. teacher's desk

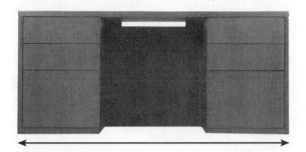

about _____ meters

4. wall

about _____ meters

5. window

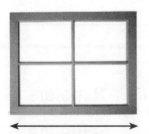

about _____ meters

6. chalkboard

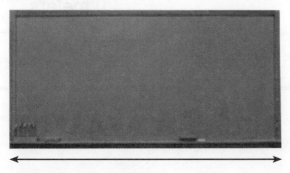

about _____ meters

PROBLEM SOLVING REAL WORLD

Write Math

Solve. Write or draw to explain.

7. Tim and Erin each placed 3 meter sticks end-to-end along the length of the bicycle rack. About how long is the bicycle rack?

about _____ meters long

8. **H.O.T.** In meters, estimate the distance from your teacher's desk to the door of your classroom.

about _____ meters

Explain how you made your estimate.

_____

_____

_____

_____

9. ⭐ **Test Prep** Which is the best estimate for the length of an adult's bicycle?

○ 2 meters

○ 5 meters

○ 8 meters

○ 20 meters

TAKE HOME ACTIVITY • With your child, estimate the lengths of some objects in meters.

FOR MORE PRACTICE:
Standards Practice Book, pp. P215–P216

Name _____

Measure and Compare Lengths

Essential Question How do you find the difference between the lengths of two objects?

COMMON CORE STANDARD CC.2.MD.4
Measure and estimate lengths in standard units.

Listen and Draw REAL WORLD

Measure and record each length.

_____ centimeters

_____ centimeters

Math Talk
Name a classroom object that is longer than the paintbrush. **Explain** how you know.

MATHEMATICAL PRACTICES

TAKE HOME ACTIVITY · Your child measured these lengths as an introduction to measuring and then comparing lengths.

Model and Draw

How much longer is the pencil than the crayon?

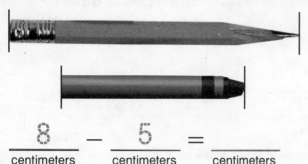

_____ 8 centimeters

_____ 5 centimeters

$$\underset{\text{centimeters}}{8} - \underset{\text{centimeters}}{5} = \underset{\text{centimeters}}{}$$

The pencil is _____ centimeters longer than the crayon.

Share and Show

Measure the length of each object. Write a number sentence to find the difference between the lengths.

☑ 1.

_____ centimeters

_____ centimeters

$$\underset{\text{centimeters}}{} - \underset{\text{centimeters}}{} = \underset{\text{centimeters}}{}$$

The string is _____ centimeters longer than the straw.

☑ 2.

_____ centimeters

_____ centimeters

$$\underset{\text{centimeters}}{} - \underset{\text{centimeters}}{} = \underset{\text{centimeters}}{}$$

The paintbrush is _____ centimeters longer than the toothpick.

On Your Own

Measure the length of each object. Write a number sentence to find the difference between the lengths.

3.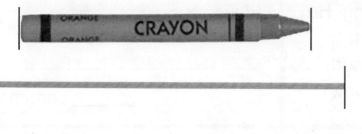

_____ centimeters

_____ centimeters

_____ − _____ = _____
centimeters   centimeters   centimeters

The yarn is _____ centimeters longer than the crayon.

___

4.

_____ centimeters

_____ centimeters

_____ − _____ = _____
centimeters   centimeters   centimeters

The string is _____ centimeters longer than the paper clip.

___

5. **H.O.T.** Use a centimeter ruler. Measure the length of your desk and the length of a book.

desk: _____ centimeters

book: _____ centimeters

Which is shorter? _____

How much shorter is it? _____

PROBLEM SOLVING REAL WORLD

Write Math

Solve. Write or draw to explain.

6. Mark has a paper strip chain that is 23 centimeters long. He unhooks 15 centimeters from the chain. What is the length of the paper strip chain now?

_____ centimeters

7. H.O.T. The yellow ribbon is 15 centimeters longer than the green ribbon. The green ribbon is 29 centimeters long. What is the length of the yellow ribbon?

_____ centimeters

8. ⭐ Test Prep Measure the length of each object.

How much longer is the crayon than the string?

○ 17 centimeters longer

○ 11 centimeters longer

○ 8 centimeters longer

○ 5 centimeters longer

TAKE HOME ACTIVITY • Have your child tell you how he or she solved one of the problems on this page.

FOR MORE PRACTICE:
Standards Practice Book, pp. P217–P218

Chapter 9 Review/Test

Vocabulary

Use the words in the box to complete the sentence.

| centimeter |
| meter |

1. One _____ is longer than

   one _____. (p. 450)

Concepts and Skills

Draw a diagram. Write a number sentence using
a ▨ for the missing number. Then solve. (CC.2.MD.6, CC.2.MD.5)

2. Mrs. Cook has a poster board that is 21 centimeters
   long. She cuts off 8 centimeters from the poster
   board. How long is the poster board now?

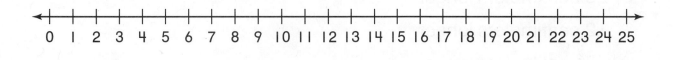

   _____

   The poster board is _____ centimeters long now.

Measure the real object to the nearest centimeter.
Then measure to the nearest meter. (CC.2.MD.2)

3. bulletin board

_____ centimeters

_____ meters

Fill in the bubble for the correct answer choice.

4. Which is the best estimate for the length of a real desk? (CC.2.MD.3)

- ○ 2 meters
- ○ 10 meters
- ○ 50 meters
- ○ 100 meters

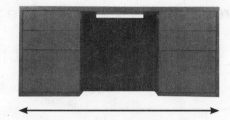

5. Use a centimeter ruler.

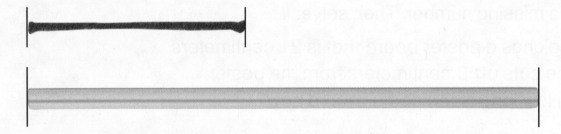

How much longer is the straw than the yarn? (CC.2.MD.4)

- ○ 20 centimeters longer
- ○ 12 centimeters longer
- ○ 8 centimeters longer
- ○ 3 centimeters longer

6. Use a centimeter ruler. Which is the best choice for the length of the toothpick? (CC.2.MD.1)

- ○ 10 centimeters
- ○ 9 centimeters
- ○ 7 centimeters
- ○ 5 centimeters

Fill in the bubble for the correct answer choice.

7. Use a centimeter ruler to measure the length of the paintbrush to the nearest centimeter.

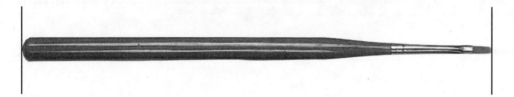

Which is the best choice for the length of the paintbrush? (CC.2.MD.1)

○ 13 centimeters

○ 18 centimeters

○ 21 centimeters

○ 23 centimeters

8. The paper clip is about 4 centimeters long. Which is the best estimate for the length of the string? (CC.2.MD.3)

○ 20 centimeters

○ 9 centimeters

○ 4 centimeters

○ 3 centimeters

Constructed Response

9. The craft stick is about 12 centimeters long.
   Circle the best estimate for the length of the string.

   6 centimeters

   9 centimeters

   11 centimeters

   Explain how you chose your estimate. (CC.2.MD.3)

   _____

   _____

   _____

Performance Task (CC.2.MD.5, CC.2.MD.2)

10. Mrs. Dillon has 2 posters. The first poster is 75 centimeters
    long. The second poster is 58 centimeters long. How much
    longer is the first poster than the second poster?
    Draw or write to show how you solved the problem.

    _____ centimeters longer

    If Mrs. Dillon measures the length of her bulletin board
    in centimeters and in meters, how will the number of
    centimeters and the number of meters be different? Explain.

    _____

    _____

    _____

Curious About Math with
Curious George

Look at the different kinds of balloons.

What are some ways you can sort these balloons?

Name _____

Show What You Know ✓

Read a Picture Graph

Use the picture graph.

Fruit We Like				
orange				
pear				

1. How many children chose pear? _____ children

2. Circle the fruit that more children chose.

Read a Tally Chart

Complete the tally chart.

Color We Like		Total
green	|||	
red	~~||||~~		
blue	~~||||~~ |||	

3. How many children chose red?

_____ children

4. Which color did the fewest children choose?

_____

Addition and Subtraction Facts

Write the sum or difference.

5. $10 - 4 =$ _____ | 6. $4 + 5 =$ _____ | 7. $6 + 5 =$ _____

8. $9 - 3 =$ _____ | 9. $5 + 7 =$ _____ | 10. $11 - 3 =$ _____

Family note: This page checks your child's understanding of important skills needed for success in Chapter 10.

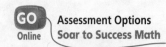

© Houghton Mifflin Harcourt Publishing Company

Vocabulary Builder

Review Words

tally marks
more than
fewer than

Visualize It

Draw **tally marks** to show each number.

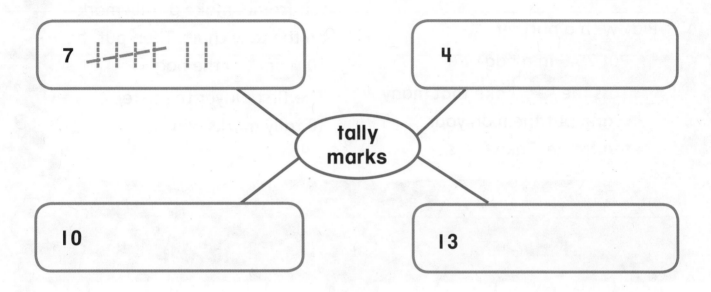

Understand Vocabulary

Write a number to complete the sentence.

1. 10 apples is **more than** _____ apples.

_____

2. 6 bananas is **fewer than** _____ bananas.

_____

3. _____ grapes is **more than** 6 grapes.

_____

4. _____ oranges is **fewer than** 5 oranges.

GO Online
• eStudent Edition
• Multimedia eGlossary

Game

Making Tens

Materials • • 25 📖
• small bag

Play with a partner.

① Put 25 📖 in a bag.

② Toss the 🎲 . Take that many 📖 and put them on your ten frame. Take turns.

③ When you have 10 📖 on your ten frame, make a tally mark on the tally chart. Then put the 10 📖 back in the bag.

④ The first player to make 10 tally marks wins.

Player 1

Player 2

Making Tens

Player	Tally
Player 1	
Player 2	

Collect Data

Essential Question How do you use a tally chart to record data from a survey?

COMMON CORE STANDARD CC.2.MD.10
Represent and interpret data.

Listen and Draw

Take turns pulling a cube from the bag.
Draw a tally mark in the chart for each cube.

Cube Colors	
Color	**Tally**
blue	
red	
green	

HOME CONNECTION • Your child made tally marks to record the color of cubes pulled from a bag. This activity prepares children for using and recording data in this chapter.

Math Talk

Explain how tally marks help you keep track of what has been pulled.

MATHEMATICAL PRACTICES

Model and Draw

You can take a **survey** to collect **data**.
You can record the data with tally marks.

Greg asked his classmates which lunch is their favorite.

Favorite Lunch	
Lunch	**Tally**
pizza	||||
sandwich	卌	
salad	|||
pasta	卌

The tally marks in the tally chart show the children's answers. Each tally mark stands for one child's choice.

Share and Show

1. Take a survey. Ask 10 classmates which pet is their favorite. Use tally marks to show their choices.

☑ 2. How many classmates chose dog?

_____ classmates

☑ 3. Which pet did the fewest classmates choose?

_____

Favorite Pet	
Pet	**Tally**
cat	
dog	
fish	
bird	

4. Did more classmates choose cat or dog? _____

How many more? _____ more classmates

470 four hundred seventy

On Your Own

5. Take a survey. Ask 10 classmates which indoor game is their favorite. Use tally marks to show their choices.

Favorite Indoor Game	
Game	**Tally**
board	
card	
computer	
puzzle	

6. How many classmates chose board game?

_____ classmates

7. Which game did the most classmates choose?

_____

8. Did more classmates choose a card game or a computer game?

_____

How many more?   _____ more classmates

9. Which game did the fewest classmates choose?

_____

10. How many classmates did not choose a board game or a puzzle? **Explain** how you know.

_____

_____

_____

_____

PROBLEM SOLVING REAL WORLD

Claire asked her classmates to choose their favorite subject. She made this tally chart.

Favorite Subject	
Subject	**Tally**
reading	~~IIII~~ I
math	~~IIII~~ IIII
science	~~IIII~~ ~~IIII~~

11. How many more classmates chose math than reading?

_____ more classmates

12. How many classmates did Claire ask?

_____ classmates

13. **H.O.T.** Write a new question about the data in the chart. Then write the answer to your question.

_____

_____

_____

14. ⭐ **Test Prep** Use the tally chart. Which statement is true?

○ 13 children voted for breakfast.

○ 35 children voted in all.

○ 12 children voted for dinner.

○ Fewer children voted for lunch than for breakfast.

Favorite Meal	
Meal	**Tally**
breakfast	~~IIII~~ III
lunch	~~IIII~~ ~~IIII~~
dinner	~~IIII~~ ~~IIII~~ II

TAKE HOME ACTIVITY • With your child, take a survey about favorite games and make a tally chart to show the data.

472 four hundred seventy-two

Read Picture Graphs

Name _____

Essential Question How do you use a picture graph to show data?

COMMON CORE STANDARD CC.2.MD.10
Represent and interpret data.

Listen and Draw REAL WORLD

Use the tally chart to solve the problem.
Draw or write to show what you did.

Favorite Hobby	
Hobby	**Tally**
crafts	卌 I
reading	IIII
music	卌
sports	卌 II

_____ more children

Math Talk
Can the chart be used to find how many girls chose music? **Explain.**

MATHEMATICAL PRACTICES

FOR THE TEACHER • Read the following problem. Mr. Martin's class made this tally chart. How many more children in his class chose sports than chose reading as their favorite hobby?

Chapter 10

Model and Draw

A **picture graph** uses pictures to show data.

Number of Soccer Games							
March	⚽	⚽	⚽	⚽			
April	⚽	⚽	⚽				
May	⚽	⚽	⚽	⚽	⚽	⚽	
June	⚽	⚽	⚽	⚽	⚽	⚽	⚽

Key: Each ⚽ stands for 1 game.

A key tells how many each picture stands for.

Share and Show

Use the picture graph to answer the questions.

Favorite Snack								
pretzels	☺	☺	☺	☺	☺	☺	☺	☺
grapes	☺	☺	☺	☺	☺	☺	☺	
popcorn	☺	☺	☺					
apples	☺	☺	☺	☺	☺	☺		

Key: Each stands for 1 child.

✓ 1. Which snack was chosen by the fewest children? _____

_____

✓ 2. How many more children chose pretzels
than apples?

_____ more children

On Your Own

Use the picture graph to answer the questions.

Number of Pencils									
Alana	\	\	\						
Teresa	\	\	\	\	\				
John	\	\	\	\					
Brad	\	\	\	\	\	\	\	\	

Key: Each \ stands for 1 pencil.

3. How many pencils do Alana and
   Brad have? _____ pencils

4. How many more pencils does Teresa
   have than Alana has? _____ more pencils

5. How many pencils do the four
   children have? _____ pencils

6. Christy has 7 pencils. Write two sentences to
   describe how her number of pencils compares
   to the data in the picture graph.

   _____

   _____

   _____

   _____

PROBLEM SOLVING REAL WORLD

Favorite Balloon Color

green	🎈	🎈	🎈	🎈				
blue	🎈	🎈	🎈	🎈	🎈			
red	🎈	🎈	🎈	🎈	🎈	🎈	🎈	
purple	🎈	🎈	🎈	🎈				

Key: Each 🎈 stands for 1 child.

7. How many children chose the color blue or chose the color green?

_____ children

8. **H.O.T.** Which three colors were chosen by a total of 13 children?

_____

9. ⭐ **Test Prep** Use the picture graph. How many pets do the three children have?

   ○ 6
   ○ 5
   ○ 4
   ○ 3

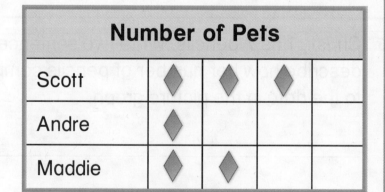

Number of Pets

Scott	◆	◆	◆	
Andre	◆			
Maddie	◆	◆		

Key: Each ◆ stands for 1 pet.

TAKE HOME ACTIVITY • Have your child explain how he or she solved Exercise 9.

FOR MORE PRACTICE:
Standards Practice Book, pp. P225–P226

Name _____

Make Picture Graphs

Essential Question How do you make a picture graph
to show data in a tally chart?

COMMON CORE STANDARD CC.2.MD.10
Represent and interpret data.

Listen and Draw

Take turns pulling a cube from the bag.
Draw a smiley face in the graph for each cube.

Cube Colors					
blue					
red					
green					
orange					

Key: Each ☺ stands for 1 cube.

HOME CONNECTION • Your child made
a graph by recording smiley faces for the
colors of cubes taken from a bag. This
activity prepares children for working with
picture graphs in this lesson.

Math Talk

Explain how you
know that the number
of smiley faces for blue
matches the number
of blue cubes.

MATHEMATICAL
PRACTICES

Model and Draw

Each picture in the graph stands for 1 flower.
Draw pictures to show the data in the tally chart.

Number of Flowers Picked	
Name	**Tally**
Jessie	|||
Inez	⊬||
Paulo	||||

Number of Flowers Picked					
Jessie	◯	◯	◯		
Inez					
Paulo					

Key: Each ◯ stands for 1 flower.

Share and Show

1. Use the tally chart to complete the picture graph.
   Draw a ☺ for each child.

Favorite Sandwich	
Sandwich	**Tally**
cheese	⊬||
ham	||
tuna	||||
turkey	|||

Favorite Sandwich					
cheese					
ham					
tuna					
turkey					

Key: Each ☺ stands for 1 child.

✔2. How many children chose tuna? _____ children

_____

✔3. How many more children chose cheese
   than ham? _____ more children

On Your Own

4. Use the tally chart to complete the picture graph.
   Draw a ☺ for each child.

Favorite Fruit	
Fruit	**Tally**
apple	|||||
plum	||
banana	||||
orange	|||

Favorite Fruit				
apple				
plum				
banana				
orange				

Key: Each ☺ stands for 1 child.

5. How many children chose banana? _____ children

6. How many fewer children chose plum
   than banana? _____ fewer children

7. Which fruit did the most children choose?
   _____

8. How many more children chose banana
   than orange? _____ more children

9. **H.O.T.** Which three fruits were
   chosen by a total of 10 children?

   _____

TAKE HOME ACTIVITY • Ask your child to explain how to
read the picture graph on this page.

Name _____

Mid-Chapter Checkpoint

Concepts and Skills

Use the picture graph to answer the questions. (CC.2.MD.10)

Favorite Season									
spring	☺	☺	☺	☺	☺	☺			
summer	☺	☺	☺	☺	☺	☺	☺	☺	
fall	☺	☺	☺	☺					
winter	☺	☺	☺	☺	☺	☺	☺		

Key: Each ☺ stands for 1 child.

1. Which season did the fewest children choose?

   _____

2. How many more children chose spring than fall?

   _____ more children

3. How many children chose a season that was not winter?

   _____ children

★ Test Prep (CC.2.MD.10)

4. James took a survey. 5 children chose green as their favorite color. Which group of tally marks should James use to show this?

   ○ |||

   ○ ||||

   ○ ⱵⱵⱵ

   ○ ⱵⱵⱵ |

Read Bar Graphs

Essential Question How is a bar graph used to show data?

COMMON CORE STANDARD CC.2.MD.10
Represent and interpret data.

Listen and Draw REAL WORLD

Use the picture graph to solve the problem.
Draw or write to show what you did.

Red Trucks Seen Last Week

Morgan	■	■	■					
John	■	■	■	■	■	■		
Cindy	■	■	■	■	■	■	■	■
Carlos	■	■	■	■				

Key: Each ■ **stands for 1 red truck.**

_____ red trucks

FOR THE TEACHER • Read this problem to children. Morgan made a picture graph to show the number of red trucks that she and her friends saw last week. How many red trucks did the four children see last week?

Math Talk
Describe how the data in the graph for John and for Cindy are different.

MATHEMATICAL PRACTICES

A **bar graph** uses bars to show data.
Look at where the bars end.
This tells how many.

There are 8 children playing soccer.

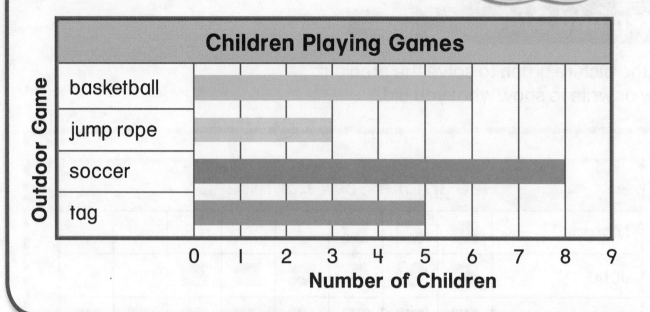

Children Playing Games

Outdoor Game: basketball, jump rope, soccer, tag

Number of Children: 0 1 2 3 4 5 6 7 8 9

Share and Show

Use the bar graph.

1. How many green marbles are in the bag?

   _____ green marbles

2. How many more blue marbles than purple marbles are in the bag?

   _____ more blue marbles

3. How many marbles are in the bag?

   _____ marbles

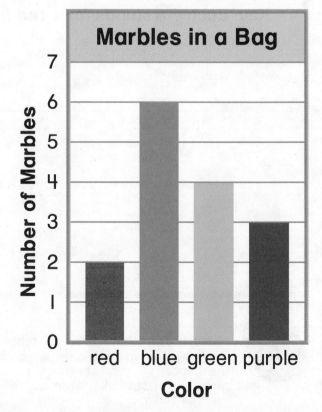

Marbles in a Bag

Number of Marbles: 0 1 2 3 4 5 6 7

Color: red blue green purple

Name _____

On Your Own

Use the bar graph.

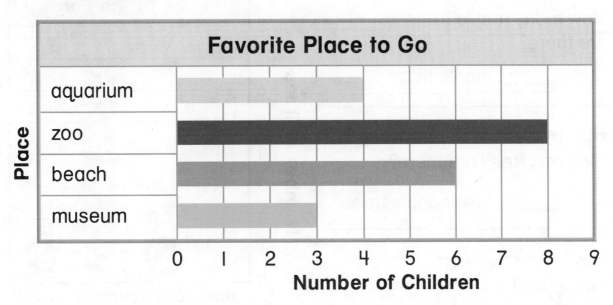

Favorite Place to Go

Place:
- aquarium
- zoo
- beach
- museum

Number of Children (0–9)

4. How many children chose the beach?

   _____ children

5. Which place did the fewest children choose?

   _____

6. How many more children chose the zoo than the aquarium?

   _____ more children

7. How many children chose a place that was not the zoo?

   _____ children

8. Find the number of children who chose the aquarium and the beach. Then find the number of children who chose the zoo and the museum. Describe how these two numbers are different.

   _____

   _____

   _____

   _____

PROBLEM SOLVING

REAL WORLD

Write Math

Use the bar graph.

9. How many maple trees are there?

_____ maple trees

10. How many fewer apple trees than oak trees are there?

_____ fewer apple trees

11. How many trees are not apple trees?

_____ trees

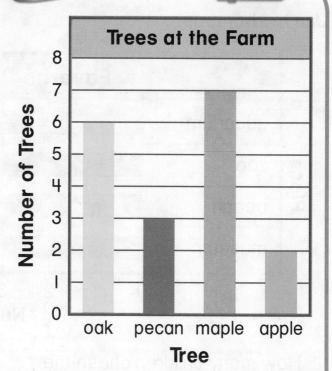

Trees at the Farm

Number of Trees

oak   pecan   maple   apple

Tree

12. H.O.T. Suppose 7 more trees are brought to the farm. How many trees would be at the farm then? Explain.

_____

_____

_____

13. ⭐ **Test Prep** Look at the bar graph above. How many oak trees are at the farm?

○ 3
○ 6
○ 7
○ 8

TAKE HOME ACTIVITY • Ask your child to explain how he or she solved Exercise 10.

FOR MORE PRACTICE:
Standards Practice Book, pp. P229–P230

Name _____

Make Bar Graphs

Essential Question How do you make a bar graph to show data?

COMMON CORE STANDARD CC.2.MD.10
Represent and interpret data.

Listen and Draw REAL WORLD

Use the bar graph to solve the problem.
Draw or write to show what you did.

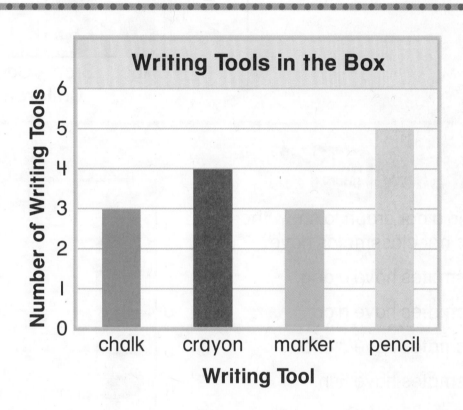

Writing Tools in the Box

(Number of Writing Tools: chalk = 3, crayon = 4, marker = 3, pencil = 5)

Writing Tool

_____ writing tools

FOR THE TEACHER • Read the following problem. Barry made this bar graph. How many writing tools are in the box?

Math Talk
Describe how the information in the graph for crayon and for marker is different.

MATHEMATICAL PRACTICES

Abel read 2 books, Brad read 4 books, Cara read 1 book, and Lynn read 3 books.

Complete the bar graph to show this data.

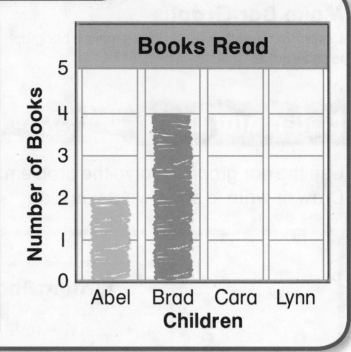

Share and Show

Ella is making a bar graph to show the kinds of pets her classmates have.

- 5 classmates have a dog.
- 7 classmates have a cat.
- 2 classmates have a bird.
- 3 classmates have fish.

1. Write labels and draw bars to complete the graph.

_____

2. How will the graph change if one more child gets a bird?

_____

_____

_____

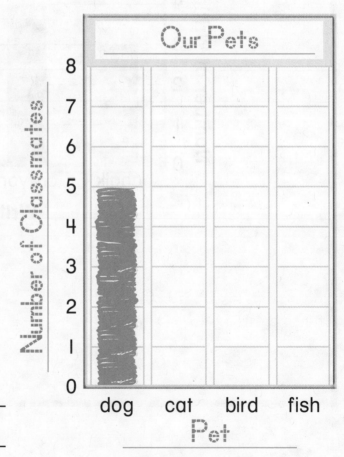

Name _____

On Your Own

Dexter asked his classmates which pizza topping is their favorite.

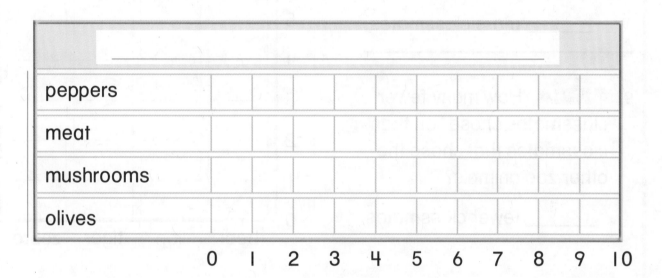

- 4 classmates chose peppers.

- 7 classmates chose meat.

- 5 classmates chose mushrooms.

- 2 classmates chose olives.

3. Write a title and labels for the bar graph.

_____

4. Draw bars in the graph to show the data.

peppers											
meat											
mushrooms											
olives											

0   1   2   3   4   5   6   7   8   9   10

_____

5. Which topping did the most classmates choose? _____

6. 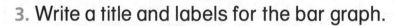 **H.O.T.** Did more classmates choose peppers and olives than meat? **Explain.**

_____

_____

_____

PROBLEM SOLVING REAL WORLD

Write Math

Cody asked his classmates which zoo animal is their favorite.

Use the data to complete the bar graph.

- 6 classmates chose bear.
- 4 classmates chose lion.
- 7 classmates chose tiger.
- 3 classmates chose zebra.

7. Write a title and labels. Draw bars.

_____

8. How many more classmates chose bear than zebra?

_____ more classmates

_____

9. **H.O.T.** How many fewer classmates chose lion than classmates that chose the other zoo animals?

_____ fewer classmates

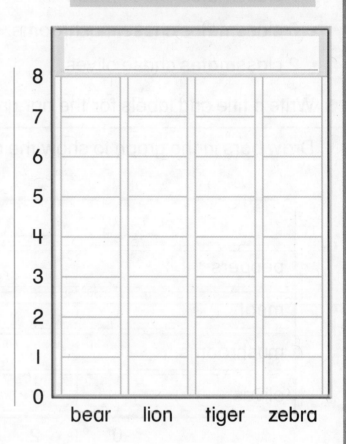

10. ⭐ **Test Prep** Look at the bar graph above. Which animal did the most classmates choose?

- ○ bear
- ○ tiger
- ○ lion
- ○ zebra

TAKE HOME ACTIVITY • Ask your child to describe how he or she used the favorite zoo animal data to complete the bar graph.

FOR MORE PRACTICE:
Standards Practice Book, pp. P231–P232

Name _____

Problem Solving • Display Data

Essential Question How does making a bar graph help when solving problems about data?

COMMON CORE STANDARD CC.2.MD.10
Represent and interpret data.

Maria recorded the rainfall in her town for four months. How did the amount of rainfall change from September to December?

September	4 inches
October	3 inches
November	2 inches
December	1 inch

🔑 Unlock the Problem

What do I need to find?

how the amount of ___rainfall___ changed from September to December

What information do I need to use?

the amount of ___rainfall___ in each of the four months

Show how to solve the problem.

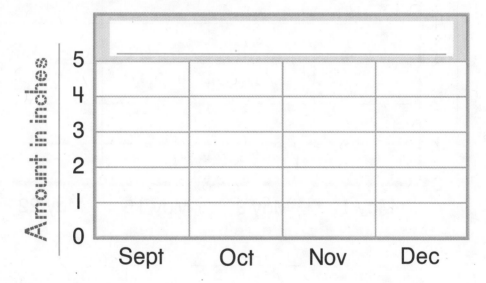

The amount of rainfall _____

_____

HOME CONNECTION • Your child made a bar graph to show the data. Making a graph helps your child organize data to solve problems.

Try Another Problem

Make a bar graph to solve the problem.

- What do I need to find?
- What information do I need to use?

I. Matthew measured the height of his plant once a week for four weeks. Describe how the height of the plant changed from May 1 to May 22.

May 1	2 inches
May 8	3 inches
May 15	5 inches
May 22	7 inches

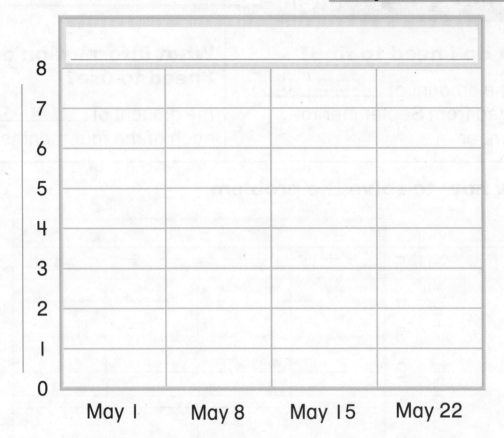

The height of the plant _____

_____

Math Talk
How many inches did the plant grow from May 1 to May 22? **Explain.**

MATHEMATICAL PRACTICES

Name _____

Share and Show

Make a bar graph to solve the problem.

2. Bianca wrote the number of hours that she practiced playing guitar in June. Describe how the amount of practice time changed from Week 1 to Week 4.

Week 1	1 hour
Week 2	2 hours
Week 3	4 hours
Week 4	5 hours

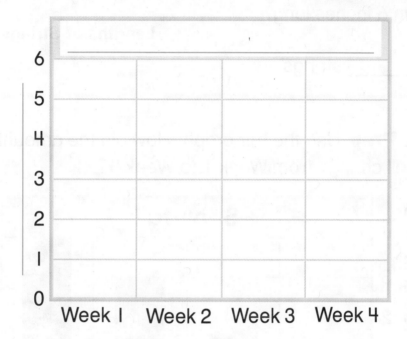

The amount of practice time _____

_____

3. If Bianca's practice time is 4 hours in Week 5, how does her practice time change from Week 1 to Week 5?

_____

_____

_____

On Your Own

Solve.

4. How many strings are 9 inches long?

_____ strings

5. **H.O.T.** How many strings are more than 6 inches long?

_____ strings

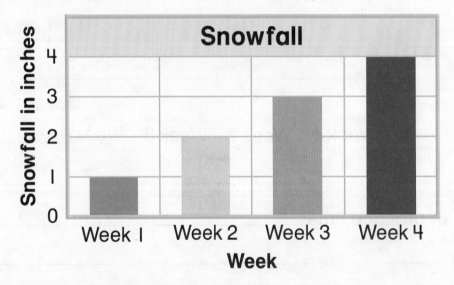

X
X X X
X X X X
X X X X
+---+---+---+---+
6   7   8   9

Lengths of Strings in Inches

6. ⭐ **Test Prep** Use the bar graph. How did the amount of snowfall change from Week 1 to Week 4?

Snowfall

Snowfall in inches

4
3
2
1
0
   Week 1   Week 2   Week 3   Week 4
              Week

○ The amount of snowfall stayed the same.

○ The amount of snowfall increased.

○ The amount of snowfall decreased.

○ The amount of snowfall decreased and then increased.

TAKE HOME ACTIVITY • Have your child explain how he or she solved Exercise 5.

FOR MORE PRACTICE:
Standards Practice Book, pp. P233–P234

Name _____

Vocabulary

Use a word in the box to complete each sentence.

| bar graph |
| picture graph |
| data |

1. You can take a survey to collect _____.
   (p. 470)

2. A _____ uses pictures to show data in a graph. (p. 474)

Concepts and Skills

Use the tally chart to complete the picture graph.
Draw a ☺ for each bird. (CC.2.MD.10)

Birds Counted at the Park	
Child	**Tally**
Reggie	IIII
Kate	HHt
Ted	II
Mandy	IIII

Birds Counted at the Park				
Reggie				
Kate				
Ted				
Mandy				

Key: Each ☺ stands for 1 bird.

3. Which child counted the most birds?

   _____

4. How many fewer birds did Ted count than Reggie counted?

   _____ fewer birds

5. How many birds did the four children count?

   _____ birds

Fill in the bubble for the correct answer choice.

6. Use the tally chart.
   How many children chose
   apple muffins? (CC.2.MD.10)

   ○ 13
   ○ 8
   ○ 7
   ○ 5

Favorite Muffin	
Muffin	**Tally**
banana	|||
blueberry	~~||||~~ ~~||||~~	
apple	~~||||~~ |||

7. Use the bar graph.
   How many more yellow toy
   cars than green toy cars
   were sold? (CC.2.MD.10)

   ○ 1
   ○ 3
   ○ 4
   ○ 5

Toy Cars Sold

Color: red, green, yellow, blue

Number of Toy Cars: 0 1 2 3 4 5

8. Use the picture graph.
   How many stickers do Megan
   and Lin have? (CC.2.MD.10)

   ○ 4
   ○ 5
   ○ 6
   ○ 7

Stickers We Have				
Shane	☺	☺	☺	
Megan	☺	☺		
Lin	☺	☺	☺	☺
Elroy	☺	☺	☺	

Key: Each ☺ stands for 1 sticker.

Name _____

Fill in the bubble for the correct answer choice.

9. Use the picture graph.
How many fewer books did
Joy read than Tony? (CC.2.MD.10)

- ○ 1
- ○ 2
- ○ 3
- ○ 5

Books We Read					
Joy	📖				
Dave	📖	📖	📖	📖	
Sasha	📖	📖	📖		
Tony	📖	📖	📖	📖	

Key: Each 📖 stands for 1 book.

10. Use the tally chart. How many
children chose truck? (CC.2.MD.10)

- ○ 5
- ○ 8
- ○ 10
- ○ 12

Favorite Toy	
Toy	**Tally**
ball	ⵑⵑⵑⵑ
truck	ⵑⵑⵑⵑ ⵑⵑⵑⵑ ‖
doll	ⵑⵑⵑⵑ ‖‖

11. Use the bar graph.
How many more mums than
roses are in the basket? (CC.2.MD.10)

- ○ 1
- ○ 2
- ○ 3
- ○ 8

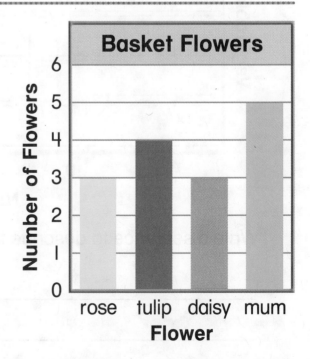

Constructed Response

12. The data for grape juice is not shown in the picture graph. If 13 children voted in all, how many pictures should there be for grape juice?

_____ pictures

Explain your answer. <small>(CC.2.MD.10)</small>

Favorite Juice				
apple	▮	▮	▮	▮
berry	▮	▮		
orange	▮	▮	▮	
grape				

Key: Each ▮ stands for 1 child.

_____

_____

Performance Task <small>(CC.2.MD.10)</small>

13. In a survey for favorite vegetable, 3 children chose squash, 4 children chose beans, 6 children chose corn, and 5 children chose carrots. Write labels and draw bars to complete the graph.

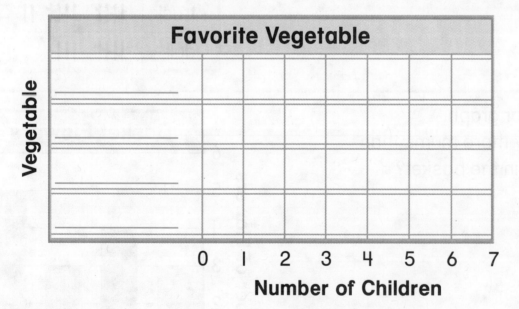

Write a sentence to describe the data in the graph.

_____

_____

A Farmer's Job

by Tami Morton

COMMON CORE

CRITICAL AREA **Describing and analyzing shapes**

A farmer's job is never done. Farmers are busy during all of the seasons of the year. They grow fruits and vegetables for people to eat.
What shapes do you see?

_____

Social Studies

498

Why is a farmer's work important?

In the spring, farmers get the fields ready.

They plow the fields and fertilize the soil.

They plant their seeds.

What shapes do you see?

Social Studies

How is a farmer's work today different from long ago?

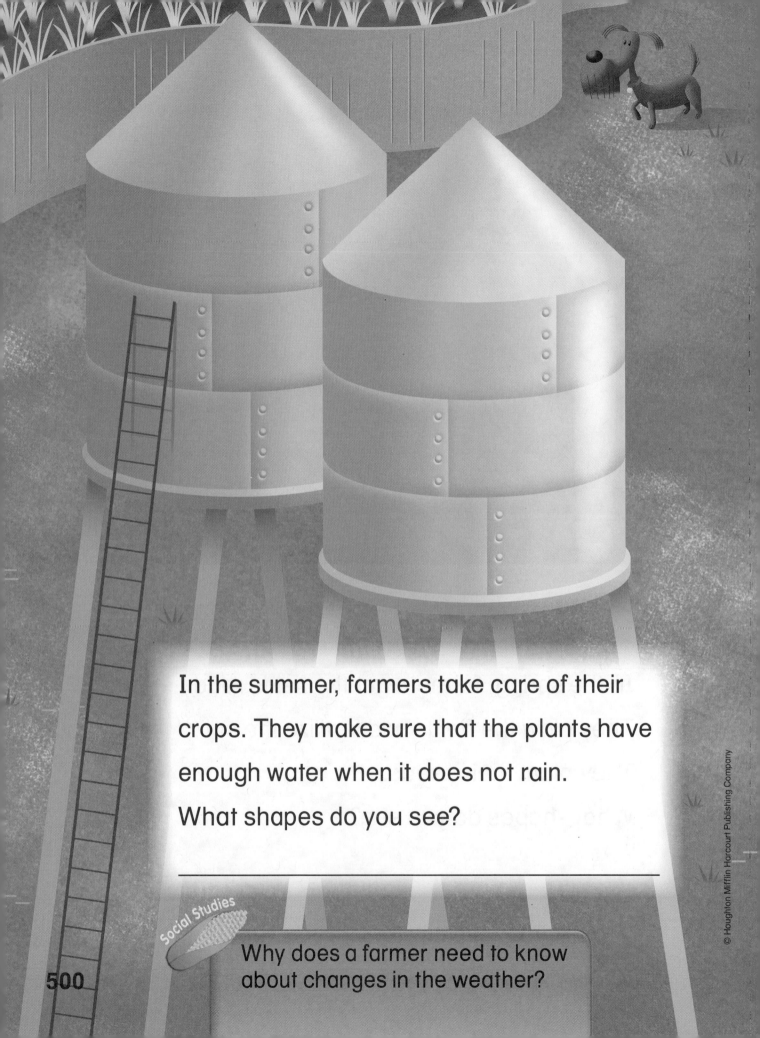

In the summer, farmers take care of their crops. They make sure that the plants have enough water when it does not rain.

What shapes do you see?

_____

Social Studies

Why does a farmer need to know about changes in the weather?

In the fall, farmers harvest many fruits and vegetables. They sell most of these fruits and vegetables to other people. What shapes do you see?

Social Studies

Why does a farmer grow more fruits and vegetables than his or her family can eat?

501

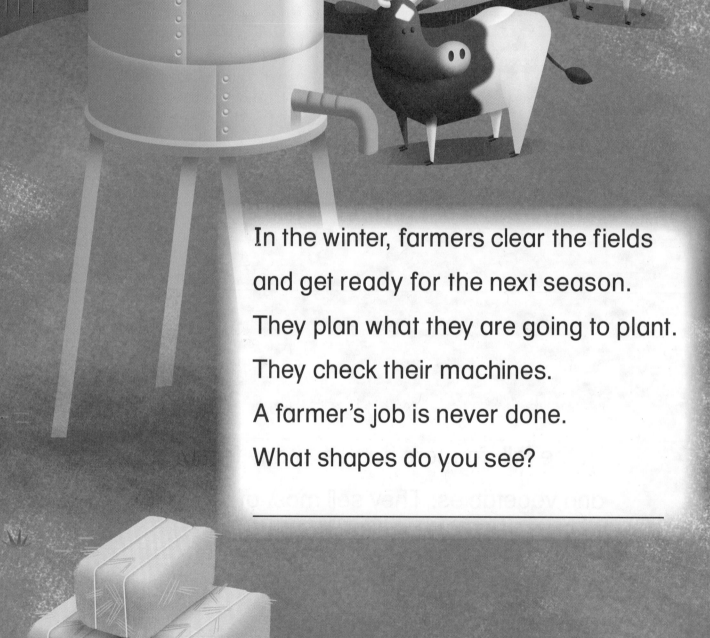

In the winter, farmers clear the fields
and get ready for the next season.

They plan what they are going to plant.

They check their machines.

A farmer's job is never done.

What shapes do you see?

_____

Social Studies

502

Why are the seasons
important to a farmer?

Write About the Story

Look at the pictures of the farm objects. Draw a picture and write your own story about the objects. Tell about the shapes that the objects look like.

Vocabulary Review

cylinder	cube
cone	circle
sphere	triangle
square	rectangle
rectangular prism	

_____

_____

_____

_____

_____

What shape do you see?

Draw a line to match the shape with the name.

• • •

• • •

cylinder   rectangular prism   circle

Circle each shape that has a curved surface.

cylinder   rectangular prism

cube   cone

sphere

 Write a riddle about a shape. Ask a classmate to read the riddle and name the shape.

Curious About Math with

Curious George

Hot air rises. A balloon filled with hot air will float up into the sky.

Some balloons look as though they have two-dimensional shapes on them. Name some two-dimensional shapes. Then draw some examples of them.

Name _____

Equal Parts

Circle the shape that has two equal parts.

1.  | 2.

Identify Three-Dimensional Shapes

3. Circle each .

4. Circle each ⬚ .

Identify Shapes

Circle all the shapes that match the shape name.

5. triangle

6. rectangle

Family note: This page checks your child's understanding of important skills needed for success in Chapter 11.

© Houghton Mifflin Harcourt Publishing Company

 Online   Assessment Options
Soar to Success Math

Vocabulary Builder

Review Words
equal parts
shape
rectangle
triangle
square

Visualize It

Draw pictures to complete the graphic organizer.

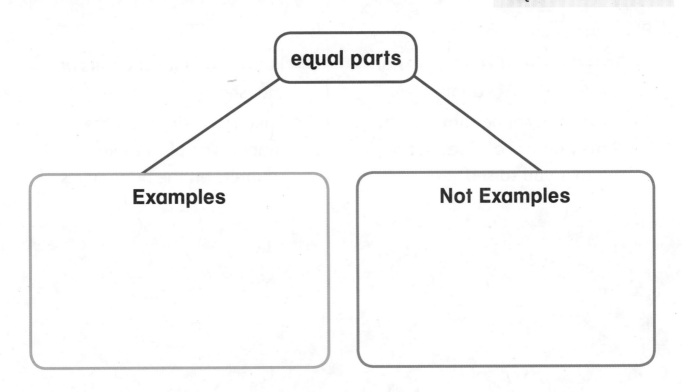

equal parts

Examples

Not Examples

Understand Vocabulary

Draw a **shape** to match the shape name.

rectangle | triangle | square

© Houghton Mifflin Harcourt Publishing Company

Chapter 11

GO Online
• eStudent Edition
• Multimedia eGlossary

five hundred seven **507**

Count the Sides

Materials • 1 • 10 ● • 10 ●

Play with a partner.

1. Toss the . If you toss a 1 or a 2, toss the again.

2. Look for a shape that has the same number of sides as the number you tossed.

3. Put one of your counters on that shape.

4. Take turns. Cover all the shapes. The player with more counters on the board wins.

Name _____

Three-Dimensional Shapes

Essential Question What objects match
three-dimensional shapes?

COMMON CORE STANDARD CC. 2.G.1
Reason with shapes and their attributes.

Listen and Draw · REAL WORLD

Draw a picture of an object that has the shape shown.

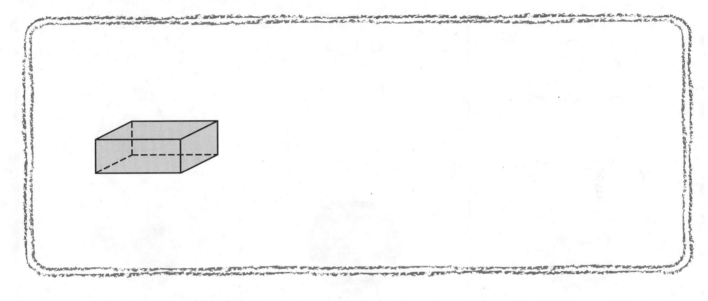

 FOR THE TEACHER • Have children look at the
first shape and name some real objects that have
this shape, such as a cereal box. Have each child
draw a picture of a real-life object that has the
same shape. Repeat for the second shape.

Math Talk
Describe how the
shapes are alike.
Describe how they
are different.

MATHEMATICAL PRACTICES

Chapter 11

five hundred nine **509**

Model and Draw

These are three-dimensional shapes.

cube

rectangular prism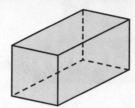

sphere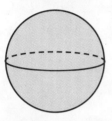

cylinder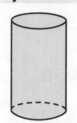

cone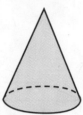

Which of these objects has the shape of a cube?

Share and Show

Circle the objects that match the shape name.

☑ 1. sphere

☑ 2. cube

510 five hundred ten

On Your Own

Circle the objects that match the shape name.

3. cylinder

4. rectangular prism

5. cone

6. cube

7. **H.O.T.** Circle the shapes that roll.
Draw an X on the shapes that do not roll.

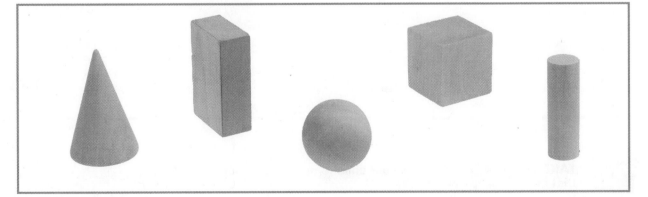

PROBLEM SOLVING REAL WORLD

Write Math

8. Reba traced around the bottom of each block. Match each block with the shape Reba drew.

9. **H.O.T.** Julio used cardboard squares as the flat surfaces of a cube. How many squares did he use?

_____ squares

10. ⭐ **Test Prep** Which of these shapes is a cube?

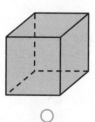

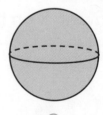

○   ○   ○   ○

TAKE HOME ACTIVITY • Ask your child to name an object that has the shape of a cube.

FOR MORE PRACTICE: Standards Practice Book, pp. P239–P240

Attributes of Three-Dimensional Shapes

Essential Question How would you describe the faces of a rectangular prism and the faces of a cube?

Lesson 11.2

COMMON CORE STANDARD CC.2.G.1
Reason with shapes and their attributes.

Listen and Draw

Circle the cones. Draw an X on the sphere.

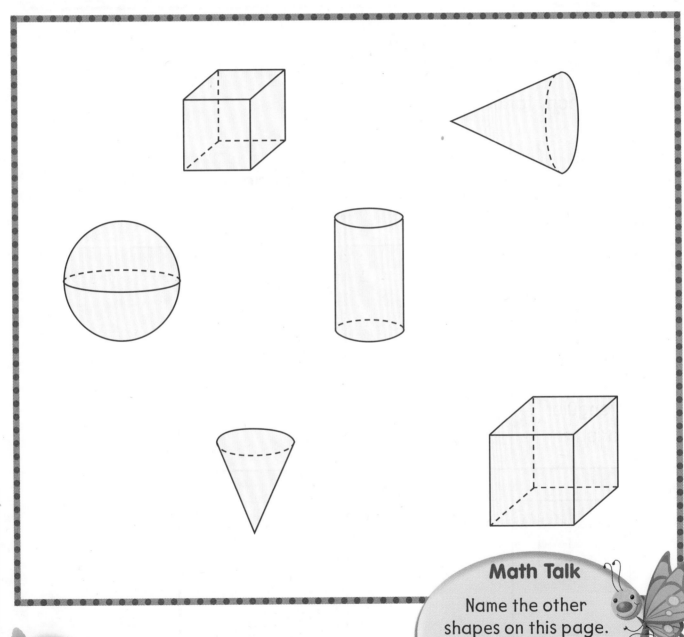

HOME CONNECTION • Your child identified the shapes on this page to review some of the different kinds of three-dimensional shapes.

Math Talk

Name the other shapes on this page. **Describe** how they are different.

MATHEMATICAL PRACTICES

Chapter 11

The **faces** of a cube are squares.

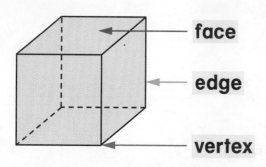

face

edge

vertex

The **vertices** are the corner points of the cube.

Share and Show

Write how many for each.

	faces	edges	vertices
✓ 1. rectangular prism	_____	_____	_____
✓ 2. cube	_____	_____	_____

On Your Own

Circle the set of shapes that are the faces
of the three-dimensional shape.

3.

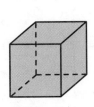

cube

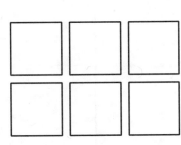

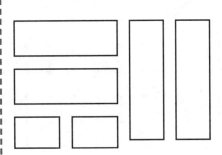

4.

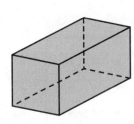

rectangular prism

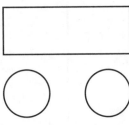

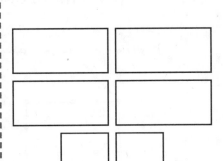

5. Look at the faces of the cube and the faces of the
   rectangular prism. **Explain** how they are different.

_____

_____

_____

_____

PROBLEM SOLVING REAL WORLD

Write Math

6. **H.O.T.** Use dot paper. Follow these steps to draw a cube.

Step 1 Draw a square. Make each side 4 units long.

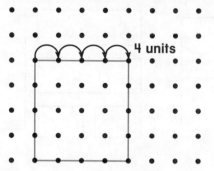

4 units

Step 2 Draw edges from 3 vertices, like this.

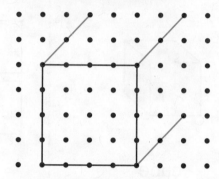

Step 3 Draw 2 more edges.

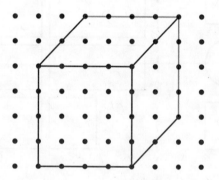

Step 4 Draw 3 dashed edges to show the faces that are not seen.

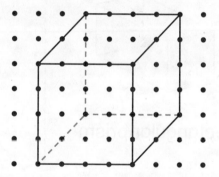

7. ⭐ **Test Prep** How many faces does a rectangular prism have?

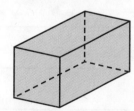

- ○ 6
- ○ 8
- ○ 12
- ○ 16

TAKE HOME ACTIVITY • Have your child tell you about the faces on a cereal box or another kind of box.

FOR MORE PRACTICE:
Standards Practice Book, pp. P241–P242

Two-Dimensional Shapes

Essential Question What shapes can you name just by knowing the number of sides and vertices?

COMMON CORE STANDARD CC.2.G.1
Reason with shapes and their attributes.

Listen and Draw

Use a ruler. Draw a shape with 3 straight sides.
Then draw a shape with 4 straight sides.

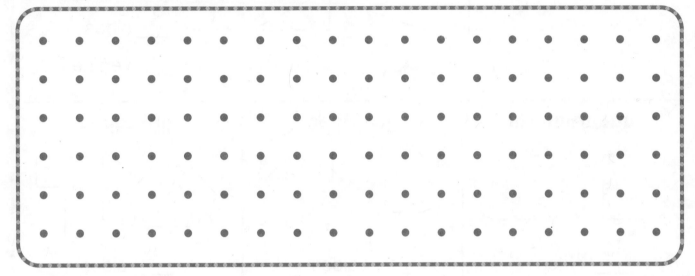

FOR THE TEACHER • Have children use rulers as straight edges for drawing the sides of shapes. Have children draw a two-dimensional shape with 3 sides and then a two-dimensional shape with 4 sides.

Math Talk

Describe how your shapes are different from the shapes a classmate drew.

MATHEMATICAL PRACTICES

Model and Draw

You can count **sides** and **vertices** to name two-dimensional shapes. Look at how many sides and vertices each shape has.

triangle

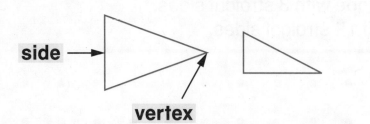

side →

vertex

_3_ sides
_3_ vertices

quadrilateral	**pentagon**	**hexagon**
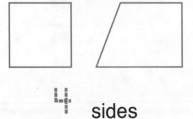	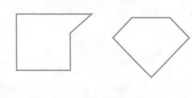	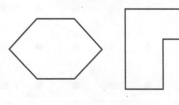
_4_ sides	____ sides	____ sides
____ vertices	____ vertices	____ vertices

Share and Show

Write the number of sides and the number of vertices.

1. triangle

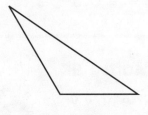

____ sides
____ vertices

✓ 2. hexagon

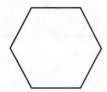

____ sides
____ vertices

✓ 3. pentagon

____ sides
____ vertices

Name _____

On Your Own

Write the number of sides and the number of vertices. Then write the name of the shape.

4.

_____ sides

_____ vertices

_____

5.

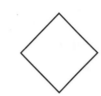

_____ sides

_____ vertices

_____

6.

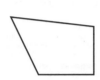

_____ sides

_____ vertices

_____

7.

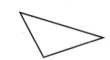

_____ sides

_____ vertices

_____

8.

_____ sides

_____ vertices

_____

9.

_____ sides

_____ vertices

_____

 Draw more sides to make the shape.

10. pentagon

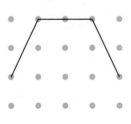

11. quadrilateral

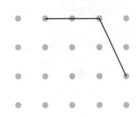

12. hexagon

PROBLEM SOLVING REAL WORLD

Write Math

Solve. Draw or write to explain.

13. Alex is making a hexagon and a pentagon with straws. He uses one straw for each side of each shape. How many straws does he need?

_____ straws

14. Mrs. Johnson buys 2 boxes of crayons. There are 8 crayons in each box. How many crayons are in the two boxes?

_____ crayons

15. ☼ **H.O.T.** ☼ Ed draws a shape that has 4 sides. It is not a square. It is not a rectangle. Draw a shape that could be Ed's shape.

16. ⭐ **Test Prep** What is the shape of this sign?

○ quadrilateral

○ hexagon

○ pentagon

○ triangle

TAKE HOME ACTIVITY • Ask your child to draw a shape that is a quadrilateral.

FOR MORE PRACTICE:
Standards Practice Book, pp. P243–P244

Name _____

Angles in Two-Dimensional Shapes

Essential Question How do you find and count angles in two-dimensional shapes?

COMMON CORE STANDARD CC.2.G.1
Reason with shapes and their attributes.

Listen and Draw

Use a ruler. Draw two different triangles.
Then draw two different rectangles.

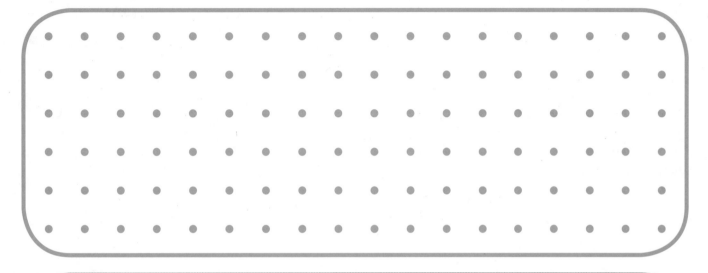

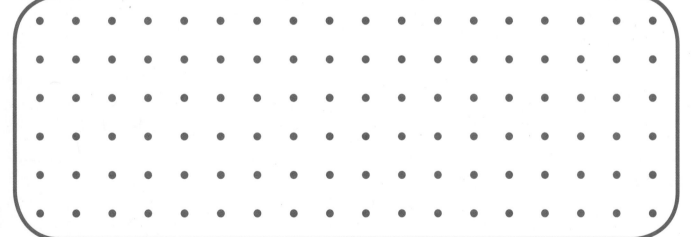

FOR THE TEACHER • Have children use pencils and rulers (or other straight edges) to draw the shapes. Have them draw two different triangles in the green box and two different rectangles in the purple box.

Math Talk
Describe a triangle and a rectangle. Tell about their sides and vertices.
MATHEMATICAL PRACTICES

Model and Draw

When two sides of a shape meet, they form an **angle**.

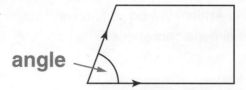

angle

This shape has 3 angles.

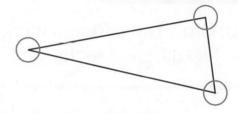

Share and Show

Circle the angles in each shape.
Write how many.

1.

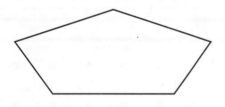

_____ angles

2.

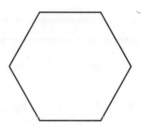

_____ angles

3.

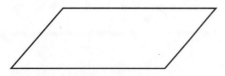

_____ angles

4.

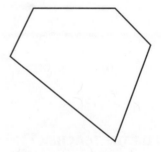

_____ angles

Name _____

On Your Own

Circle the angles in each shape.
Write how many.

5.

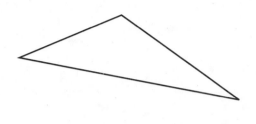

_____ angles

6.

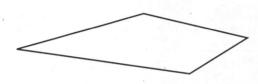

_____ angles

7.

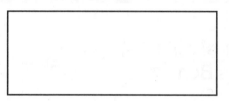

_____ angles

8.

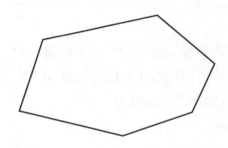

_____ angles

H.O.T. Draw more sides to make the shape.
Write how many angles.

9. pentagon

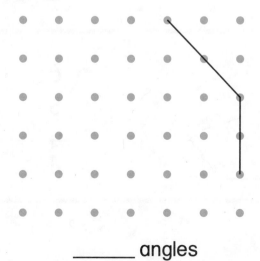

_____ angles

10. quadrilateral

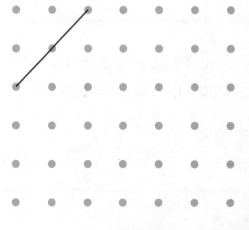

_____ angles

PROBLEM SOLVING REAL WORLD

Write Math

11. Amy drew 2 two-dimensional shapes that had 7 angles in all. Draw shapes Amy could have drawn.

12. **H.O.T.** Ben drew 3 two-dimensional shapes that had 11 angles in all. Draw shapes Ben could have drawn.

13. ⭐ **Test Prep** How many angles does this shape have?

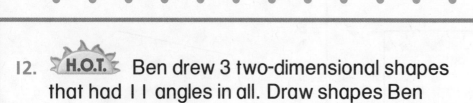

○ 6
○ 5
○ 4
○ 3

TAKE HOME ACTIVITY • Ask your child to draw a shape with 4 sides and 4 angles.

FOR MORE PRACTICE:
Standards Practice Book, pp. P245–P246

Name _____

Sort Two-Dimensional Shapes

Essential Question How do you use the number of sides and angles to sort two-dimensional shapes?

COMMON CORE STANDARD CC.2.G.1
Reason with shapes and their attributes.

Listen and Draw

Make the shape with pattern blocks.
Draw and color the blocks you used.

Use one block.

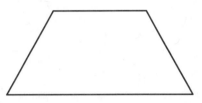

Use two blocks.

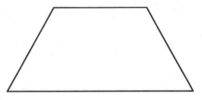

Use three blocks.

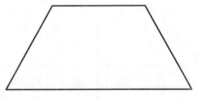

FOR THE TEACHER • Tell children that the shape shown three times on the page is a trapezoid. Have children use pattern blocks to make the trapezoid three times: with one pattern block, with two pattern blocks, and then with three pattern blocks.

Math Talk
Describe how you could sort the blocks you used.

MATHEMATICAL PRACTICES

Model and Draw

Which shapes match the rule?

Shapes with more than 3 sides	Shapes with fewer than 5 angles

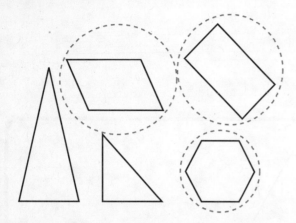 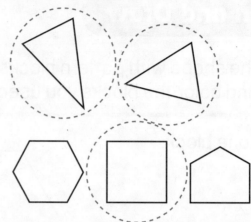

Share and Show

Circle the shapes that match the rule.

1. Shapes with 5 sides

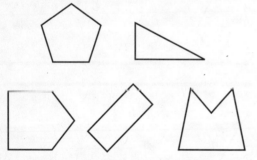

2. Shapes with more than 3 angles

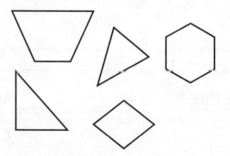

✓3. Shapes with fewer than 4 angles

✓4. Shapes with fewer than 5 sides

526 five hundred twenty-six

On Your Own

Circle the shapes that match the rule.

5. Shapes with 4 sides

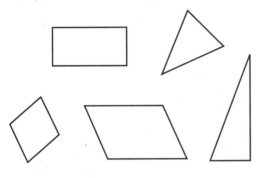

6. Shapes with more than 4 angles

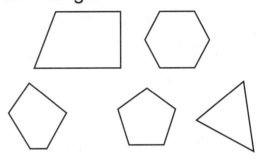

7. Shapes with fewer than 4 angles

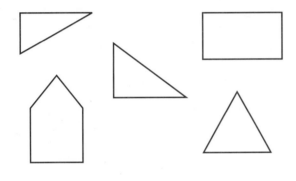

8. Shapes with fewer than 5 sides

9. **H.O.T.** Draw three shapes that match the rule. Circle them. Then draw two shapes that do not match the rule.

Shapes with fewer than 5 angles

PROBLEM SOLVING

Write Math

10. Sort the shapes.
   • Use red to color the shapes with more than 4 sides.
   • Use blue to color the shapes with fewer than 5 angles.

11. **H.O.T.** Jay plays baseball. He sees that home plate has the shape of a pentagon. How many angles does home plate have?

____ angles

12. ⭐ **Test Prep** Which of these shapes has fewer than 4 angles?

TAKE HOME ACTIVITY • Ask your child to draw some shapes that each have 4 angles.

FOR MORE PRACTICE: Standards Practice Book, pp. P247–P248

© Houghton Mifflin Harcourt Publishing Company

Name _____

Partition Rectangles

Essential Question How do you find the total number of same-size squares that will cover a rectangle?

COMMON CORE STANDARD **CC.2.G.2**
Reason with shapes and their attributes.

Listen and Draw

Put several color tiles together. Trace around the shape to draw a two-dimensional shape.

HOME CONNECTION • After putting together tiles, your child traced around them to draw a two-dimensional shape. This activity is an introduction to partitioning a rectangle into several same-size squares.

Math Talk
Is there a different shape that can be made with the same number of tiles? **Explain.**

MATHEMATICAL PRACTICES

Trace around color tiles. How many square tiles cover this rectangle?

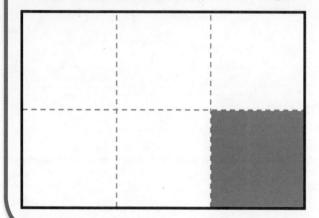

Number of rows: ___2___

Number of columns: ___3___

Total: _____ square tiles

Share and Show

Use color tiles to cover the rectangle.
Trace around the square tiles. Write how many.

1.

Number of rows: _____

Number of columns: _____

Total: _____ square tiles

2.

Number of rows: _____

Number of columns: _____

Total: _____ square tiles

Name _____

On Your Own

Use color tiles to cover the rectangle.
Trace around the square tiles. Write how many.

3.

Number of rows: _____

Number of columns: _____

Total: _____ square tiles

4.

Number of rows: _____

Number of columns: _____

Total: _____ square tiles

5. **H.O.T.** Mary started to cover
this rectangle with ones blocks.
Explain how you would estimate
the number of ones blocks that
would cover the whole rectangle.

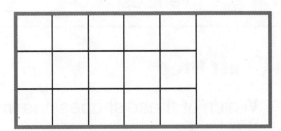

_____

_____

TAKE HOME ACTIVITY · Have your child describe what
he or she did in this lesson.

© Houghton Mifflin Harcourt Publishing Company

Chapter 11 · Lesson 6

FOR MORE PRACTICE:
Standards Practice Book, pp. P249–P250

Name _____

Concepts and Skills

Circle the objects that match the shape name. (CC.2.G.1)

1. cylinder		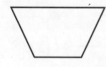		
2. cube				

Write the number of sides and the number of vertices. (CC.2.G.1)

3. quadrilateral	4. pentagon	5. hexagon
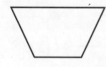		
_____ sides	_____ sides	_____ sides
_____ vertices	_____ vertices	_____ vertices

 Test Prep

6. Which of these shapes has more than 4 angles? (CC.2.G.1)

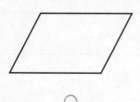   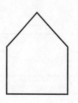      

  ◯   ◯   ◯   ◯

Name _____

Equal Parts

Essential Question What are halves, thirds, and fourths of a whole?

COMMON CORE STANDARD CC.2.G.3
Reason with shapes and their attributes.

Listen and Draw

Put pattern blocks together to match the shape of the hexagon. Trace the shape you made.

FOR THE TEACHER • Have children place a yellow hexagon pattern block on the workspace and make the same shape by using any combination of pattern blocks. Discuss how they know if the outline of the blocks they used is the same shape as the yellow hexagon.

Math Talk
Describe how the shapes you used are different from the shapes a classmate used.

MATHEMATICAL PRACTICES

Model and Draw

The green rectangle is the whole.
It can be divided into equal parts.

There are 2 **halves**.
Each part is a half.

There are 3 **thirds**.
Each part is a third.

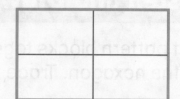

There are 4 **fourths**.
Each part is a fourth.

Share and Show

Write how many equal parts there are in the whole.
Write **halves**, **thirds**, or **fourths** to name the equal parts.

1.

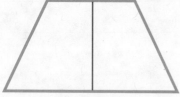

____ equal parts

_____

2.

____ equal parts

_____

3.

____ equal parts

_____

4.

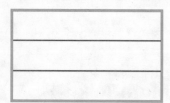

____ equal parts

_____

☑5.

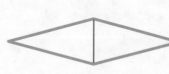

____ equal parts

_____

☑6.

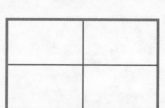

____ equal parts

_____

On Your Own

Write how many equal parts there are in the whole.
Write **halves**, **thirds**, or **fourths** to name the equal parts.

7.

_____ equal parts

_____

8.

_____ equal parts

_____

9.

_____ equal parts

_____

10.

_____ equal parts

_____

11.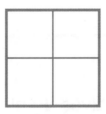

_____ equal parts

_____

12.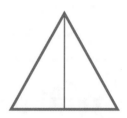

_____ equal parts

_____

13.

_____ equal parts

_____

14.

_____ equal parts

_____

15.

_____ equal parts

_____

PROBLEM SOLVING

Write Math

16. Sort the shapes.

- Draw an X on shapes that do **not** show equal parts.

- Use red to color the shapes that show thirds.

- Use blue to color the shapes that show fourths.

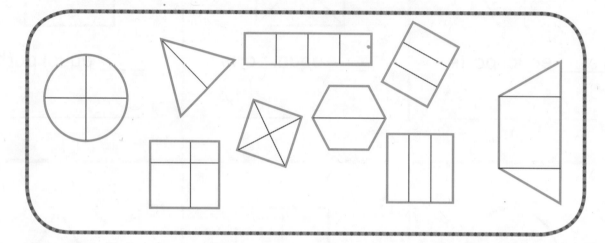

17. **H.O.T.** Draw to show halves. Explain how you know that the parts are halves.

_____

_____

18. ⭐ **Test Prep** Which shape has parts that are fourths?

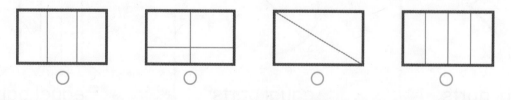

TAKE HOME ACTIVITY • Ask your child to fold one sheet of paper into halves and another sheet of paper into fourths.

FOR MORE PRACTICE:
Standards Practice Book, pp. P251–P252

Name _____

Show Equal Parts of a Whole

Essential Question How do you know if
a shape shows halves, thirds, or fourths?

COMMON CORE STANDARD CC.2.G.3
Reason with shapes and their attributes.

Listen and Draw

Circle the shapes that show equal parts.

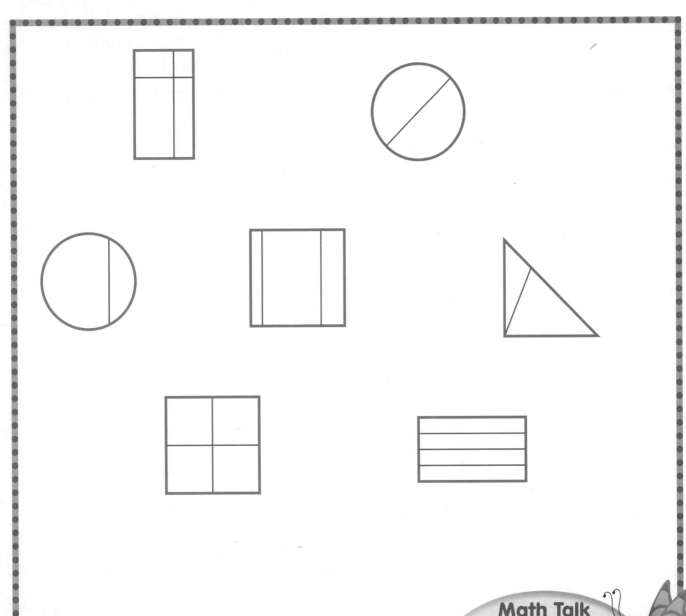

Math Talk
Does the
triangle show
halves? **Explain.**

MATHEMATICAL
PRACTICES

HOME CONNECTION · Your child completed
this sorting activity with shapes to review
the concept of equal parts.

Chapter 11

Model and Draw

You can draw to show equal parts of a whole.

halves 2 equal parts	thirds 3 equal parts	fourths 4 equal parts
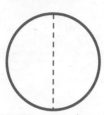	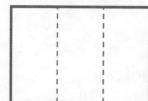	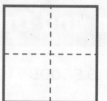
There are 2 halves in a whole.	There are 3 thirds in a whole.	There are 4 fourths in a whole.

Share and Show

Draw to show equal parts.

1. thirds	2. halves	3. fourths
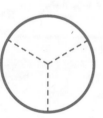		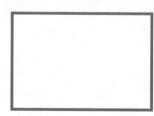

4. halves	✓ 5. fourths	✓ 6. thirds
		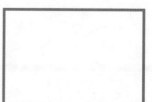

Name _____

On Your Own

Draw to show equal parts.

7. halves

8. fourths

9. thirds

10. thirds

11. halves

12. fourths

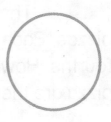

13. halves

14. thirds

15. fourths

16. Does this shape show thirds?
Explain.

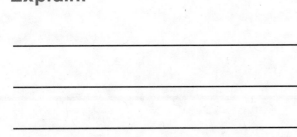

_____

_____

_____

PROBLEM SOLVING REAL WORLD

Write Math

Solve. Write or draw to explain.

17. Mrs. Blackwell has one muffin. She cuts the muffin into halves. How many pieces of muffin does she have?

_____ pieces

18. **H.O.T.** There are two square pizzas. Each pizza is cut into fourths. How many pieces of pizza are there?

_____ pieces

19. ⭐ **Test Prep** A piece of ribbon is cut into thirds. How many pieces of ribbon are there?

○ 2
○ 3
○ 4
○ 6

TAKE HOME ACTIVITY · Have your child explain how he or she solved Exercise 18.

FOR MORE PRACTICE:
Standards Practice Book, pp. P253–P254

Name _____

Describe Equal Parts

Essential Question How do you find a half of, a third of, or a fourth of a whole?

COMMON CORE STANDARD CC.2.G.3
Reason with shapes and their attributes.

Listen and Draw

Find shapes that show fourths and color them green.
Find shapes that show halves and color them red.

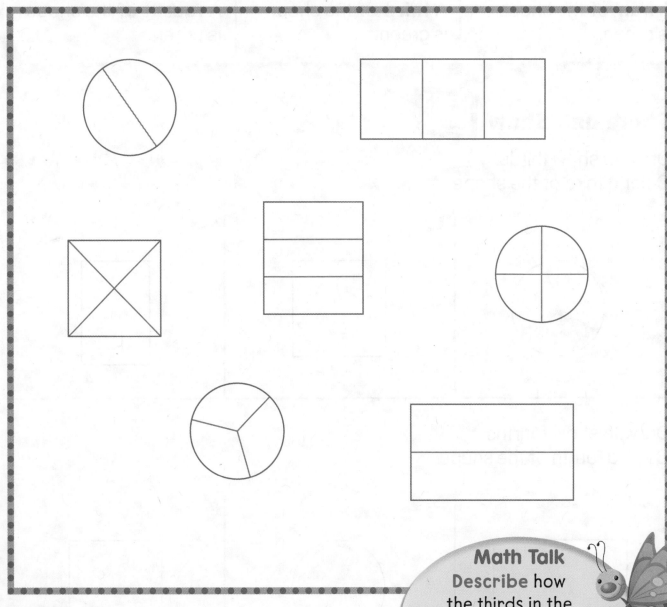

Math Talk
Describe how the thirds in the unshaded shapes compare to each other.

MATHEMATICAL PRACTICES

HOME CONNECTION · Your child identified the number of equal parts in shapes to review describing equal parts of a whole.

Model and Draw

These are some ways to show and describe an equal part of a whole.

> I of 4 equal parts is called a **quarter of** that shape.

2 equal parts

A **half of** the shape is green.

3 equal parts

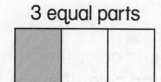

A **third of** the shape is green.

4 equal parts

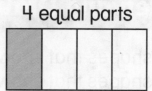

A **fourth of** the shape is green.

Share and Show

Draw to show thirds.
Color a third of the shape.

1.

2.

✓3.

Draw to show fourths.
Color a fourth of the shape.

4.

5.

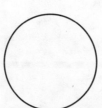

✓6.

On Your Own

Draw to show halves.
Color a half of the shape.

7.

8.

9.

Draw to show thirds.
Color a third of the shape.

10.

11.

12.

Draw to show fourths.
Color a fourth of the shape.

13.

14.

15.

PROBLEM SOLVING

16. Circle all the shapes that have a quarter of the shape shaded.

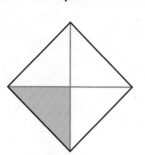
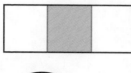
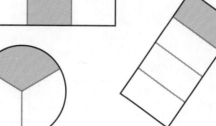
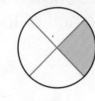

17. 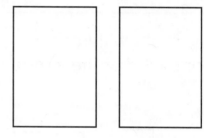 **H.O.T.** Two posters are the same size. A third of one poster is red, and a fourth of the other poster is blue.

Is the red part or the blue part larger? Draw and write to explain.

_____

_____

_____

_____

18. ⭐ **Test Prep** Which of these has a third of the shape shaded blue?

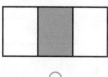
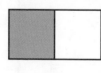
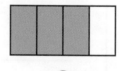
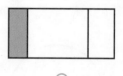

○   ○   ○   ○

TAKE HOME ACTIVITY • Draw a square. Have your child draw to show thirds and color a third of the square.

FOR MORE PRACTICE:
Standards Practice Book, pp. P255–P256

Name _____

Problem Solving • Equal Shares

Essential Question How can drawing a diagram help when solving problems about equal shares?

COMMON CORE STANDARD CC.2.G.3
Reason with shapes and their attributes.

There are two sandwiches that are the same size. Each sandwich is divided into fourths, but the sandwiches are cut differently. How might the two sandwiches be cut?

🔑 Unlock the Problem REAL WORLD

What do I need to find?

how the sandwiches

could be cut

What information do I need to use?

There are _____ sandwiches.
Each sandwich is divided

into _____.

Show how to solve the problem.

HOME CONNECTION · Your child drew a diagram to represent and solve a problem about dividing a whole in different ways to show equal shares.

© Houghton Mifflin Harcourt Publishing Company

Try Another Problem

Draw to show your answer.

- What do I need to find?
- What information do I need to use?

1. Roger has two square sheets of paper that are the same size. He wants to cut each sheet into halves. What are two different ways he can cut the sheets of paper?

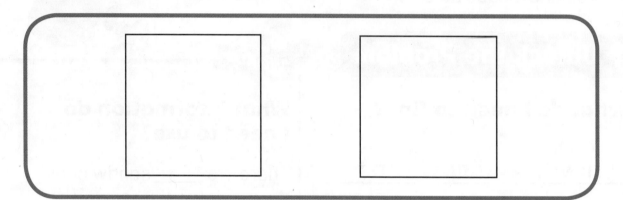

2. Dana has two pieces of cloth that are the same size. She needs to divide each piece into thirds. What are two different ways she can divide the pieces of cloth?

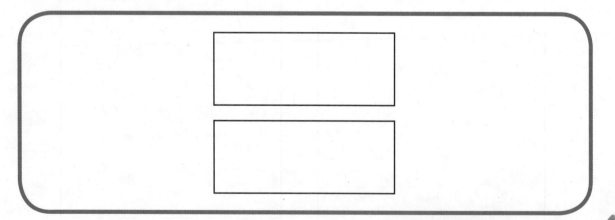

Math Talk

In Problem 2, **explain** how a third of the two pieces of cloth are alike and how they are different.

MATHEMATICAL PRACTICES

Name _____

Share and Show

Draw to show your answer.

✓ 3. Brandon has two pieces of toast that are the same size. What are two different ways he can divide the pieces of toast into halves?

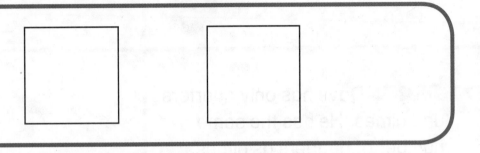

✓ 4. Mr. Rivera has two small cakes that are the same size. What are two different ways he can cut the cakes into fourths?

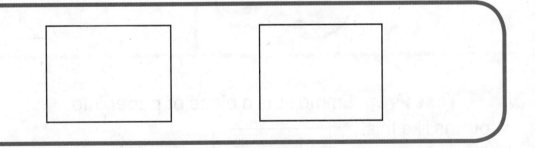

5. Erin has two ribbons that are the same size. What are two different ways she can divide the ribbons into thirds?

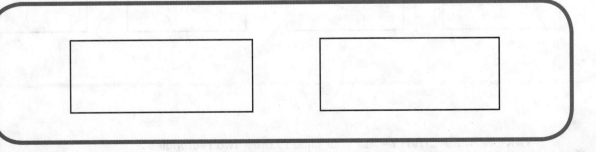

© Houghton Mifflin Harcourt Publishing Company

On Your Own

Solve. Write or draw to explain.

6. Patty has 75 beads in a box. 28 beads are red and the rest are blue. How many blue beads does Patty have?

_____ blue beads

7. **H.O.T.** Dave has only quarters and dimes. He has the same number of quarters as dimes. The total value of his coins is 70¢. What coins does Dave have?

_____ quarters

_____ dimes

8. ⭐ **Test Prep** Emma cuts a piece of paper into fourths like this.

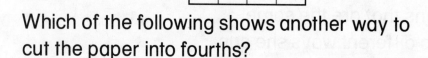

Which of the following shows another way to cut the paper into fourths?

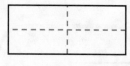   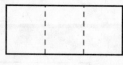   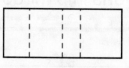   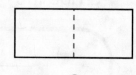

○   ○   ○   ○

TAKE HOME ACTIVITY · Ask your child to draw two rectangles and show two different ways to divide them into fourths.

FOR MORE PRACTICE:
Standards Practice Book, pp. P257–P258

✓ Chapter 11 Review/Test

Vocabulary

Use a word in the box to complete each sentence.

third of
fourth of
sphere
pentagon

1. A basketball has the shape of

   a _____. (p. 510)

2. A _____ has 5 sides and 5 angles. (p. 518)

3. One of three equal parts of a shape is

   a _____ the shape. (p. 542)

Concepts and Skills

Circle the shapes that match the rule. (CC.2.G.1)

4. Shapes with more than 3 angles	5. Shapes with fewer than 5 sides
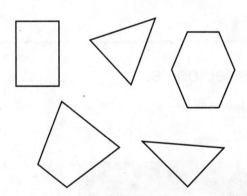	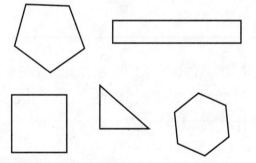

Draw to show equal parts. (CC.2.G.3)

6. thirds	7. halves	8. fourths

Fill in the bubble for the correct answer choice.

9. Which of these shapes is a cube? (CC.2.G.1)

 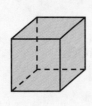 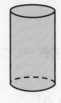 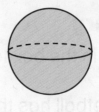

○   ○   ○   ○

10. Which of these shapes has 5 angles? (CC.2.G.1)

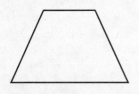   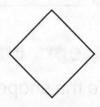

○   ○   ○   ○

11. Max used square color tiles to cover this rectangle. How many square color tiles did he use to cover the rectangle? (CC.2.G.2)

○ 2
○ 4
○ 6
○ 8

Fill in the bubble for the correct answer choice.

12. How many faces does a cube have? (CC.2.G.1)

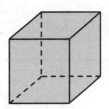

- ○ 2
- ○ 4
- ○ 6
- ○ 8

13. James drew a shape that has 4 sides and 4 angles. What is this shape called? (CC.2.G.1)

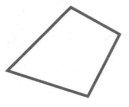

- ○ triangle
- ○ quadrilateral
- ○ hexagon
- ○ pentagon

14. There is one pizza. If the pizza is cut into fourths, how many pieces of pizza will there be? (CC.2.G.3)

- ○ 2
- ○ 3
- ○ 4
- ○ 5

Constructed Response

15. Reggie makes a pentagon and a quadrilateral with toothpicks. He uses one toothpick for each side of a shape. How many toothpicks does he use?

Draw or write to explain your answer. (CC.2.G.1)

_____ toothpicks

Performance Task (CC.2.G.3)

16. Keira has two poster boards that are the same size. She wants to divide each poster board into fourths. What are two different ways that she can divide the poster boards into fourths?

Suppose Keira also has a banner that she wants to divide into thirds. Describe what she should do.

_____

_____

_____

Picture Glossary

addend sumando

$$5 + 8 = 13$$

addends

bar graph gráfica de barras

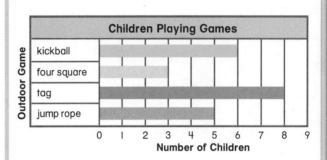

A.M. a.m.

Times after midnight and before noon are written with **A.M.**

11:00 A.M. is in the morning.

cent sign signo de centavo

53¢

↑

cent sign

angle ángulo

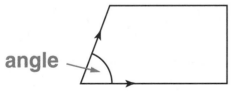

angle

centimeter centímetro

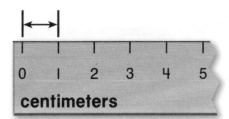

centimeters

compare comparar

Use these symbols when you **compare**: >, <, =.

241 > 234

123 < 128

247 = 247

cylinder cilindro

cone cono

data datos

Favorite Lunch	
Lunch	**Tally**
pizza	IIII
sandwich	IIII I
salad	III
pasta	IIII

The information in this chart is called **data**.

cube cubo

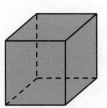

decimal point punto decimal

$1.00
↑
decimal point

difference diferencia

$$9 - 2 = 7$$

     ↑
difference

dollar dólar

One **dollar** is worth 100 cents.

digit dígito

0, 1, 2, 3, 4, 5, 6, 7, 8, and 9 are **digits**.

dollar sign signo de dólar

$1.00

↑
dollar sign

dime moneda de 10¢

A **dime** has a value of 10 cents.

edge arista

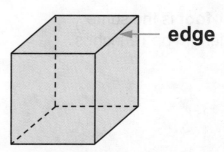

An **edge** is formed where two faces of a three-dimensional shape meet.

even par

2, 4, 6, 8, 10, . . .

even numbers

---

face cara

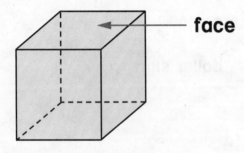

face

Each flat surface of this cube is a **face**.

---

foot pie

1 **foot** is the same length as 12 inches.

---

fourth of cuarto de

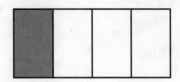

A **fourth of** the shape is green.

---

fourths cuartos

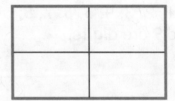

This shape has 4 equal parts. These equal parts are called **fourths**.

---

half of mitad de

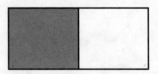

A **half of** the shape is green.

halves mitades

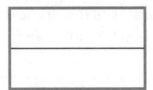

This shape has 2 equal parts. These equal parts are called **halves**.

hexagon hexágono

A two-dimensional shape with 6 sides is a **hexagon**.

hundred centena

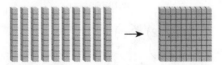

There are 10 tens in 1 **hundred**.

inch pulgada

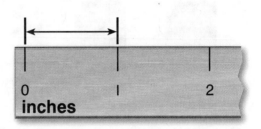

is equal to (=) es igual a

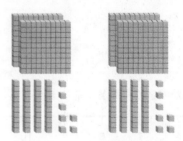

247 **is equal to** 247.
247 = 247

is greater than (>) es mayor que

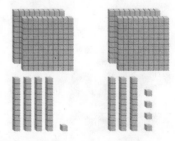

241 **is greater than** 234.
241 > 234

is less than (<) es menor que

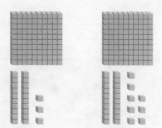

123 **is less than** 128.

123 < 128

line plot diagrama de puntos

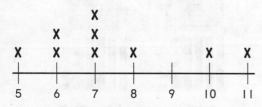

Lengths of Paintbrushes in Inches

measuring tape cinta métrica

meter metro

I **meter** is the same length as 100 centimeters.

midnight medianoche

Midnight is 12:00 at night.

minute minuto

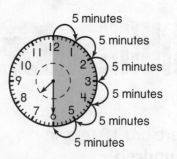

5 minutes
5 minutes
5 minutes
5 minutes
5 minutes
5 minutes

There are 30 **minutes** in a half hour.

nickel moneda de 5¢

A **nickel** has a value of
5 cents.

noon mediodía

Noon is 12:00 in the
daytime.

odd impar

1, 3, 5, 7, 9, 11, . . .

odd numbers

penny moneda de 1¢

A **penny** has a value of
1 cent.

pentagon pentágono

A two-dimensional shape
with 5 sides is a **pentagon**.

picture graph gráfica con
dibujos

Number of Soccer Games							
March	⚽	⚽	⚽	⚽			
April	⚽	⚽	⚽				
May	⚽	⚽	⚽	⚽	⚽	⚽	
June	⚽	⚽	⚽	⚽	⚽	⚽	⚽

Key: Each ⚽ stands for 1 game.

P.M. p.m.

Times after noon and before midnight are written with P.M.
11:00 P.M. is in the evening.

---

quadrilateral cuadrilátero

A two-dimensional shape with 4 sides is a **quadrilateral**.

---

quarter moneda de 25¢

A **quarter** has a value of 25 cents.

quarter of cuarta parte de

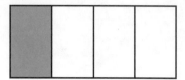

A **quarter of** the shape is green.

---

quarter past y cuarto

8:15

15 minutes after 8
quarter past 8

---

rectangular prism prisma rectangular

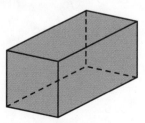